PROFESSIONAL
EMBEDDED ARM DEVELOPMENT

INTRODUCTION xxi

➤ **PART I**   **ARM SYSTEMS AND DEVELOPMENT**

CHAPTER 1   The History of ARM 3
CHAPTER 2   ARM Embedded Systems. 13
CHAPTER 3   ARM Architecture. 29
CHAPTER 4   ARM Assembly Language 53
CHAPTER 5   First Steps. 73
CHAPTER 6   Thumb Instruction Set 107
CHAPTER 7   Assembly Instructions 121
CHAPTER 8   NEON 145
CHAPTER 9   Debugging 159
CHAPTER 10 Writing Optimized C 175

➤ **PART II**   **REFERENCE**

APPENDIX A Terminology 193
APPENDIX B ARM Architecture Versions 199
APPENDIX C ARM Core Versions 205
APPENDIX D NEON Intrinsics and Instructions. 215
APPENDIX E Assembly Instructions 221

INDEX 247

PROFESSIONAL

Embedded ARM Development

PROFESSIONAL

Embedded ARM Development

James A. Langbridge

wrox™
A Wiley Brand

Professional Embedded ARM Development

Published by
John Wiley & Sons, Inc.
10475 Crosspoint Boulevard
Indianapolis, IN 46256
www.wiley.com

Copyright © 2014 by John Wiley & Sons, Inc., Indianapolis, Indiana

ISBN: 978-1-118-78894-3
ISBN: 978-1-118-78901-8 (ebk)
ISBN: 978-1-118-88782-0 (ebk)

10 9 8 7 6 5 4 3 2 1

ACQUISITIONS EDITOR
Mary James

PROJECT EDITOR
Christina Haviland

TECHNICAL EDITORS
Jean-Michel Hautbois
Chris Shore

PRODUCTION EDITOR
Christine Mugnolo

COPY EDITOR
San Dee Phillips

EDITORIAL MANAGER
Mary Beth Wakefield

FREELANCER EDITORIAL MANAGER
Rosemarie Graham

ASSOCIATE DIRECTOR OF MARKETING
David Mayhew

MARKETING MANAGER
Ashley Zurcher

BUSINESS MANAGER
Amy Knies

VICE PRESIDENT AND EXECUTIVE GROUP PUBLISHER
Richard Swadley

ASSOCIATE PUBLISHER
Jim Minatel

PROJECT COORDINATOR, COVER
Patrick Redmond

PROOFREADER
Nancy Carrasco

TECHNICAL PROOFREADER
Stephan Cadene

INDEXER
Robert Swanson

COVER DESIGNER
Ryan Sneed

COVER IMAGE
Background: PhotoAlto
Images/Fotosearch

For my loving girlfriend, Anne-Laure, who put up with entire weekends spent on my PC (while she spent her weekend on her laptop, sending me encouraging electronic messages). Thank you for supporting me when I should have been paying attention to you.

For my wonderful daughter, Eléna. Thank you for letting daddy work when I really should have spent more time playing with you, and despite what I might have said at the time, thank you for unplugging my computer when I ignored you for too long. Your smiles and first words are what powered me through the late nights and tight deadlines.

ABOUT THE AUTHOR

JAMES A. LANGBRIDGE does not like talking about himself in the third person, but he will try anyway. James was born in Singapore, and followed his parents to several countries before settling down in Nantes, France, where he lives with his partner and their daughter.

James is an embedded systems consultant and has worked for more than 15 years on industrial, military, mobile telephony, and aviation security systems. He works primarily on low-level development, creating bootloaders or optimizing routines in assembly, making the most of small processors. When not on contract, James trains engineers on embedded systems, or he makes new gizmos, much to the dismay of his partner.

James wrote his first computer program at age six and has never stopped tinkering since. He began using Apple IIs, ZX80s and ZX81s, before moving on to BBC Micros and the Amiga, before finally having no other option but to use PCs.

ABOUT THE TECHNICAL EDITORS

CHRIS SHORE is the Training and Education Manager at ARM Ltd, based in Cambridge, UK. He has been responsible for training ARM's global customer base for over 13 years, delivering nearly 200 training courses per year on everything from chip design to software optimization. Chris has taught classes on every continent except Antarctica — opportunities there are limited, but surely it's only a matter of time! He is a regular speaker at industry conferences.

Following graduation with his degree in Computer Science from Cambridge University, Chris worked as a software consultant for over 15 years, primarily in embedded real-time systems, before moving to ARM in 1999. He is a Chartered Engineer and Member of the Institute of Engineering and Technology, and he sits on the Industry Advisory Board of Queen Mary College, London. In his free time he keeps bees, tries to play the guitar, and is always looking for ways to visit new countries.

JEAN-MICHEL HAUTBOIS lives in France and has been developing software professionally, or as a hobbyist, for more than 15 years. He is currently employed as an embedded Linux consultant with Vodalys, and is the architect of his company's main video product which was developed on an ARM-based SoC. He is involved in the decision-making process when a new hardware product needs to be created and performance is critical. In his free time Jean-Michel likes to travel, and he enjoys spending time with his wife and newborn son.

ACKNOWLEDGMENTS

I CAN'T FIND THE WORDS to thank everyone who has helped me with this project. It all started with the questions of junior developers; I hope I've answered your questions. The LinkedIn ARM group has been an excellent source of information, both by the questions asked and the quality of the answers. I would like to thank everyone at ARM who has helped me. My thanks especially to my two technical editors, Chris Shore and Jean-Michel Hautbois; without your help, this book would not have been possible. My thanks also to Philippe Lançon for your support, to Atmel and Silicon Labs for your boards and your time, and to all my friends and family who helped me with this project. And, of course, the Wiley team, who helped me every time I had a question or a doubt, and who put up with me. To Christina Haviland, Mary James, San Dee Phillips, and everyone else who helped me — thank you.

CONTENTS

INTRODUCTION   *xxi*

PART I: ARM SYSTEMS AND DEVELOPMENT

CHAPTER 1: THE HISTORY OF ARM   3

The Origin of ARM   3
Why Acorn Decided to Create a New Processor   5
Why Acorn Became ARM   5
Why ARM Doesn't Actually Produce Microprocessors   6
ARM Naming Conventions   7
How to Tell What Processor You Are Dealing With   8
Differences between ARM7TDMI and ARM926EJ-S   9
Differences between ARM7 and ARMv7   10
Differences between Cortex-M and Cortex-A   11
Manufacturer Documentation   11
What Is ARM Doing Today?   11
Summary   12

CHAPTER 2: ARM EMBEDDED SYSTEMS   13

ARM Embedded Systems Defined   15
What Is a System on Chip?   15
What's the Difference between Embedded Systems
and System Programming?   16
Why Is Optimization So Important?   17
What Is the Advantage of a RISC Architecture?   19
Choosing the Right Processor   21
What Should You Start With?   22
What Boards Are Available?   23
What Operating Systems Exist?   24
Which Compiler Is Best Suited to My Purpose?   25
Getting Ready for Debugging   26
Are There Any Complete Development Environments?   26
Is There Anything Else I Need to Know?   27
Summary   28

CHAPTER 3: ARM ARCHITECTURE 29

Understanding the Basics 29
    Register 30
    Stack 31
    Internal RAM 31
    Cache 31
Getting to Know the Different ARM Subsystems 33
    Presenting the Processor Registers 33
    Presenting the CPSR 35
    Calculation Unit 37
    Pipeline 37
    Tightly Coupled Memory 39
    Coprocessors 39
Understanding the Different Concepts 40
    What Is an Exception? 40
    Handling Different Exceptions 42
    Modes of Operation 43
    Vector Table 44
    Memory Management 45
Presenting Different Technologies 47
    JTAG Debug (D) 47
    Enhanced DSP (E) 47
    Vector Floating Point (F) 48
    EmbeddedICE (I) 48
    Jazelle (J) 48
    Long Multiply (M) 48
    Thumb (T) 49
    Synthesizable (S) 49
    TrustZone 49
    NEON 50
    big.LITTLE 50
Summary 51

CHAPTER 4: ARM ASSEMBLY LANGUAGE 53

Introduction to Assembly Language 53
Talking to a Computer 54
Why Learn Assembly? 55
    Speed 55
    Size 56
    Fun! 57
    Compilers Aren't Perfect 57

Understanding Computer Science through Assembly 58
Shouldn't You Just Write in Assembly? 58
Uses of Assembly 59
Writing Bootloaders 59
Reverse Engineering 59
Optimization 60
ARM Assembly Language 60
Layout 61
Instruction Format 61
Condition Codes 62
Updating Condition Flags 65
Addressing Modes 66
ARM Assembly Primer 69
Loading and Storing 69
Setting Values 69
Branching 69
Mathematics 70
Understanding an Example Program 70
Summary 71

CHAPTER 5: FIRST STEPS 73

Hello World! 74
Taking the World Apart 77
Hello World, for Real This Time! 79
Software Implementation 81
Memory Mapping 83
Real World Examples 85
Silicon Labs STK3800 85
Silicon Labs STK3200 89
Atmel D20 Xplained Pro 95
Case Study: U-Boot 102
Machine Study: Raspberry Pi 103
Boot Procedure 103
Compiling Programs for the Raspberry Pi 104
What's Next? 105
Summary 105

CHAPTER 6: THUMB INSTRUCTION SET 107

Thumb 108
Thumb-2 Technology 109
How Thumb Is Executed 109

Advantages of Using Thumb   110
Cores Using Thumb   111
ARM-Thumb Interworking   113
Introduction to Thumb-1   113
   Register Availability   114
   Removed Instructions   114
   No Conditionals   114
   Set Flags   114
   No Barrel Shifter   115
   Reduced Immediates   115
   Stack Operations   115
Introduction to Thumb-2   115
   New Instructions   116
   Coprocessor   117
   DSP   118
   FPU   118
Writing for Thumb   118
Summary   119

CHAPTER 7: ASSEMBLY INSTRUCTIONS   121

Movement   122
   MOV   122
   MVN   122
   MOVW   123
   MOVT   123
   NEG   123
   Example: Loading a 32-Bit Constant from
   the Instruction Stream   123
Arithmetic   125
   ADD   125
   ADC   126
   SUB   126
   SBC   126
   RSB   126
   RSC   127
   Example: Basic Math   127
Saturating Arithmetic   127
   QADD   128
   QSUB   128
   QDADD   128
   QDSUB   129

Data Transfer	**129**
LDR	129
STR	130
Example: memcpy	130
Logical	**130**
AND	131
EOR	131
ORR	131
BIC	131
CLZ	131
Compare	**131**
CMP	132
CMN	132
TST	132
TEQ	132
Branch	**132**
B	133
BL	133
BX	133
BLX	134
Example: Counting to Zero	134
Example: Thumb Interworking	134
What Is MOV pc, lr?	135
Multiply	**135**
MUL	135
MLA	135
UMULL	136
UMLAL	136
SMULL	136
SMLAL	136
Divide	**136**
SDIV	137
UDIV	137
Multiple Register Data Transfer	**137**
STM	138
LDM	139
Barrel Shifter	**139**
LSL	139
LSR	140
ASR	140

ROR   140
RRX   140
Stack Operations   140
  PUSH   141
  POP   141
  Example: Returning from a Subroutine   141
Coprocessor Instructions   141
  MRC   141
  MCR   142
Miscellaneous Instructions   142
  SVC   142
  NOP   143
  MRS   143
  MSR   143
Summary   143

CHAPTER 8: NEON   **145**

What Are the Advantages to NEON?   145
What Data Types Does NEON Support?   147
Using NEON in Assembly   147
  Presenting the Registers   147
  Loading and Storing Data   148
  Optimized memcpy   152
  NEON Instructions   152
Using NEON in C   153
  Presenting Intrinsics   154
  Using NEON Intrinsics   155
  Converting an Image to Grayscale   156
Summary   158

CHAPTER 9: DEBUGGING   **159**

What Is a Debugger?   159
  What Can a Debugger Do?   160
  ARM Debugging Capabilities   160
Types of Debugging   162
  Loops   162
  Routines   163
  Interrupt Controllers   163
  Bootloaders   163

Debuggers	**163**
GNU Debugger	163
J-Link GDB Debugger	165
Example Debugging	**165**
Infinite Loop	165
Unknown Exception	167
Dividing by Zero	168
In-Depth Analysis	**169**
Data Abort	169
Corrupted Serial Line	170
64-Bit Calculations	172
A Timely Response	173
Summary	**174**

CHAPTER 10: WRITING OPTIMIZED C	**175**

Rules for Optimized Code	**175**
Don't Start with Optimization	176
Know Your Compiler	176
Know Your Code	176
Profiling	**176**
Profiling Inside an Operating System	177
Profiling on a Bare Metal System	178
C Optimizations	**180**
Basic Example	180
Count Down, Not Up	182
Integers	183
Division	183
Don't Use Too Many Parameters	184
Pointers, Not Objects	185
Don't Frequently Update System Memory	185
Alignment	185
Assembly Optimizations	**186**
Specialized Routines	186
Handling Interrupts	186
Hardware Configuration Optimizations	**187**
Frequency Scaling	187
Configuring Cache	188
Summary	**190**

PART II: REFERENCE

APPENDIX A: TERMINOLOGY   193

Branch Prediction	193
Cache	193
Coprocessors	194
CP10	195
CP11	195
CP14	195
CP15	195
Cycle	195
Exception	195
Interrupt	196
Jazelle	196
JTAG	196
MIPS	196
NEON	196
Out-of-Order Execution	197
Pipeline	197
Register	197
SIMD	197
SOC	197
Synthesizable	197
TrustZone	198
Vector Tables	198

APPENDIX B: ARM ARCHITECTURE VERSIONS   199

ARMv1	200
ARMv2	200
ARMv3	200
ARMv4	201
ARMv5	201
ARMv6	202
ARMv6-M	202
ARMv7-A/R	203
ARMv7-M	203
ARMv8	203

APPENDIX C: ARM CORE VERSIONS   205

ARM6	205
ARM7	205

ARM7TDMI   206

ARM8   206

StrongARM   206

ARM9TDMI   207

ARM9E   207

ARM10   207

XScale   208

ARM11   208

Cortex   208

APPENDIX D: NEON INTRINSICS AND INSTRUCTIONS   **215**

Data Types   215

Lane Types   216

Assembly Instructions   216

Intrinsic Naming Conventions   220

APPENDIX E: ASSEMBLY INSTRUCTIONS   **221**

ARM Instructions   221

Thumb Instructions on Cortex-M Cores   234

INDEX   ***247***

INTRODUCTION

IN THE WORLD OF EMBEDDED SYSTEMS, you can't work for long without working on an ARM CPU. ARM CPUs are known for their low electric power consumption, making them ideal for mobile embedded systems. Since 2012, virtually all PDAs and smartphones contain ARM CPUs, and ARMs account for 75 percent of all 32-bit embedded systems and 90 percent of embedded RISC systems. In 2005, 98 percent of more than one billion mobile phones sold used at least one ARM processor. You can find ARM processors in mobile phones, tablets, MP3 players, handheld games consoles, calculators, and even computer peripherals such as Bluetooth chips and hard disk drives.

With more than 1 billion ARM processors shipped every 2 months, it is surprising to know that ARM does not actually make processors, but rather designs the core, and ARM partners use those designs to make their own processors, adding external devices and peripherals or modifying the core for speed or power consumption benefits. By working closely with manufacturers, ARM has created a huge ecosystem. The result is an amazing range of processors, used for all types of devices in all classes of devices, and all running using a common architecture, enabling developers to switch easily from one processor to another.

ARM processors are by no means tiny processors with limited performance; they range from micro-controller devices used in the smallest of systems all the way to 64-bit processors used in servers.

This book introduces you to embedded ARM systems, how to get them up and running, how to develop for this platform, and some of the devices available in this huge ecosystem.

WHO THIS BOOK IS FOR

This book is primarily for developers who want to start in the embedded field. A basic understanding of C is required for most examples, but no assembly knowledge is required.

This book is also for developers who want better knowledge of the internals of a processor and to understand what goes on deep inside the core.

WHAT THIS BOOK COVERS

This book covers the advances in technology for ARM processors and focuses on the more recent ARMv7 architecture, for Cortex-A, Cortex-R, and Cortex-M devices. If you use the Cortex range of processors, you will feel at home, but if you use ARM Classic cores, you can also find information and a listing of the differences between architectures and platforms.

HOW THIS BOOK IS STRUCTURED

This book is designed to give as much information as possible to someone who does not have working experience with ARM processors. To understand ARM's philosophy, it is necessary to understand where ARM came from and how the ARM processor was born. This book then covers all aspects of an embedded project: understanding the processor and the extensions, understanding assembler, creating your first program using a more familiar C, and then continuing to debugging and optimization.

Chapter 1, "The History of ARM," gives an outline of the fascinating history of ARM; where it came from and why it is where it is today.

Chapter 2, "ARM Embedded Systems," gives an explanation on what an embedded system is and a presentation of the strong points of an ARM system.

Chapter 3, "ARM Architecture," lists the different elements that compose an ARM processor and how to use them effectively.

Chapter 4, "ARM Assembly Language," gives an introduction to ARM assembly and explains why understanding assembly is so important.

Chapter 5, "First Steps," presents some simulators and real-world cards to write programs, both to get an ARM processor started and to use as a basis for more complex programs. This chapter also presents some real-world scenario projects.

Chapter 6, "Thumb Instruction Set," presents the Thumb mode and also the Thumb-2 extension. Cortex-M processors use only Thumb mode, but Thumb can also be used on every modern processor where code density is important.

Chapter 7, "Assembly Instructions," presents a list of assembly instructions in ARM's Unified Assembly Language, and explains their use with easy-to-follow programs.

Chapter 8, "NEON," presents NEON, ARM's advanced Single Instruction Multiple Data processor and shows how you can use it to accelerate mathematically intensive routines.

Chapter 9, "Debugging," describes debugging, what is required to debug a program, and what you can achieve. It uses several real-world examples.

Chapter 10, "Writing Optimized C," describes the final part of any application—optimization. With some simple examples, you will learn how to write optimized code, and understand what happens deep inside the processor to implement further optimization.

Appendix A, "Terminology," explains some of the words and terms you will encounter when working on embedded systems, and more specifically, ARM embedded systems.

Appendix B, "ARM Architecture Versions," lists the different ARM Architectures that exist, and explain what each version brought in terms of technological advancement, but also which processor belongs to which architecture.

Appendix C, "ARM Core Versions," looks closer at the ARM cores, and presents the changes in each processor. Discussing briefly each processor from ARM6 onwards, it goes into more detail for modern Cortex-class processors.

Appendix D, "Neon Intrinsics and Instructions," lists the different instructions available for ARM's NEON engine, and also presents the intrinsics used to perform NEON calculation in an optimized way, using C.

Appendix E, "Assembly Instructions," lists the different assembly instructions used in UAL, with a description of each, as well as a list of Thumb instructions used on different Cortex-M class processors.

WHAT YOU NEED TO USE THIS BOOK

Most people imagine an embedded system surrounded with costly electronics and expensive software licenses, but the truth is that you can start embedded development with little investment. To start, you need a development computer. Examples are given for Linux, but you can also use Windows and MacOS. Royalty-free compilers are proposed, and you can use a free ARM simulator for your first programs, but later, a small ARM system is advisable: either an evaluation board from a manufacturer (two are presented), or you can use an inexpensive small-factor computer, such as a Raspberry Pi or an Arduino Due.

To run the samples in the book, you need the following:

➤ Linux development computer

➤ Mentor Graphics compiler suite

➤ Atmel SAM D20 Xplained Pro evaluation board

➤ Silicon Lab's STK3200 and STK3800 evaluation boards

➤ Raspberry Pi

The source code for the samples is available for download from the Wrox website at:

www.wiley.com/go/profembeddedarmdev

CONVENTIONS

To help you get the most from the text and keep track of what's happening, we've used a number of conventions throughout the book.

> **NOTE** *Notes indicate notes, tips, hints, tricks, and asides to the current discussion.*

As for styles in the text:

➤ We *highlight* new terms and important words when we introduce them.

➤ We show keyboard strokes like this: Ctrl+A.

➤ We show filenames, URLs, and code within the text like so: `persistence.properties`.

➤ We present code in this way:

```
We use a monofont type with no highlighting for most code examples.
```

SOURCE CODE

As you work through the examples in this book, you may choose either to type in all the code manually or to use the source code files that accompany the book. All the source code used in this book is available for download at `www.wrox.com`. Specifically for this book, the code download is on the Download Code tab at:

`www.wrox.com/go/profembeddedarmdev`

You can also search for the book at `www.wrox.com` by ISBN (the ISBN for this book is 978-1-118-78894-3) to find the code. And a complete list of code downloads for all current Wrox books is available at `www.wrox.com/dynamic/books/download.aspx`.

At the beginning of Chapter 5, you will find a list of the major code files for the chapter. Throughout the chapter, you will also find references to the names of code files available for download.

Most of the code on `www.wrox.com` is compressed in a .ZIP, .RAR archive, or similar archive format appropriate to the platform.

After you download the code, decompress it with your favorite compression tool. Alternatively, you can go to the main Wrox code download page at `www.wrox.com/dynamic/books/download.aspx` to see the code available for this book and all other Wrox books.

ERRATA

We make every effort to ensure that there are no errors in the text or in the code. However, no one is perfect, and mistakes do occur. If you find an error in one of our books, like a spelling mistake or faulty piece of code, we would be grateful for your feedback. By sending in errata, you may save another reader hours of frustration, and at the same time, you can help us provide higher quality information.

To find the errata page for this book, go to:

`www.wrox.com/go/profembeddedarmdev`

Then click the Errata link. On this page you can view all errata that has been submitted for this book and posted by Wrox editors.

If you don't spot "your" error on the Book Errata page, go to www.wrox.com/contact/techsupport.shtml and complete the form there to send us the error you have found. We'll check the information and, if appropriate, post a message to the book's errata page and fix the problem in subsequent editions of the book.

P2P.WROX.COM

For author and peer discussion, join the P2P forums at http://p2p.wrox.com. The forums are a web-based system for you to post messages relating to Wrox books and related technologies and interact with other readers and technology users. The forums offer a subscription feature to e-mail you topics of interest of your choosing when new posts are made to the forums. Wrox authors, editors, other industry experts, and your fellow readers are present on these forums.

At http://p2p.wrox.com, you will find a number of different forums that will help you, not only as you read this book, but also as you develop your own applications. To join the forums, just follow these steps:

1. Go to http://p2p.wrox.com and click the Register link.

2. Read the terms of use and click Agree.

3. Complete the required information to join, as well as any optional information you want to provide, and click Submit.

4. You will receive an e-mail with information describing how to verify your account and complete the joining process.

> **NOTE** *You can read messages in the forums without joining P2P, but to post your own messages, you must join.*

After you join, you can post new messages and respond to messages other users post. You can read messages at any time on the web. If you would like to have new messages from a particular forum e-mailed to you, click the Subscribe to this Forum icon by the forum name in the forum listing.

For more information about how to use the Wrox P2P, be sure to read the P2P FAQs for answers to questions about how the forum software works, as well as many common questions specific to P2P and Wrox books. To read the FAQs, click the FAQ link on any P2P page.

PART I
ARM Systems and Development

➤ **CHAPTER 1:** The History of ARM

➤ **CHAPTER 2:** ARM Embedded Systems

➤ **CHAPTER 3:** ARM Architecture

➤ **CHAPTER 4:** ARM Assembly Language

➤ **CHAPTER 5:** First Steps

➤ **CHAPTER 6:** Thumb Instruction Set

➤ **CHAPTER 7:** Assembly Instructions

➤ **CHAPTER 8:** NEON

➤ **CHAPTER 9:** Debugging

➤ **CHAPTER 10:** Writing Optimized C

1

The History of ARM

WHAT'S IN THIS CHAPTER?

➤ The beginnings of Acorn

➤ How Acorn became ARM

➤ ARM naming conventions

➤ ARM processor architecture

In the late 1970s, the computer industry was going through a period of huge change and substantial growth. Up until that time, computers were the size of a room and took dozens of people to operate. The ENIAC weighed 30 tons, took up a surface of 1,800 square feet (167 square meters), and required 150 kilowatts of energy. Huge technological advances were being made, and people started talking about the possibility of creating a computer that didn't weigh more than 2 tons. Then, the transistor revolution happened. Suddenly, all the power held in a room full of electronics (some would say electrics) could be put into a single microchip, just a few centimeters squared. Businesses could afford to have multiple systems; schools bought computers for research and education; and even families could finally enjoy personal computing. The 1970s saw the birth of some of the major players in computers: Apple Computer, Atari, Commodore, and Acorn, to name but a few. It would take only a few years to see some of the mythical names in personal computing: The Amiga, the Atari ST, and the Commodore 64, for example — gift-giving hasn't been the same since.

THE ORIGIN OF ARM

In late 1978, Hermann Hauser and Chris Curry founded Acorn Computers, Ltd. in Cambridge, UK. Initially working as a consultancy group, Hauser and Curry obtained a contract from Ace Coin Equipment to develop a microprocessor-based fruit machine. After an initial research and development phase, Hauser and Curry chose a MOS Technology 6502 processor for the job. The 6502 was produced in 1974 and was one of the most reliable processors available at that time, which would soon revolutionize the computer industry.

The 6502 was an 8-bit microprocessor that was by far the cheapest microprocessor at the time, while still remaining comparable to competing designs. The 6502 was easy to program, and its overall speed was good. The 6502 was also well known for its low interrupt latency, making it good at handling interrupt-driven events. The 6502 had a simplistic design; it had "only" 3,510 transistors. (Intel's 8085 had 6,500, the Zilog Z80 had 8,500, and the Motorola 6800 had 4,100.) It also had comparatively few registers, requiring frequent RAM access.

The 6502 went on to power some of the most famous names in computing history: the Apple II series, the Atari 2600, and the Commodore VIC-20, among others.

Acorn Computers won multiple contracts and continued to use the 6502 for its projects, capitalizing on its knowledge of this microprocessor.

With its experience with the 6502, Acorn went on to develop the Acorn System 1. It was designed by Sophie Wilson and was based on the 6502. It was a small system (for the time) and was launched into the semi-professional market. With a $96.43 (£65) price tag, it was accessible not only to professionals in laboratories, but also to enthusiasts. It consisted of two simple boards: the top one holding a hex keypad and a small seven-segment LED display standing on a ribbon cable, the bottom one carrying the processor and support circuitry. The simple ROM monitor enabled memory to be edited and software to be stored on cassette tapes. Most were sold as self-assembly kits. With each success, Acorn launched a new System, up to the System 5 in 1983, still featuring a 6502, but rack-mounted, including a disk controller, video card, and RAM adapters.

Acorn then released the Acorn Atom — a personal computer that still used the 6502. By now, Acorn had an excellent knowledge of the 6502, allowing it to push the processor to its limits and sometimes even beyond. Acorn's experience with the 6502 was legendary. However, the 6502 was becoming an old processor, and technological advancements meant that faster processors were available.

From here, Acorn shifted slightly; internal discussions debated on which market to pursue. Curry wanted to target the consumer market, while many other factions did not believe in the consumer market and wanted to target a more professional target, namely laboratories. Several research projects were launched, including the possibility of a 16-bit computer, but Hauser suggested a compromise, an improved 6502-based machine with more expansion capabilities: the Proton.

At the time, the British Broadcasting Corporation, the BBC, took an interest in the microcomputer market and began the BBC Computer Literacy Project. Television episodes on microelectronics and the predicted impact of computers in industry were designed to be made available to students, who had no time to design their own computer system. The BBC wanted a computer to go with their television series and started to look for candidate systems.

The BBC had a long list of subjects that it wanted to demonstrate in its series; graphics capabilities, sound and music, teletext, external I/O, and networking were all requirements. Several companies competed for the contract, and the Proton project was an ideal candidate. The only problem was the Proton didn't actually exist. It was only in the design stage; it wasn't prototyped. Acorn had little time, only 4 days, and spent those 4 days working night and day, prototyping the design, and getting the Proton ready to show to the BBC Finally, only hours before the meeting with the BBC, the Proton was ready. All the hard work done during that week paid off; not only was the Proton the only machine to meet the BBC's specifications, it also exceeded them. Acorn was awarded the contact, and the project's name was changed. The BBC Micro was born.

The BBC Micro sold so well that Acorn's profits rose from a little more than $4,800 (£3000) to more than $13.6 million (£8.5 million) in July 1983. Acorn anticipated the total sales of the BBC Micro to be approximately 12,000 units, but after 12 years, more than 1.5 million units were sold. By 1984, Acorn claimed sales of 85 percent of the computers in British schools, with deliveries of 40,000 units a month. The BBC Micro was extremely well designed for its use; a robust keyboard that could withstand anything children could throw at it (literally), a carefully designed interface, and the right machine at exactly the right time.

Why Acorn Decided to Create a New Processor

Acorn was now faced with a major problem; almost all its projects had been done on a 6502, so it knew the hardware well. When seeking a new processor to replace the aging 6502, it found that other processors just weren't up to the job. Graphics systems were emerging, and it was clear that the 6502 couldn't keep up in the graphics field. The Motorola 68000 was a 16/32-bit microprocessor that was used in many family and business computers, but slow interrupt response times meant that it couldn't keep up with a communication protocol that the 6502 had no problem running.. Numerous processors were studied and excluded. One by one, the processors on the market were studied, analyzed, and rejected. Finally, the list ran out, and Acorn was left with no choice; if it wanted to do things its way, it had to make its own processor.

Creating processors wasn't necessarily something new; it was the golden age of multipurpose CPUs, and several companies were designing CPUs, using little more than transparent film and pens, but what Acorn was about to do went well beyond simply designing a new CPU with 4000 transistors; ARM set out to create a 32-bit processor.

The project was started in October 1983, with Sophie Wilson designing the instruction set and Steve Furber doing the hardware design using BBC Micros to model and develop the chip, and on April 26, 1985, the first Acorn RISC Machine processor was born, the ARM1. It also worked perfectly the first time, which was rather exceptional for a processor that was basically designed by hand.

The primary application of the ARM1 was to be a coprocessor on BBC Micros and to help create the ARM2. Subsequent chips were sold as specialized coprocessors, or as development boards linked onto BBC Masters. It was in 1987 when the first ARM-based computer was sold, the Acorn Archimedes.

Why Acorn Became ARM

With the education market starting to fall off, Acorn's priority was to open new markets and to promote its processor design. VLSI, Acorn's partner, had been tasked with finding new applications for ARM processors, and Hauser had a separate company, Active Book, that was developing a mobile system based on an ARM2 CPU. Apple Computer's Advanced Technology Group (ATG) contacted Acorn and started to study ARM processors. Apple's ATG objective was to create an Apple II-like computer, but the project was abandoned for fear of creating too much confusion with Macintosh systems. However, the final report stated that ARM processors were extremely interesting — both their initial design and their power usage and processing power ratio.

Later, Apple Computers again studied the ARM processor. Apple had set strict requirements for its Newton project; requiring a processor that had specific power consumption, performance, and cost, but also a processor that could be completely stopped at any given moment by freezing the system clock. Acorn's design came closest to Apple's requirements but didn't quite fill them. A number of changes were required, but Acorn lacked the resources necessary to make the changes. Apple helped Acorn develop the missing requirements, and after a short collaboration, it was decided that the best move would be to create a new, separate company. In November 1990, with funding from VLSI, Acorn, and Apple, ARM was founded.

Why ARM Doesn't Actually Produce Microprocessors

ARM's original mission wasn't to create a processor but to create an architecture. The subtle difference is that the strategy was not to deliver a CPU with written specifications to a client but more to become a partner, providing a solution to clients who would build their own chips incorporating that solution.

Typical processor designers also manufacture their own processors and let others design systems using their processors and other external components. In some cases, the processor designer also includes peripherals, allowing for a more embedded approach, but it means that a choice must be made between all the processors available.

ARM has a different approach. Although ARM processors are one of the best sellers worldwide, ARM doesn't actually make its own chips; it licenses its intellectual property to other companies. Some of the major players in the field create their own ARM chips: Intel, Nvidia, STMicroelectronics, Texas Instruments and Samsung, to name but a few. This is one of the strong points for ARM; a multitude of ARM-powered processors exist, and they vary greatly in their use and operation. Small ARM-powered processors exist with limited options (few I/O ports, small memory sizes, and so on) and can be found on small systems (ARM-powered processors are common on Bluetooth adapters, for example). And complete systems exist, too, containing everything needed for a small computer. Freescale's i.MX6 processors, for example, contain a DDR controller, ATA controller, Ethernet, flash memory, USB and video controllers, all on one chip, greatly reducing the need for external components.

Another example can be found with Apple Computer, Inc. Apple had clear requirements for the processor that would power the iPhone and iPad but weren't convinced by what was available at the time. Apple knew that it needed an ARM core for the excellent power-to-energy ratio, but existing solutions either had too many peripherals or too few. Apple's sense of perfection is legendary, so it settled for a different option; it made its own core. By becoming an ARM licensee, it was given the tools necessary to make a custom core; not just by the peripherals surrounding the core, but also with custom cache sizes optimized for speed or power-saving. The result is the A4 processor and subsequent generations.

Just like with Apple, you can create your own ARM-powered chip. ARM technology can be licensed in two formats: synthesizable or hard macro. In hard macro format the cell is provided, and external components can be added around the existing cell. In synthesizable format ARM IP is delivered electronically and can be integrated into an ASIC chip using different parameters: cache size, optimizations, or debug options. There is more work to be done, but it also enables greater creativity and differentiation.

Today, the amount of chip manufacturers proposing (or using) ARM-powered systems is overwhelming. Most of the major manufacturers are ARM licensees. Samsung makes the Exynos line of CPUs, and Nvidia makes the Tegra line of chips. You can find both of these in high-end tablets, and the Exynos is even used in a Chromebook. NEC, Panasonic, NXP, Freescale, and STMicroelectronics are but a few to license ARM cores. Currently, 273 companies have licensed the ARM9 core, and more than 100 have a license to the latest Cortex-A technology.

ARM's strategy to not produce processors but to sell IP means that it can concentrate on what it does best: developing extremely power efficient performance processors. ARM spends almost all its R&D creating processor cores, and because the costs are spread across a number of licensees, ARM core licenses are cost-effective. The end result for engineers is a market full of low-power processors with excellent compatibility. Do you want a processor that can run a small Linux distribution for an embedded project? Well, the choice is yours. There are dozens of processors and System On a Chip (SoC) designs available, and the hardest part will not be to find a processor that fits your project; the hard part will be choosing which one you will go with.

ARM NAMING CONVENTIONS

ARM processors have had a relatively consistent naming convention since their start, but the naming convention can be a little confusing. You must understand the difference between a processor and an architecture.

An *architecture* is a design. It is the combination of years of research that forms a base technology. An architecture can define the programmer's model, covering all aspects of the design. The programmer's model defines registers, addressing, memory architecture, basic operation, and indeed all aspects of the processor, as well as modifications from previous architectures.

A *processor* is a device. It depends on an architecture but also adds other features that may not be common to all devices using a particular architecture. The most common example is the processor pipeline; all processors in the same architecture version can use the same instructions (because they are defined in the architecture), but the pipeline may well be different for each processor; it is not specified in the architecture reference.

An architecture has several processors, all of them using the same basic features, but each processor has a slightly different configuration. An architecture reference says whether a cache system is defined, but each processor may have different cache sizes or configurations. In all cases, the use of cache, the general layout, and anything necessary for its use are defined by the architecture. When studying a processor, it is essential to know two details: which processor family this device belongs to and which architecture the processor is based on.

How to Tell What Processor You Are Dealing With

Although processor names may vary, all ARM cores share a common naming convention, and there have been two main naming conventions during the lifetime of the architecture. Classic ARM cores have the name ARM{x}{labels}, with later variants adopting a name of the form ARM{x}{y}{z} {labels}. Since 2004, all ARM cores have been released under the Cortex brand and have names in the form Cortex-{x}{y}.

The first cores, known as classic processors, use the naming conventions listed in Table 1-1. The first number (x) corresponds to the core version. The second and third numbers (y and z) correspond to the cache/MMU/MPU information and cache size, respectively.

TABLE 1-1: ARM Processor Numbering

X	Y	Z	DESCRIPTION	EXAMPLE
7			ARM7 core version	ARM7
9			ARM9 core version	ARM9
10			ARM10 core version	ARM10
11			ARM11 core version	ARM11
	1		Cache, write buffer and MMU	ARM710
	2		Cache, write buffer and MMU, Process ID support	ARM920
	3		Physically mapped cache and MMU	ARM1136
	4		Cache, write buffer and MPU	ARM940
	5		Cache, write buffer and MPU, error correcting memory	ARM1156
	6		No cache, write buffer	ARM966
	7		AXI bus, physically mapped cache and MMU	ARM1176
		0	Standard cache size	ARM920
		2	Reduced cache	ARM1022
		6	Tightly Coupled Memory	ARM1156
		8	As for ARM966	ARM968

The letters after a processor name are called the label and indicate what optional extensions are available on the processor, as shown in Table 1-2.

TABLE 1-2: ARM Label Attributes

ATTRIBUTE	DESCRIPTION
D	Supports debugging via the JTAG interface. Automatic for ARMv5 and above.
E	Supports Enhanced DSP instructions. Automatic for ARMv6 and above.
F	Supports hardware floating point via the VFP coprocessor.
I	Supports hardware breakpoints and watchpoints. Automatic for ARMv5 and above.
J	Supports the Jazelle Java acceleration technology.
M	Supports long multiply instructions. Automatic for ARMv5 and above.
T	Supports Thumb instruction set. Automatic for ARMv5 and above.
-S	This processor uses a synthesizable hardware design.

For newer cores, known as Cortex, the naming convention is different, and easier to follow. There are three Cortex families: Cortex-A, Cortex-R, and Cortex-M.

The Cortex-A family is the computer family; the Application processors. They are designed as fully functional computers, capable of running complex operating systems directly. They are used in mobile telephones, tablets, and laptops.

The Cortex-R family is the fast reacting family, the Real-time processor series. They are often less powerful than the Cortex-A series, but are much more reactive to external stimuli. They adapt better to demanding situations, having lower interrupt latency and more deterministic real-time response, and are often used in critical systems where data interpretation is essential. They are found in medical devices, car systems, and low-level device controllers, such as hard drive controllers.

The Cortex-M family is the ultra-low-powered, small form-factor family, the Micro-controller series. It generally operates at a lower performance point than the A or R series but can run well over 100 MHz. It is usually built into microcontrollers with multiple input and output lines and is designed for small factor systems that rely on heavy digital input and output. The Cortex-M family is found in robotic systems and small consumer electronics and has even been found embedded in data transfer cables. It is often used as support processors in larger devices, for instance, it is not uncommon to find a Cortex-M processor handling power management in a larger application-class device.

Differences between ARM7TDMI and ARM926EJ-S

Traditional naming is useful to know exactly what is available on a processor core. In this case, it serves to compare an ARM7TDMI to an ARM926EJ-S. The ARM926EJ-S was one of the most-used cores, but how does it vary to an ARM7TDMI, or even an ARM1136J-S? How can you tell?

By using the previous tables, you can get a better understanding of the two processors. The ARM7TDMI is an ARM7 core, and because it does not have the {y} or {z} numbering, that means that it does not have any cache or write buffer. For example, the ARM710 core does have cache, because it has {y} numbering.

Also onboard the ARM7TDMI are four architectural options: T, D, M, and I. T indicates that this core supports the Thumb instruction set; D indicates that this core enables for enhanced debugging via a JTAG port; M indicates that this core supports long multiplication; and finally, I means that this core supports advanced breakpoints and watchpoints.

Also of interest is that the ARM7TDMI belongs to the ARMv4T architecture.

In summary, the ARM7TDMI enables easy debugging and includes some advanced features. However, it does not have any cache or buffering, which might be a problem for some applications, but not all. It also does not have an MMU. The ARM7TDMI powered most of Apple's iPod series, dozens of mobile telephones (especially from Nokia), the Game Boy Advance, most Samsung micro-SD cards, and numerous embedded projects.

The ARM926EJ-S, one of the most popular classic cores along with the ARM7TDMI, belongs to the ARM9 family. Because {y} is 2 and {z} is 6, you know that this processor includes cache and an MMU, and also includes Tightly Coupled Memory. The 926EJ-S also has two options: E meaning that this core includes enhanced DSP instructions, and J meaning that it includes Jazelle Java acceleration technology. The -S at the end of the processor name means that it is delivered as VHDL source code, which is compiled and synthesized by the licensee.

The ARM926EJ-S belongs to the ARMv5TE architecture. Because ARMv5TE includes the Thumb instruction set, this processor also includes Thumb. It is not necessary to specify the extension at the end of the processor name. Because it belongs to the ARMv5 architecture, it also automatically supports JTAG debugging, breakpoints, and long multiplication. In short, the ARM926EJ-S supports all the options that the ARM7TDMI had. The ARM926EJ-S went on to power an entire line of mobile telephones, home and business network devices, and some graphing calculators.

The ARM926EJ-S was a great choice when upgrading from ARM7TDMI systems. They were binary compatible, but the ARM926EJ-S had even better energy efficiency and much higher performance. However, some projects encountered a small problem when comparing the two processors; at equivalent clock rate with all caches disabled on the ARM926EJ-S, the ARM9 was noticeably slower than the ARM7TDMI. The ARM926EJ-S was designed with cache in mind, and it is extremely important to run the ARM926EJ-S with cache enabled, as specified in the Programmer's Model.

Differences between ARM7 and ARMv7

This is a common question — and a common mistake. There is no comparison possible; the ARM7 is a core, whereas ARMv7 is an architecture.

The ARM7 is a generation of processor designs; some of the most famous cores include the ARM7, ARM7TDMI, and ARM7EJ. The fact that the core name contains the number 7 does not mean that it belongs to the seventh architecture, far from it. Indeed, all three belong to different architectures: the ARM7 belongs to the ARMv3 architecture, the ARM7TDMI belongs to ARMv4T, and the more recent ARM7EJ belongs to ARMv5TE.

More recent cores from ARM use the Cortex naming convention and are easier to categorize.

Differences between Cortex-M and Cortex-A

Using the new naming convention from ARM, it is easier to immediately tell what a core is designed for. There are three branches in the Cortex family: the Cortex-A, the Cortex-R, and the Cortex-M. Bonus points are awarded to anyone noticing that, again, ARM managed to use the same three letters.

A Cortex-A, for Application, is probably connected to a large amount of memory and runs at a relatively high clock speed. It is designed to handle large amounts of applications, while running a complete operating system. It can be used as the primary processor on mobile devices that require fast computational power, while using little power. You can find the Cortex-A in mobile phones, tablets, digital cameras, and just about any consumer mobile device.

A Cortex-M, on the other hand, designed for the microcontroller world, has much less memory, runs at a slower clock speed but requires far less energy to run and is much smaller. It is often used to control hardware devices or to be an interface between hardware and another processor. (Most Bluetooth USB keys have a Cortex-M processor inside.)

These two cores can be used for separate functions, but often they are used together. A smaller Cortex-M could take some of the work of a larger Cortex-A by handling device connection, data output, or power supply regulation.

MANUFACTURER DOCUMENTATION

There are two things to know about the processor that you use:

➤ Processor family

➤ Architecture version

ARM provides two documents: the processor manual, called the Technical Reference Manual, and the architecture, called the Architecture Reference Manual.

The Architecture Reference Manual lists all the features common to an architecture version, including, but not limited to, assembly instructions, processor modes, memory management systems, and other subsystems. The Technical Reference Manual gives more detailed information about the options and internal information about the current CPU but does not go into architecture details.

For a system on a chip device, the manufacturer normally has extensive documentation. The SoC will be based on an ARM core and ARM architecture, so ARM's documentation will be necessary, but the manufacturer will also produce a document listing all the electrical characteristics and input/output information, together with any custom or proprietary peripherals that have been included.

WHAT IS ARM DOING TODAY?

Today, you are in the middle of a mobile revolution. You are no longer tied to cables, in some cases even for recharging mobile devices. The amount of mobile devices has exploded, and with those figures, the amount of processors. Today, with the phenomenal amount of ARM licensees, companies are building bigger and better chips. The Samsung Exynos Octa serves as an example of previously unheard of designs. On one single chip, there are two clusters of processors, a quad-core Cortex-A7 and a quad-core Cortex-A15, for a total of eight cores, and also a graphics processor, as well as numerous peripherals.

CPUs are not the only technology that ARM licenses. One of its concerns when moving away from the 6502 was the chip's inability to provide good graphics (for the time). Although some embedded systems do not have a screen, others depend heavily on one. A tablet today is only as good as the CPU inside the tablet, but also only as good as the graphics chip. Having a fast CPU isn't everything; if the web page isn't displayed fluidly, the system is considered to be useless. ARM develops and licenses Mali graphics processors, achieving more graphics power than some desktop-based graphics cards, while using ultra-low power.

ARM is also heavily focused on its new architecture: ARMv8. ARMv8 is a huge step forward because it introduces 64-bit capability to the ARM ecosystem, while maintaining 32-bit support. ARMv8 will open a new market for ARM. Although the low power Cortex-A57 processor could be integrated into a mobile telephone or a tablet, it can also be used on servers, with multiple vendors already working on solutions using ARM technology. A typical server room presents one of the biggest IT costs of any company; the amount of electricity used by servers is phenomenal. Server processors are power hungry, but they also create a lot of heat that has to be evacuated quickly; estimates say that 25 percent of the electricity used is for cooling. Because ARM processors are low-powered and run cool, they are the ideal candidate.

SUMMARY

In this chapter, I have explained the beginnings of Acorn, how the company became ARM, and what prompted ARM to create a new processor. After years of developing processors, ARM created two different naming conventions, and they have been explained, as well as the architecture system that different processors belong to. It is also important to explain the changes between the different processors, and the processor attributes.

In the next chapter, I will go deeper into what an ARM embedded system is, what makes them different from other systems, and what you will need to know before beginning a new project.

2

ARM Embedded Systems

WHAT'S IN THIS CHAPTER?

➤ Understanding the concept of an embedded system

➤ Understanding why ARM processors are used in embedded systems

➤ Choosing the right processor for the job

➤ Getting the necessary tools

➤ Knowing the different products used for embedded development

Imagine you're scheduled for a big project, one of the company's strategic sales. You've just finished a project, and you take the weekend off to relax. On your way home, you go to the store to pick up one of the latest computer games you've heard about. On the box, you see the system requirements — a guide to what is needed to play the game in optimal conditions. Looks like your home computer is up to it, so you buy the game and go home. Sure enough, the game does run, but on the box it says that the game requires 4 gigabytes of memory, but 8 is recommended. You have only 4, and you can feel that it is a little slow from time to time. Never mind, the shop is only 5 minutes away! You return and buy another 4 gigabytes of memory. When you return, you open up the computer, install the memory, and turn the computer back on. The system beeps, the screen flickers, and within a few seconds, the screen tells you that you now have 8 gigabytes of memory. The operating system fires up, and after a few seconds, you can run your game. And yes, it is much faster; you have no excuse not getting past the first level!

A lot has happened here. A few months ago, a team of developers were creating this game. Someone, somewhere, had to make a choice. Out of all the possible combinations, how did you decide what the minimum requirements should be? The company probably has statistics from previous games to know what their users use. It might have done a survey to know what most people use. It might even have boldly said, "Everyone should have x amount of memory." It has all happened before. On most systems, this isn't a problem because memory can be swapped out, and more can be added. This is also mostly true for the CPU, the graphics card, or the hard disk, some of the other things that are normally noted on a system requirement sheet. In this case, you decided to add some memory, effectively doubling what you had.

Monday morning, and with a good dose of caffeine, it is time to go to the office to learn more about this new project. It is an aeronautic project; a major company wants to outsource one of its sensors on a new drone. Your bosses believe that your team is up for the job. This is a system that will be attached to an existing drone to monitor air quality coming from different sensors and to record it. You need input from air sensors, temperature sensors, a GPS unit to record where samples came from, and possibly a few other sources that will be added during the project. (This is the sort of phrase that can send shivers down your spine.) Your company hasn't yet won the contract; this is only a research and development product. You are in competition with at least two other companies, so how do you win the contract? You will be judged on several factors:

➤ **Cost of the system** — Naturally, it wants the cheapest solution possible. Using expensive components can result in beautifully fast products, but it all comes at a price. The question here is, "What is really needed?"

➤ **Size of the finished product** — This product will go onto a drone that has only limited space.

➤ **Weight** — Again, a drone can hold only a certain amount of weight.

➤ **Power Consumption** — The less it uses, the more is available for other systems. The drone is also probably electric; although you don't know that for sure. Making a system that uses the last amount of power possible could give you the winning edge.

➤ **Speed** — You will be taking measurements, and the more measurements you can take, the better the system can perform.

With that in mind, the company has made some strategic decisions. There was probably a great deal of talk in meetings as to what was actually needed. What factor do you concentrate on? What is needed, and what factor can give you the edge, if you concentrate on it? Remember, most of the hardware will be decided at the start of the project. As a developer, you should know what to work on from the start. A few changes will probably be made (it is rare that hardware isn't changed slightly during development), but you already know what you will use.

The specifications are simple: one ARM processor, 2 MB of RAM, and 2 MB of ROM, 16 digital input lines, 8 digital output lines. You will also use an SD card for data storage, but the CPU you chose doesn't have a native SD controller; you must make your own. This isn't actually a problem. It does mean more work for the developers, but the chips that came with an SD controller were more expensive and much larger. You can use some of your digital outputs and inputs for this task.

That's it! Your team is ready to go. Now be careful how you program; the system has 2 MB of RAM and 2 MB of ROM, and that cannot change. Adding more memory would mean adding more chips, increasing size, weight, cost, and electrical use. Don't worry; on this sort of system, 2 MB is more than enough and can even enable you to put extended features in. The same goes for the amount of input and output lines that were made available. In theory you need only half, but it is a good thing that you have more available because the client asked for a new feature halfway through the project. The data was to be sent by Wi-Fi to a receiving station when the drone flew over it. One of your competitors didn't have enough input and output lines planned ahead and couldn't continue the project without changing its hardware, and preferred to cancel the project.

The ideal processor does not exist; if it did, everyone would use it. The ideal processor would have an astronomical amount of calculation power, running on battery power for months, with little or no heat being produced. Unfortunately, that will not be happening any time soon. The embedded world is all about trade-offs. By sacrificing one characteristic, you can augment another.

ARM EMBEDDED SYSTEMS DEFINED

There are various definitions of what an embedded system is. Some people talk about small factor systems; others talk about a system stripped of all the unwanted options. An intelligent water meter is an embedded system; it is lightweight and has only what is needed. It controls a larger system. More specifically, it does only one thing, and it does it well. This brings the question, "Is a mobile telephone an embedded system?" Engineers will argue over this. Some would say "yes" because the device is custom designed and made (no two mobile telephones have the same factor mainboard), and it has a specific task in mind: to place and receive telephone calls. Some would argue "no" because these devices have become so powerful, are like personal computers, and have complete operating systems, and end users can install software that places them in a new category: mobile devices.

Luckily for developers, the definition is much simpler. Unlike working on standard computer applications, the developer knows exactly what the application will run on.

An ARM-embedded system is an electronic system with an ARM-powered core, with fixed hardware specifications. The processor could be a standalone ARM-powered processor or possibly a system on chip. In both cases, the system is designed with a single task in mind, regardless of the electronic components used.

What Is a System on Chip?

Some embedded systems are as small as possible, containing only the absolutely essential components for the application. The advantage of such a system is often cost and often power conservation. For other designs, you can use a system on a chip (SoC); a single chip contains a processor and almost all the components needed for an entire system — and often much more than is required. Both are available, and both have their advantages. A few years ago, SoC systems were prohibitively expensive, but with today's market and the amount of processors made, some SoC chips can be made relatively cheaply, and in some cases, cheaper than having a simple processor and adding hardware to meet your needs. The amount of research and development needed to create a printed circuit board with all the necessary components often outweighs the advantage of having a single chip (coupled with some memory). However, SoC chips mean more transistors, so greater power requirements. They also mean little R&D cost because large semi-conductor companies invest heavily in these chips; therefore, they also invest heavily in making software. Most SoC systems have complete support for at least one full operating system, often several. Installing an operating system onto a working board can often be done in little more than minutes.

ARM's first attempt at SoC was the ARM250, based on the ARMv2a architecture. The ARM250 was used in budget versions of the Archimedes A3000 and A4000 computers. It did not have any cache, but it did contain the ARM core, a memory controller, a video controller, and an I/O controller integrated directly into one piece of silicon. The use of ARM250 meant that the mainboard was less complex, but initial supply problems meant that early machines had a mezzanine board above the CPU, essentially simulating an SoC.

Today, things are different. ARM still licenses cores, but the licensees often create amazing SoC systems, including literally everything needed for a single-board computer. Freescale's iMX 6 series processor contains a DDR controller, four USB2.0 ports, gigabit Ethernet, PCI Express, a GPU, and much more, alongside a quad-core Cortex A9, all on one single chip. The Chinese device-maker Hiapad has created the Hi-802, a tiny complete system only just larger than a USB key, connecting directly to the HDMI port of a television or monitor, which has USB to plug in a keyboard and mouse and integrates Bluetooth, an SD slot, and Wi-Fi. Of course, there are also cheaper versions; a device called the U2 has been selling for as little as $20US, containing a 1.5 GHz Cortex A8, containing again a wireless network card, HDMI interface, USB, ports, and SD-card support.

Manufacturers often have different philosophies concerning SoC chips, and care must be taken when deciding which system to use. Freescale has always been known to make energy-efficient systems, at the cost of slightly degraded processing power. Nvidia, with its Tegra series, have always made multimedia its priority. Samsung makes some of the fastest SoC chips with its Exynos series. Each product range has its advantage, and time must be taken to analyze the best choice possible.

Another term that is sometimes employed is SiP, short for System in Package. SiP often includes several chips in one; combining the processor, random access memory, and flash memory.

If your project requires specific hardware and you cannot find a suitable solution on the market, there is always another solution. FPGA SoCs are chips that have an integrated ARM core and enough logic cells to complete your design. The advantage of this sort of platform is the ability to have as much logic as possible on a single chip and entirely adapted to your solution.

What's the Difference between Embedded Systems and System Programming?

There is a big difference between the two previous systems. When creating a PC application, it is rarely known on what system it will be used. Perhaps this is a server application, and the client has given all the systems details of its servers, but nothing guarantees that this won't change in time. Perhaps it is a desktop application for cataloging a film collection. It could be installed on anything, from an entry-level netbook to a high-end system. Or perhaps it is a game, requiring a fast system, but some clients won't have the required configuration for it to run optimally. What should be considered to be the minimum?

Embedded systems are often different. They are defined beforehand and cannot be changed. Developers usually know exactly what processor will be used, the amount of memory that will be available, and all the external systems that will be connected. There will not be a memory upgrade; there will not be a processor change. Your computer system will probably change over time; a new graphics card might be added, or the processor might be upgraded. On the other hand, your mobile telephone will stay the same until the day you decide to change it. The only option you may have is to put in a bigger flash card, but that will change only the external storage amount and will not change the system itself. Your intelligent water meter will probably never change; it will have to do its job for decades.

An embedded system is designed with a particular use in mind, whereas a system is designed to be flexible and to meet a wide range of end-user needs. When designing a personal computer, it is impossible to know exactly what it will be used for, and therefore expansion possibilities must be designed. System programming is often less rigid, with fewer constraints. Embedded systems are different, since all the constraints are known right from the start.

Why Is Optimization So Important?

One of the main design criterion for an embedded system is its price. You can spend hundreds, if not thousands, of dollars for a computer system that will enable you to do everything you need today, and part of what you need tomorrow, but the tiny embedded computer inside your microwave will often be designed to be as cheap as possible, to the cent. To achieve this, studies are done to estimate the minimum amount of system resources necessary. Typically, you will not need the fastest processor, you will not need the fastest memory, and you will not need the largest amount of memory available.

During a job interview, I asked candidates some trick questions. Imagine that I wanted to design a space vehicle that could get me into orbit and land me safely again. What would you suggest? Most suggested medium- to high-end processors for their power and speed; with a decent amount of system memory. 500 MHz and 512 Mb were a common answer. Then I told them that the only computer system I had available was a 1 mega-hertz processor, with 512KB of memory. Any chance of getting into orbit? Most candidates shifted uneasily in their chairs, one or two laughed. No, it isn't possible. The system specifications are far too low. The system would be horribly slow, and there just isn't enough memory to keep all the calculations.

Ironically, the specifications that I gave are higher than the IBM AP-101, the flight computer used by the B-52 bomber and NASA's space shuttle program. When you hear the word computer today, you immediately imagine a large system, with numerous expansion cards and subsystems. On the contrary, embedded systems should be as simple as possible, including only the hardware required to complete its task, and nothing more. Having a smaller program also means there is less to go wrong. We've all had to reboot our work computer because of a problem, but with a flight control computer, this isn't an option. Put simply, it must work. To do more with less, you have to be careful and optimize.

A processor is all about crunching numbers — anything a processor does, such as reading input, decoding audio, encoding video, and copying memory. Everything is just a lot of numbers. Contrary to what you were told in school, some numbers are faster than others.

Modern CPUs can deal with a lot of different numbers. The most common is the unsigned integer. Integers can also be signed, but that changes the maximum and minimum values.

Other formats exist, like floating point numbers, but while some processors provide acceleration for floating-point numbers, some implement this entirely in software; you must either create your own libraries, or use existing libraries.

In embedded systems, it is vitally important to know exactly what type of number to use and what range you need. When dealing with a system designed to handle monetary transactions, you might be tempted to use floating-point numbers to deal with the decimal point, but this is overkill just to print $12.46. Also, surprisingly, floating-point numbers don't necessarily have the precision required for reliable monetary transactions. In this case, you might prefer to use integer numbers for their speed and precision, and instead of counting pounds/euros/dollars, you can prefer to count pennies/cents. $12.46 will become 1246, and the name of the variable should reflect that.

This happens often; some sensors will return an integer: a digital representation of the loudest sound recorded from a microphone, or a pressure sensor that will return atmospheric pressure. In both cases, these devices will return data within a certain range, using integers instead of floating-point numbers. If the device has to output a floating-point number (for example, the atmospheric pressure in millibars), the programmer will have to specifically convert the sensor output.

Also, think about the size you need. An unsigned 32-bit integer's maximum size is 4,294,967,295, but if you are making a vending machine, then $40 million is quite a lot of money for a chocolate bar and a soda. You could put the value into an unsigned 16-bit integer, with a maximum value of 65535, or maybe even an unsigned 8-bit integer uint8 for micro-transactions, with a maximum value of 255. However, this presents another problem: access. ARMs are good at reading in 32-bit values since the ALU is also 32-bits wide; reading 8-bits of data, involves masking and shifting to deal with overflow and maintain the correct sign, which can slow down the calculation. Although perfectly feasible, this comes at a small price. It is up to you what you need and what the technical constraints are.

Doing calculations on integers is extremely fast; in most cases, all operations are done in a single cycle. Integers cannot be used for everything, so for more precise mathematics, floating point numbers were also introduced.

Y2K

In the 1950s, computers were used widely for banking and statistics. Banking was simply creating a list of transactions: a date and the amount. Memory was extremely expensive at the time, and no one could have imagined a single SD card that could hold more data than any single bank possessed. It might even have contained all the data of a country and still leave some room. Terabytes wasn't even in the realm of dreams; most companies were using standard IBM punch cards, containing a staggering 80 characters. Having more memory on a card wasn't an option; the IBM punch card became an industry standard, and at the time there was no need for anything bigger. Memory itself was expensive, and one of the machines used to read them, the IBM 1401, shipped in 1959 with a standard 2 K of RAM. 16 K versions were available, and few systems were upgraded to 32 K. Those that were upgraded were done so by special request only. The low-end 1401 shipped with 1 k of memory.

To maximize memory efficiency, repetitive numbers were omitted. One of the first numbers to disappear was the "19" in every date. Instead of writing 1960, operators would just write 60. Who would have thought that by doing this, they were creating a major international problem 40 years later?

In 1958, Bob Bemer, from IBM, tried to alert some major companies about this programming error and spent 20 years attempting to change the situation. No one listened. In the 1970s, people started talking about a future problem, but we had to wait until the mid-1990s to actually hear about it. Suddenly people started realizing that in a few years' time, we would be in 2000, not in 1900. Computers, still presuming that the first two figures were 19 would switch back to 1900, or possibly 19100? A general panic ensued, with some people thinking that airplanes would fall out of the sky, that electrical generators would shut down (possibly exploding just before), and that life as we knew it would stop. In the end, nothing happened, apart from some humorous messages on the Internet, with clocks showing "Welcome! We are the 1st January, 1900." Operating systems managed to cheat a little; computer vendors sold more computers than ever before; and today, in a world in which memory costs a fraction of the cost that it used to, we calculate dates using a different system. That doesn't mean that we are safe. In 2038 we will be confronted by a different problem with more or less the same origins, but we won't make the same mistake twice. Systems and programs will be changed long before.

What Is the Advantage of a RISC Architecture?

This is one of the most common debates, and one that has forced major companies in separate directions. What should you use? Reduced Instruction Set Computing (RISC) or Complex Instruction Set Computing (CISC)?

In the 1960s, computers weren't what they are today. Academics and students rarely approached a computer; at the time it took armies of technicians to keep a computer the size of a room up and running. Academics would hand punch cards to computer operators and wait for the results, sometimes hours or days later. Punch cards could contain up to 80 characters, the equivalent of one line of code. For multiple lines of code, the academic would hand over multiple cards. The system operator would then feed these cards into the computer, wait for the result, and then return the results to the academic. The processor speed wasn't an important factor; compared to the time it took to collect the cards, feed them into the system, get the results and return them to the programmer, execution time was a mere fraction.

When punch cards were replaced with other means such as floppy disks, more memory, or more hard drives, then the computer spent more time calculating, and suddenly the easiest way to increase the speed of a computer was to increase the speed of the processor or its capacity to execute instructions. Two philosophies were competing: one was to increase the number of instructions by adding more specialized instructions, and the other was to decrease processor complexity, therefore allowing it to run faster.

A common misunderstanding of the term "reduced instruction set computer" is the mistaken idea that the processor has a smaller set of instructions. Today, some RISC processors have larger instruction sets than their CISC counterparts. The term "reduced" was intended to describe the fact that the amount of work any single instruction accomplishes is reduced (typically one data element per cycle), compared to the "complex instructions" of CISC CPUs where instructions may take dozens of data memory cycles to complete a single instruction.

RISC processors will typically have fewer transistors dedicated to core logic, allowing designers more space to increase the size of the register set, and to increase internal parallelism. In 1982, the Berkeley RISC project delivered their first RISC-I processor. At 44,420 transistors (compared to over 100,000 for CISC counterparts) and 32 instructions, it outperformed any single-chip design at the time.

The trend continued, with more and more specialized instructions being added to processors. A single instruction could now handle extremely complex calculations and also specific calculations. In the 1990s, personal computers were used for just about anything. Complete systems were sold with TV acquisition cards, complex audio creation systems, 3-D graphics, and power calculations. A specific system may have targeted either the consumer market, the business market, or the server market, but the CPU inside remained mostly the same. Processors had to adapt to just about any situation, so more and more complex instructions were added. This created a rather interesting case; some systems never used some of the instructions. Adding instructions to a processor means adding transistors, making the processor more complicated, and therefore more expensive. The original Intel 8086 processor was the beginning of the modern PC era; it was released in 1978 and contained 29,000 transistors. Just more than 10 years later, in 1989, Intel released the 80486, with a total of 1,180,000 transistors. In 2000, Intel released the Pentium 4, containing 42,000,000 transistors. In 2011, Intel's six-core Core i7 processor packed a whopping 2,270,000,000 transistors. However, these figures can be eclipsed by other systems. In 2011, AMD's Tahiti graphics processor was comp0sed of 4,300,000,000 transistors, and in the same year, Xilinx's Virtex-7 FPGA contained 6,800,000,000 transistors. Although the cost of fabricating processors has gone down drastically, the time needed to create such chips, the amount of waste created by defective silicon, and the time needed to rigorously test all the processor's functions means that prices are still high. At the same time, a single Core i7 processor today has more calculation power than most countries in the 1960s.

Enter ARM, with its Reduced Instruction Set Computing (RISC) technology and philosophy. RISC may be seen as a step backward from the days when CISC helped, but the same criteria do not exist today. In the 1960s, DEC sold 12-kilobyte memory modules for $4,600, roughly $35,000 in 2012. With that amount of money, today you could have close to 7 terabytes of memory, if you could find a system that could support that much RAM.

ARM's philosophy is radically different. ARM believes that having fewer instructions is better. Just like Lego, you can make some amazing things by using the simplest of building blocks. So, instead of highly specialized instructions, RISC systems have few instructions. Reducing the silicon on the chip means lower costs, but especially lower power consumption. So, if the constraints that were present in 1960 are no longer present, why is CISC still used? Well, one of the reasons is backward compatibility. No one expected the PC architecture to expand the way it did, and on today's high-end Core i7 CPUs, you still have a heritage from the original 8086. It would take far too much engineering to suddenly re-create all the software available for PC computers and suddenly change them to a new architecture. There are, of course, exceptions. Apple Computer Inc. had machines running under the PowerPC architecture and switched to x86. Linux has packages for just about any MMU-enabled chip. The rest of the world will stick to the x86 architecture because it has served it well. The x86 architecture doesn't face the same challenges as ARM does. For power consumption, you aren't faced with the same challenges. Today, ultrabooks can boast 8 hours of battery life, which is normally more than enough for most uses. On a 14-hour flight, you probably won't use a laptop for more than 4 hours and prefer to watch a film and try to catch up on some sleep. On that same flight, there is an Emergency Locator Transmitter (ELT). If something happens to the flight, the ELT can broadcast a distress message containing the coordinates, for several weeks, and it has to work right the first time. Power consumption is critical for this sort of application, and the code goes through rigorous testing.

Today, both RISC and CISC exist, and continue to grow. RISC dominates the embedded field (especially where power consumption is a major factor). CISC continues to dominate the desktop field. However, that trend seems to be changing. Intel is working on an x86 chip for the mobile phone sector, and several OEMs have expressed interest in an ARM-based server.

CHOOSING THE RIGHT PROCESSOR

On embedded systems, it is critically important to know what your processing needs are. On mobile systems, it is just as important but sometimes even more difficult to establish.

For embedded systems, too much processing power is often as bad as too little. If your processor isn't powerful enough, you can have a hard time getting your software to run. In the best case, you can spend a long time optimizing. In the worst case, it won't run. Using a faster processor means more power consumption, more heat, and most likely, a more expensive solution.

Choosing a processor for a mobile device is often much harder. Some users are still locked into the "gigahertz syndrome," wanting the fastest processors, but only judging them on their clock speed. Most consumers probably prefer a 1.6 GHz device over a 1.4 GHz device, even if some of them will never use a program that takes full advantage of the speed difference.

In today's world, mobile devices are more and more present. How many people can spend a day without a mobile phone, or spend a long-haul flight without a tablet? The advances in CPUs over the last 40 years have been incredible. In 1971, the Intel 4004, the world's first general-purpose microprocessor, ran at 108 kHz and was estimated at 0.06 MIPS. In 2011, Intel's i7 3960X had a total of 177,730 MIPS, almost 3 million times that of the 4004. Of course, MIPS alone cannot accurately judge a microprocessor, but it shows just how much the technology has advanced. Unfortunately, battery technology has advanced, but not in line with processors.

The first line of mobiles phones was bulky. The first use of a mobile phone was in 1973, using a prototype that weighed more than a kilogram, which had only 30 minutes of talk time, after which a recharge of 10 hours was required. Although sufficient for that time (where most "mobile" phones were in fact car phones), it didn't take long for users to need much better battery life and lighter batteries. Today, a consumer judges a mobile device by lots of criteria, including battery life. Few people want to buy a high-end tablet with a high-end CPU, lots of RAM, and a terabyte of storage if it lasts only 1 hour. CPUs, being the heart of modern systems, have also made great progress in power consumption. An Intel Pentium at 75 MHz consumes 8 Watts of power, about the same amount as an Intel Atom N550, a dual-core processor clocked at 2GHz. Of course, the Atom has far less processor power than an i7, but the processor was designed specifically for low-powered devices and has made it into an entire generation of netbooks. To achieve low power consumption, Intel invested heavily, reducing the thickness of the silicon wafers for all of its microprocessors, and also by changing the core design. An Atom is still compatible with previous x86 processors, so there is no software change needed. However, the core was heavily changed. Atom processors, like many other x86 processors, actually convert x86 instructions into micro-ops, effectively RISC-style instructions.

ARM processors, from the start, were designed to be simple. They were made to be simple, and the number of transistors in a single CPU has always been significantly lower than other comparable CPUs on the market. Fewer transistors means less power. They were also designed with mobility in mind, and that paid off because ARM6 was used on the Apple Newton Messagepad. Over the years, ARM has made improvements to maximize MIPS per watt and also to lower heat production.

There are several ways to reduce power on a system. One of the most used is frequency scaling; when a processor is not used at 100 percent, it can scale back its frequency and therefore use less energy. On the same lines, some device makers underclock their processors, setting their frequency lower to what they are supposed to run on. ARM also has a rather unique solution, using its big .LITTLE technology. This solution contains two separate processors, both binary-compatible. One core is power-efficient but slower than the second processor, which is designed to handle more complex and demanding programs at the cost of increased power usage.

WHAT SHOULD YOU START WITH?

To begin development on an ARM system, you need relatively few things, all of which are readily available.

From a hardware point of view, there are a few questions that need to be asked. Will you need specific hardware, or does a system already exist? There are several all-in-one ARM systems on the market, ranging from tiny systems running at just a few dozen megahertz to large systems that can run a full OS running at more than a gigahertz. If none of these fit your requirements, or if your production is large enough, you can create your own board with a processor or a SoC of your choice.

Evaluation boards are a great way to start a project, and there are hundreds available for just about any size or requirement. ARM provides several boards suited for several types of applications. Starter boards are a great way to get to know a system and to prototype your project. They offer great debugging features, and a huge amount of documentation is available. When you are ready, you can make your own system or look for an existing system.

ARM provides several evaluation boards. The ARM Versatile Express boards provide excellent training for the Cortex A cores or soft-core Cortex-M. The Versatile range was previously used for Classic processors — from the ARM7TDMI processor up to the ARM1176. The KEIL series are more oriented toward the micro-controller domain and also includes some classic cores.

As well as ARM-based evaluation boards, almost all chip makers have their own evaluation boards. Freescale has some excellent evaluation boards for its iMX line of SoCs, complete with just about every type of connector you can think of. Infineon has a range of clever modular systems, and Texas Instruments has some small-factor systems.

Evaluation systems are useful, but they will not be used for long. They have numerous outputs that will not be used later and tend to take up more space than is required. When you finish evaluating a board, you now need to decide if you want to create your own board, or if you will use a pre-existing system. There are multiple ARM-based systems that are not evaluation boards. Moxa creates an impressive amount of industrial systems, and one of my previous clients had a stock of Moxa 7420 systems and builds its software around those systems. The Moxa 7420 is an XScale board running at 533 MHz and has eight serial ports, two Ethernet ports, USB connectivity and CompactFlash storage, along with 128 Mb of RAM and 32 Mb of ROM. With this impressive system, the client reacted quickly to market needs by developing software and a hardware solution for industrial systems on a platform that it knew well.

As explained previously, you need to think carefully about your project and know in advance what is required. Do you need a video controller? How about a SATA controller? An industrial system might not need either but would have a more specific requirement, for example, a CAN bus.

What Boards Are Available?

Probably the most important part of a project is the board. There are several ways to go depending on your project or requirements. Evaluation boards are an excellent way to start if you decide to use one particular processor, but there are some good general purpose boards available. Following is a list of just a few boards available.

Although it is impossible to list them all, there are a number of places to look for such information. ARM has an impressive line of evaluation boards, and more information can be found on their website here:

```
http://www.arm.com/products/tools/development-boards/index.php
```

Keil, ARM's tool company, also makes numerous development boards that fit in well with its line of development tools, found here:

```
http://www.keil.com/boards/
```

Arduino Due

Arduino boards are mostly known for their 8-bit single-board computers and are an excellent way to get into the fields of electronics and embedded development. The Arduino family comes with a complete range of shields, ranging from I/O ports to SD-card storage. Arduinos have been used for a huge amount of projects, from aquarium control to robotics to automated lawnmowers.

Although an entire generation of Arduinos has been using 8-bit PIC microcontrollers, the Arduino Due uses a Cortex-M microcontroller. These boards are not designed for processing power, even if the ARM CPU is clocked at 84 MHz, but they are designed for electronic projects based on I/O. They have 54 digital I/O ports, which can each be programmed as input or output. They have 12 analog inputs and 2 analog outputs.

You can find Arduinos in a lot of projects based on robotics or sensors, simply because the processor is so heavily based on I/O. It is also hugely popular because it is based on a Cortex-M and is therefore energy-efficient. It is not uncommon to see an Arduino Due run on battery power, and it has been used on mobile robotics, or even autopilot systems for remote controlled planes.

Raspberry Pi

In 2012, the Raspberry Pi Foundation released the Raspberry Pi, a credit card-sized single-board computer designed for teaching computer science. Two versions currently exist; Model-A and Model-B, which could possibly be a cultural reference to the BBC Micro, the computer ARM originally designed for school computer science. Thirty years later, ARM-based systems were back in British schools, and indeed schools around the world, teaching children the basics of computer science.

The revolution didn't stop there. Raspberry Pis were such a success that it was difficult to get hold of them in the beginning. People were buying them as a general-purpose computer, for tinkering, for use as DIY NAS boxes, or just about anything. They have been used for home automation by using an I2C bus, for home media players using the hugely popular XBMC, or for play. Mojang ported the hugely popular game *Minecraft* to the Raspberry Pi.

Raspberry Pi is a basic computer with all the functionality required for basic systems. It has either 256 Mb or 512 Mb of RAM, one or two USB ports, video output via RCA, HDMI or DSI, audio output, 10/100 Ethernet for the Model B, and an SD slot for the filesystem. There is no on-board storage; the operating system has to be placed onto an SD card. The system is based on an ARM1176JZF-S running at 700MHz with overclocking possibilities.

Raspberry Pi lacks the I/O possibilities of Arduino, but that was never its intention. Raspberry Pi has enough hardware to boot a Linux system and teach computer science. However, that does not mean that it has no I/O; it does have two I/O ports with GPIO lines. However, of all the GPIO lines available on the processor, one-third are not connected, and some are reserved for the SD card reader and an SPI port. There are numerous projects using the IO lines, but most of these are educational boards mainly focused on turning LEDs on and off.

Beagleboard

The Beagleboard is a large system compared to the Raspberry Pi and the Arduino. It is based on a Cortex-A8 and has more system functionality than the Raspberry Pi. It has complete video out capabilities, four USB ports, Ethernet, Micro-SD, a camera port, and an expansion port. Although mainly designed for software projects, it does have some I/O capability. The Beagleboard is the computer of the ARM-based development boards. If you are looking for raw processing power above all, this is the system to use.

Beaglebone

The Beaglebone is a light version of the Beagleboard. It still has the crunching power and speed of a Beagleboard but is slightly more I/O-oriented. It has more output pins and lacks an HDMI connector.

Just like the Arduino, the Beaglebone has capes — add-on cards that extend I/O capabilities or add system functionality. There are LCD touch-screen capes, battery capes, and wireless and extended I/O capes. There are also breakout boards, which enable you to create your own circuits.

What Operating Systems Exist?

If a CPU is the heart of a hardware embedded system, an operating system is the brain. An operating system enables you to concentrate on your program by abstracting the hardware details. You can concentrate on building your application while letting the operating system handle the hardware technicalities. Memory configuration, networking, and peripheral I/O can be handled directly by the operating system. Multiple choices exist, each with their strong points.

Linux

Linux has been ported to just about any MMU-enabled processor that exists and has been used on ARM systems for decades. Linux has a huge user base, and the possibility of compiling a home-kernel is a major advantage for embedded systems. You can leave out large sections of the kernel for hardware that you do not need and leave in only the strict minimum. When adding new hardware, there are lots of resources necessary for adding drivers, and it is possible that in the open-source community someone has already developed such a driver.

VxWorks

VxWorks is a real-time operating system designed and developed by Wind River. It has a multitasking kernel and has multiprocessor support. It is used in a lot of mission-critical systems, where reliability is premium. It powers the on-board computers for the Airbus A400 and powers the radar warning system for the F/A-18 Hornet. VxWorks power numerous space projects. One of the most famous uses is in the Mars Curiosity rover, where VxWorks was considered to be the only system reliable enough to be placed onto a rover that was sent 350 million miles away, in an environment where nobody can ever perform a hardware update.

Android

Android is a Linux-based operating system, designed initially by Android Inc. and later bought by Google. Most Android development is done for a Java runtime environment, but the Android operating system is open source and freely available. However, before the JVM is launched, there are multiple applications written in C, and of course the Linux kernel, with lots of work needed on low-level systems.

iOS

Apple fans will be slightly disappointed. iOS does run on Apple-specific, ARM-powered processors with Apple extensions; however, the operating system is proprietary, meaning that you cannot have access to boot-time code. Apple iOS applications are written in Objective-C; however, you can write in assembly in iOS applications, either by writing inline code, or even by adding an assembly S file. This allows for some highly optimized applications.

Which Compiler Is Best Suited to My Purpose?

Again, several solutions exist. The GNU compiler does an excellent job and is readily available on just about every platform. ARM also has a compiler. Although not free, it has the advantage of having all ARM's knowledge in a single executable file and can heavily optimize your project.

GNU Compiler Collection

The GNU compiler is the entry level C/C++ compiler. GCC was originally a C compiler, named the GNU C Compiler and was released in 1987. Since then, it has been renamed the GNU Compiler Collection because it now supports many more languages, including different forms of C (C++, Objective-C, and Objective-C++) as well as other languages (Fortran, Ada, Go, and so on). Today, GCC has been released for Linux, Windows, MacOS, and even RiscOS. Some companies consider GCC to be essential to the success of their platform.

GCC naturally supports ARM architectures and has support for different ARM processors and architectures. Instead of compiling for generic ARM, it can be fine-tuned for different architectures, either using or omitting technology as needed. It has full support for the entire ARM Classic collection, the Cortex series, and even the more recent 64-bit Cortex-A53. If you are curious, you can write a small program and see how it would be compiled for an ARM2.

Sourcery CodeBench

Sourcery CodeBench is a complete environment with an IDE, debugger, libraries, and support. The Lite Edition, however, has only the command-line tools, namely a custom version of the GCC. Changes are first made in Sourcery CodeBench before being returned to GCC.

Sourcery CodeBench Lite is a complete toolchain, including the compiler, linker, debugger, and just about any tool required to compile C, C++, and assembly.

ARM Compiler

Nobody knows ARM processors better than ARM and it has also released the ARM Compiler, the result of more than 20 years of knowledge. This compiler is designed specifically for ARM processors and includes some of the most advanced optimization techniques available. Although this is a professional solution that requires a license, it has exceptional optimization techniques that far surpass GCC.

Getting Ready for Debugging

Debug solutions exist for ARM cores or for ARM-based chips. One of the references in the ARM world is Lauterbach, with its Trace32 solution. Different modules exist enabling assembly-level debugging and displaying internal and external peripherals, hardware breakpoints, and trace solutions. It is possible to debug with only a serial line, and in some cases that is exactly what you have to do. However, more professional solutions can leverage the work load considerably by increasing bandwidth and adding advanced trace functionality.

Lauterbach Trace32

Lauterbach produces some extremely good hardware debuggers, notably the PowerDebug and PowerTrace series. These devices can effectively debug in assembly or higher languages such as C and C++. The interface has excellent support for watching variables and displaying memory contents and traces. It has full MMU support, enabling the full display of entries and registers. All the CPU registers and attached peripherals can be controlled directly. Some of the biggest names in the embedded field use Lauterbach devices in their engineering departments.

Are There Any Complete Development Environments?

Yes, there are complete solutions that exist, including an IDE, compiler toolchain, and debug tools, all in one package.

ARM DS-5

ARM has its own complete development environment: the ARM Development Studio. At the time of writing, the current version is DS-5.

The DS-5 environment is a professional solution with the Eclipse IDE as a central point and excellent debugging tools, all coupled with the ARM compiler. When coupled with a DSTREAM hardware debugger, it becomes a capable solution with a huge trace buffer that enables long-time traces to be run, even on fast targets. If hardware is not yet available, software emulation is possible with a specialized emulator.

The ARM DS-5 solution also has an option for power monitoring with a device that can read voltage and current, and link capture data with other captures so that you can know when and why a device changes its power settings, and know what portion of code uses the most battery.

The DS-5 solution is a professional solution aimed at engineering teams that work on bleeding-edge applications that must have the upper-hand in code efficiency. Solutions of this quality are not cheap, but ARM has managed to make the price extremely reasonable, and everything you need is contained in a single package.

You can find more information at `http://www.arm.com/products/tools/software-tools/ds-5/index.php`.

ARM DS-5 Community Edition

Compared to the professional DS-5 solution, this version is also managed by ARM but has some limitations and does not come with the ARM compiler. It does, however, come with function profiling, process tracing, and a limited set of performance counters. Debugging is done with software because there is no hardware debugger included, but GDB is a powerful tool, and the DS-5 CE completes that beautifully.

DS-5 CE is maintained by ARM and has the same quality as the professional build, but with open source tools and limited functionality. It is a great platform to begin working on to get used to the DS-5 environment The ARM forums are the place to look for information and to ask questions.

Is There Anything Else I Need to Know?

Some systems, such as the Raspberry Pi, come with everything needed to get a working ARM system up and running in seconds. Other systems, such as evaluation boards, may require more specialized electronics but are normally acquired by laboratories containing specialized equipment.

There are two devices that are more or less considered to be essential: a serial port and a digital voltmeter.

Modern systems can communicate either by Ethernet or USB, but embedded systems almost always have a serial port. Using a serial port is much easier than using any other device such as I2C or CAN. With a serial device, you put bytes into a specific register, and that is just about it. For this reason, and because there is little software needed to make it function, almost all embedded devices have a serial terminal.

A digital voltmeter is often useful for verification reasons to verify if an output is set to the right level or if an input is set to logic level 1. It is useful for debugging but not for analysis; other devices exist for that.

Depending on your budget, an oscilloscope can be extremely valuable to a project. Looking at a signal and not just reading the output from a voltmeter enables some advanced debugging. A power supply can also be useful, but because most modern boards use a USB power supply, it is only useful when adding electronics on a breadboard or for homemade designs.

SUMMARY

In this chapter, I have presented embedded systems and shown how ARM processors can be suited for a wide range of projects, from the smallest project to the most powerful project. In an example project, I demonstrated how important it is to plan ahead and to select the right processor. I presented some of the tools required for an embedded project, such as the operating system, compiler, and debugger, and also showed just some of the ARM-powered boards that are available on the market.

In the next chapter, I will talk more about an ARM processor — the internal systems that must be understood, the different operation modes, memory management, and the start-up sequence of an ARM processor.

3

ARM Architecture

WHAT'S IN THIS CHAPTER?

➤ Understanding the basic terms

➤ Understanding a processor

➤ ARM processor internals

➤ Understanding program flow and interruption

➤ The different technologies

It doesn't matter if you are talking about an ARM processor, a 68k or even an x86 processor; they all have some common subsystems. There are slight differences in the way some subsystems are accessed, or the amount of subsystems present, but all processors retain the same basic principle, no matter what architecture. Following is a brief explanation of the core technology found in all modern processors, before going deeper into the specific details that make ARM processors what they are.

UNDERSTANDING THE BASICS

Everything in a computer is a number — text, images, sounds — everything is written down as a collection of numbers. A computer's job is to take some data and run operations on it; put simply, take some numbers, and do some mathematical computations.

The Colossus was the first programmable digital electronic computer, used in Britain during World War II to help in the cryptanalysis of the Lorenz cipher code, a cryptocode used by the German High Command to communicate with its armies. Colossus didn't actually completely decrypt messages; it was used to break Lorenz key settings using specialized code. Colossus could outperform humans both in terms of speed and reliability, and by the end of the war ten Colossus computers were in service.

While the Colossus was programmable, it was not a general purpose computer. It was designed with a specific task in mind and could not be programmed for another task, only programmed for different calculations on the same cipher. Programming was accomplished by setting up plugs and switches before reading in a cipher.

In America, the ENIAC was announced in 1946 and was used mainly to calculate ballistic trajectory, but was also used as a calculator for the hydrogen bomb project. What made it unique was its capacity of branching, or executing computer code depending on a previous result. Instead of a calculator simply adding numbers together, a computer could conditionally execute; take this number and multiply it by 2. Is the result less than 0? If it isn't, then subtract 20; otherwise, add 10. For ballistics, a computer could be told to continue calculating the speed, distance, and height of the projectile and to continue as long as the height is above sea level.

To function, a computer needs several things:

➤ A processor, on which all the work will be done

➤ Memory, to store information

➤ Input and output, to get information and to return it to the user (or activate outputs depending on certain conditions)

The processor is the ARM core. It might be an ARM Classic processor, such as an ARM11, or a Cortex, for example a Cortex-A8.

The memory might be more complicated. There are often several types of memory on an embedded system. There might be large amounts of DDR storage available, but DDR requires an initialization sequence, and therefore, memory. ARM systems often come with a small amount of internal memory (enough to start the system and to initialize any external systems) such as DDR memory, or possibly flash memory to read the operating system from.

Input and output can be almost anything and are either directly on the processor or SoC, or specific components mapped to external addresses.

Register

A CPU register is a small amount of fast memory that is built directly into the CPU and is used to manipulate data. ARM CPUs are load/store architecture, meaning that all calculation done on a CPU is done directly onto registers. First, the CPU reads from main memory into a register before making calculations, and possibly writing the value out into main memory. No instructions operate directly onto values in main memory. This might sound inefficient, but in practice it isn't; it saves having to write to main memory after each operation. It also significantly simplifies the pipeline architecture, something that is crucial for RISC processors.

At first glance, it might be surprising that there are so few registers on a system, but with a bit of careful work, most routines can be created using few registers. ARM processors actually have more registers than some.

Stack

The *stack* is a memory location in which temporary data is put and retrieved when needed. It is a LIFO: Last In, First Out. Some card games use a stack; a place in which cards can be put and retrieved but only in a specific order; the last card placed is the first one out. To get to a specific card, you must first remove all the other cards above it. The stack works in the same way.

The stack is primarily used when executing subroutines. When entering a subroutine, care must be taken to ensure that some registers retain their initial value, and to do that, their contents are placed onto the stack. So long as care is taken to take back the same amount of elements as was put into the stack, then the same values will always be read back.

The stack can fill up quickly, depending on the situation. During complicated calculations, variables must be pushed onto the stack to make room for new data. When calling a subroutine with complex arguments, they are often pushed onto the stack, and in the case of an object, the entire object is pushed onto the stack. This can result in huge increases in the stack size, so care must be taken to ensure that the stack does not overflow.

Internal RAM

Not all processors have internal RAM, but most do. It is often small compared to system memory, but it serves its purpose. On a typical system, there might be as much as 512 megabytes of external DDR memory, but DDR memory takes time to initialize. You need to do lots of steps to get DDR memory up and running, and in the meantime you cannot do your job with registers alone. Therefore, most ARM processors have a minimal amount of internal RAM, where you can transfer a program and run it, therefore setting up critical systems before switching to DDR memory. Internal RAM is also usually much faster than external RAM.

Cache

Early CPUs read instructions directly from the system memory, but when considering the time it takes to read data from the system memory compared to a processor cycle time, it was clear that a large portion of the CPUs' time was spent waiting for data to arrive. Writing data to the system memory was often even worse. Something had to be done, and so cache memory was developed.

CPU technology advancements mean that the speed of CPUs has grown many times in comparison to the access speed of main memory. If every instruction on a CPU required a memory access, the maximum speed of a CPU would be the maximum speed of the system memory. This problem is known as the *memory bottleneck*.

Cache memory is made from a special sort of memory, SRAM. SRAM, or Static RAM, has a speed advantage over DRAM, or Dynamic RAM. Unlike DRAM, SRAM does not need to be refreshed and can hold data indefinitely provided that it remains powered. SRAM provides high speed, but the cost is prohibitively high, so only a small amount of SRAM is available; main system memory is rarely SRAM.

Cache memory is used to store information recently accessed by a processor. Several layers of cache may be implemented: Cache (Level 1) is the closest to the CPU and the fastest. It is often relatively small, varying between 4 KB and 64 KB in size. L2 cache (Level 2) is often slightly slower than L1 but also much larger. L2 cache can be in the range of 128 KB all the way to 4 MB or more.

There are two distinct cache architectures: Von Neumann (or unified) and Harvard. *Unified cache* is a single memory cache used for all memory zones. *Harvard cache* separates instruction cache and data cache. The separate caches are often referred to as D-cache (data cache) and I-cache (instruction cache). Harvard architectures have physically separate signals for storage for code and data memory, and Von Neumann architectures have shared signals and memory for code and data.

On boot, caches are disabled but not necessarily invalidated; they must be specifically set up and configured to function.

Read Cache Strategy

Cache memory is designed to avoid lengthy reads and writes, by reading in sections of memory into cache upon first use in the hope that future reads can then read from cache. If the processor requests some data, it first checks the cache. If it finds the data available, it is called a *cache hit*, and the data will be available immediately without having to read data from external RAM. If the data is not available, it is a *cache miss*, and the relevant data must be read from the system memory into the cache. Instead of reading in a single value, a cache line is read in.

Although this can be useful for some portions of the system memory, there are locations in which you do not want cache to operate at all. Caching the serial port could be disastrous; instead of reading from the serial register, you would constantly be reading the cache and presuming that no data is available. That is where memory management comes in — you can program specific memory zones to be cacheable or non-cacheable.

Memory management is done by the Memory Management Unit (MMU) or, for some systems, the Memory Protection Unit (MPU). For some Cortex-M systems, neither MMU nor MPU is available, and the cacheable attributes or memory regions are part of the fixed architectural map.

Of course, using this strategy, you are soon presented with a problem. When a cache-miss is encountered and the cache is full, what happens? In this case, one of the cache entries has to be evicted, leaving place for a new entry. But which one? This is one of the subjects on optimization; the trick is to know which cache entries will be used in the future. Because it is extremely difficult to know what will be used and what won't, one of the cache eviction strategies is LRU, or Least-Recently Used. By using this technique, the most recently accessed cache will remain, and older entries will be deleted. Careful planning can help optimize systems by defining which sections of memory are cacheable and which ones aren't.

Write Cache Strategy

Write-cache strategy is comparable to read-cache strategy, but there is a difference. Writing to cache can effectively speed up operation, but sooner or later the external memory needs to be updated, and you must first think about how to do that. There are two possible policies: write-through and write-back.

When writing data with the write-through policy, data is written to the cache, and at the same time written to system memory. Subsequent reads will read from the cache. Write-back cache is slightly different from write-through. Initially, writing is done only to the cache; writing to external memory is postponed until the cache blocks are to be replaced or updated with new content. Cache lines that have been modified are marked as *dirty*. Write-back does have speed advantages but is more complex to implement and also has a drawback. A read miss in a write-back cache (requiring a block to be replaced by a data read) often requires two memory accesses: one to write the dirty cache line to system data and one to read system data into a new cache line.

GETTING TO KNOW THE DIFFERENT ARM SUBSYSTEMS

After having shown the basics, I will now show some of the subsystems on ARM processors. They are the components that make up an ARM processor, and are essential components to an ARM core.

Presenting the Processor Registers

An ARM core can be thought of as having 16 32-bit general registers; named r0 to r15. In reality, however, there are several more because some registers are mode-specific. They are known as *banked registers*. Registers r0 to r7 are the same across all CPU modes; they are never banked. Registers r8 to r12 are the same across all CPU modes, except for FIQ. r13, r14, and r15 are unique to each mode and do not need to be saved.

As you can see in Figure 3-1, when switching from User Mode to Fast Interrupt Mode, you still have the same registers r0 to r7. That means that the values that were in r0 to r7 are still there, and when returning from Fast Interrupt, you return to where you were before the interrupt, and that portion of code expects to find the same values. However, r8 to r14 are "banked," meaning that these registers are used only inside your current mode of operation. The original r8 to r14 are still there and will be visible after you exit the fast interrupt. The advantage of this is speed; on returning, the registers must be set to their original values.

In normal programming, the user can freely access and write registers r0 to r12. r13, r14, and r15 are reserved for special purposes. The ARM coding conventions (the AAPCS, Procedure Call Standard for the ARM Architecture) state that when calling a subroutine, the arguments are passed in the first four registers (r0 to r3), and return values are also passed in r0 to r3. A subroutine must preserve the contents of the registers r4-r11. It is up to the subroutine to see if it necessary to push registers to the stack, or if it is possible to make required calculations on the first four registers. Whatever the decision, on returning, the caller function must have the result in r1, and the contents of r4 to r12 must be preserved.

r0 to r3

Normally, the first four registers, r0 to r3, are used to pass arguments to a function. After these four registers have been used, any further arguments must be placed onto the stack. This can be configured with a compiler option. r0 is also used as the return value of a function. If the return value is more than 32-bits wide, r1 is also used. A program must assume that any function call will corrupt r0 to r3.

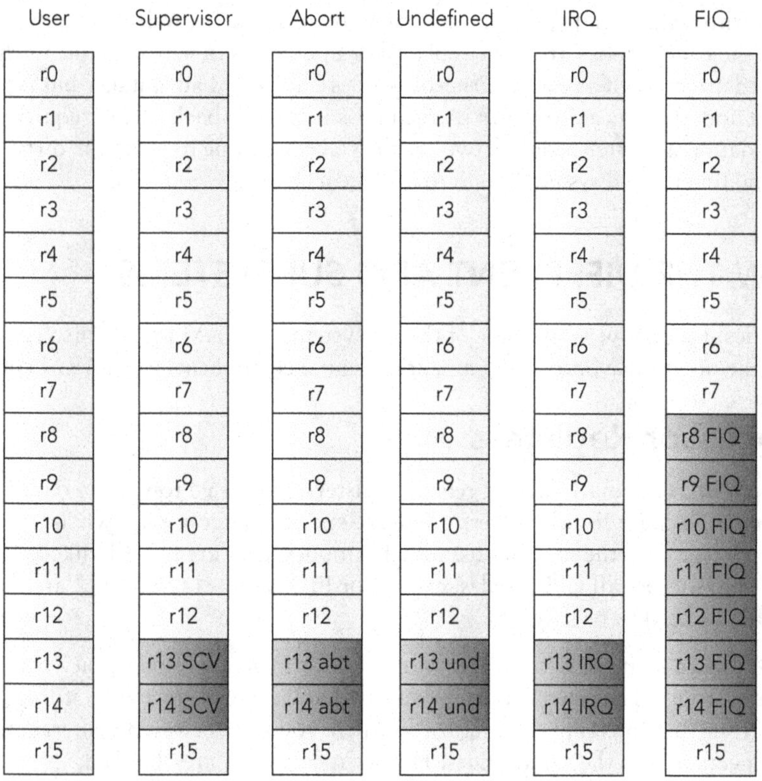

User	Supervisor	Abort	Undefined	IRQ	FIQ
r0	r0	r0	r0	r0	r0
r1	r1	r1	r1	r1	r1
r2	r2	r2	r2	r2	r2
r3	r3	r3	r3	r3	r3
r4	r4	r4	r4	r4	r4
r5	r5	r5	r5	r5	r5
r6	r6	r6	r6	r6	r6
r7	r7	r7	r7	r7	r7
r8	r8	r8	r8	r8	r8 FIQ
r9	r9	r9	r9	r9	r9 FIQ
r10	r10	r10	r10	r10	r10 FIQ
r11	r11	r11	r11	r11	r11 FIQ
r12	r12	r12	r12	r12	r12 FIQ
r13	r13 SCV	r13 abt	r13 und	r13 IRQ	r13 FIQ
r14	r14 SCV	r14 abt	r14 und	r14 IRQ	r14 FIQ
r15	r15	r15	r15	r15	r15

FIGURE 3-1: ARM Registers in different modes

r4 to r11

r4 to r11 are general purpose registers and can be used for any calculation, but they must be preserved by a function if their values are changed.

r12

r12 is sometimes known as the IP register and can be used as an interprocess scratch register. The exact use depends heavily on the system being used, and in some cases, it is used as a general purpose register. If you use an operating system, refer to the operating system guide as to the usage of r12. If you are creating a bare metal system, you can use r12 as you see fit.

The AAPCS states that r12 may be corrupted by any function call, so programs must assume that it will not be preserved across a call.

r13: The Stack Pointer

The stack pointer is an important register. r13 has a special function; it is the stack pointer. Just like the other registers, it is possible to read and write to this register, but most dedicated instructions will change the stack pointer as required. It is necessary to set up this register by writing the correct address, but after that, it is no longer necessary to directly change this register. Thumb even forbids changing the stack pointer, with the exception of add and subtract.

When entering a function, r4 to r11 need to be returned to their initial values before leaving. To do that, use the PUSH and POP instructions, both of which modify the SP as required. Of course, it is not efficient to automatically PUSH and POP all the registers; therefore, the compiler will look and see what is to be done and will operate only on the registers that need to be saved, for example:

```
subroutine   PUSH {r0-r3,r12,lr} ; Push working registers and the link register
             BL my_function
             ; my_function will return here
             POP {r0-r3,r12,pc} ; Pop working registers, r12 and the PC
```

r14: The Link Register

r14 holds the value of the Link Register, the memory address of an instruction to be run when a subroutine has been completed. Effectively, it contains the memory address to return to after you finish your task. When the processor encounters a branch with link instruction, a BL, r14 is loaded with the address of the next instruction. When the routine finishes, executing BX returns to where the program was.

Here is an example:

```
AREA      subrout, CODE, READONLY    ; Name this block of code
ENTRY                   ; Mark first instruction to execute
start     MOV     r0, #10            ; Set up parameters
          MOV     r1, #3
          BL      doadd              ; Call subroutine

[ ... ]

doadd     ADD r0, r0, r1 ; Subroutine code
          BX lr; Return from subroutine

          END ; Mark end of file
```

r15: The Program Counter

r15 holds the value of the Program Counter, the memory address of the next instruction to be fetched from memory. It is a read/write register; it can be written to, as is sometimes the case when returning from a branch instruction, modifying the address of the next instruction to be executed.

There is, however, a trick. Although technically the PC holds the address of the next instruction to be loaded, in reality it holds the location of the next instruction to be loaded into the pipeline, which is the address of the currently executing instruction plus two instructions. In ARM state, this is 8 bytes ahead, and in Thumb state it is 4 bytes. Most debuggers will hide this from you and show you the PC value as the address of the currently executing instruction, but some don't. If, during your debugging session, the PC points to something that doesn't seem related, check the documentation to see what the PC is supposed to show.

Presenting the CPSR

The CPSR is technically a register but not like the registers r0 to r15. The CPSR, short for Current Program Status Register, is a critical register that holds the status of the running program and is updated continuously. It contains condition code flags, which may be updated when an ALU operation occurs. Compare instructions automatically update the CPSR. Most other instructions do not automatically update the CPSR but can be forced to by adding the s directive after the instruction.

The ARM core uses the CPSR to monitor and control internal operations. The CPSR holds the following, among others:

➤ Current processor mode

➤ Interrupt disable flags

➤ Current processor state (ARM, Thumb, Jazelle, and so on)

➤ Data memory endianness (for ARMv6 and later)

➤ Condition flags

CPSR specifications may vary slightly from one architecture to another as ARM implements new features.

If the CPSR is the Current PSR, the SPSR is the Saved PSR. When an ARM processor responds to an event that generates an exception, the CPSR is saved into the SPSR. Each mode can have its own CPSR, and when the exception has been handled, the SPSR is restored into the CPSR, and program execution can continue. This also has the advantage of returning the processor to its exact previous state.

Understanding Condition Flags

The ALU is connected directly to the CPSR and can update the CPSR registers directly depending on the result of a calculation (or comparison).

N – Negative

This bit is set if the result of a data processing instruction was negative.

Z – Zero

This bit is set if the result was zero.

C – Carry

This bit is set if the result of an operation was greater than 32 bits.

V – Overflow

This bit is set if the result of an operation was greater than 31 bits, indicating possible corruption of the signed bit in signed numbers.

In 2's complement notation, the largest signed 32-bit number a register can hold is 0x7fffffff, so if you add 0x7fffffff and 0x7fffffff, you can generate an overflow because the result is larger than a signed 32-bit number, but the Carry (C) is not set because you do not overflow an unsigned 32-bit number.

Interrupt Masks

Interrupt masks are used to stop (or allow) specific interrupt requests from interrupting the processor. It is often useful to disable interrupts for specific tasks before re-enabling them. When servicing an IRQ, further IRQs are disabled and FIQs are not modified. When servicing a fast interrupt, FIQs and IRQs are disabled; that way, critical code cannot be interrupted. When the interrupt operation is over, the SPSR is restored and the processor is returned to its previous state (with the previous settings for interrupts).

On some cores, there is a special interrupt that cannot be disabled — NMI, or Non-maskable Interrupt.

Calculation Unit

The calculation unit, as shown in Figure 3-2, is the heart of an ARM processor.

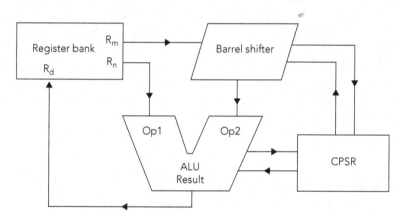

FIGURE 3-2: ARM Calculation Unit

The Arithmetic Logic Unit (ALU) has two 32-bit inputs. The first comes directly from the register bank, and the second one comes from the shifter. The ALU is connected to the CPSR and can shape the calculation output depending on the CPSR contents and also update CPSR contents according to the results of a calculation. For example, if a mathematical operation overflows, the ALU can update the CPSR directly.

You must understand that ARM cores in ARM mode do not actually need shift instructions, contrary to many other processors. Instead, the barrel shifter can perform a shift during an instruction by specifying a shift on the second operator directly inside an instruction. In Thumb mode, the instructions are simplified and shift instructions do exist.

Pipeline

The pipeline is a technique used in the design of ARM processors (and others) to increase instruction throughput. Instead of having to fetch an instruction, decode the instruction, and then execute it, you can do all three at the same time but not on the same instruction.

Imagine a factory. Imagine a worker inside the factory making a family computer. He first gets the mainboard and puts it inside the chassis. Then he takes the processor and puts it on the mainboard. Then he installs the RAM, and finally, he installs the graphics card. One worker has made the entire computer; one person is responsible for the entire chain. That isn't how they are made, though; computer manufacturers rely on assembly lines. One person will put the mainboard inside the chassis, and instead of continuing to the next task, he will repeat the process. The next worker on the assembly line will take the work of the first person and install the processor onto the mainboard, and again, the next task will be performed by someone else. The advantage is that each task is simplified, and the process can be greatly accelerated. Since each task is simple it can be easily duplicated, making several lines, parallelizing fabrication, and doubling the output.

Although making a desktop PC might seem relatively simple, imagine the complexity of a laptop computer, a flat-screen TV, or a car. Each task, although simple compared to the entire product, is still complex.

A CPU pipeline works in the same way. For example, one part of the processor constantly fetches the next instruction, another part "decodes" the instruction that has been fetched, and finally, another part executes that instruction. CPUs are driven by a clock; by doing more things on each clock pulse, you can increase the throughput of the CPU, and since each operation is made simpler, it becomes easier to increase the clock speed, further increasing throughput.

The advantage is, or course, speed. However, there are disadvantages of a pipelined system, notably stalls. A stall occurs when a pipeline cannot continue doing work as normal. For example, Figure 3-3 shows a typical six-stage pipeline.

Fetch	Issue	Decode	Execute	Memory	Write
Branch predict Fetch	Decode Co-pro	Register read Decode	Shift Multiply	Memory	Reg write

FIGURE 3-3: ARM six stage pipeline

Stage 3 accesses any operands that may be required from the register bank. After the calculation is done, in stage 6, you can write the results back into the register bank. Now suppose you have this:

```
MOV r5, #20
MOV r8, [r9]
ADD r0, r1, r2
SUB r0, r0, r3
MOV r4, r6
MVN r7, r10
```

Each instruction is run sequentially. The first Move instruction moves the value 20 into r5. The second Move instruction requires a fetch from memory, and assuming that this data is not located in cache, it can take some time. However, the data will be written into r8, and the instructions behind it do not require r8, so they would be stalled, waiting for an instruction to finish without even requiring the result.

There are different techniques to avoid stalls. One of the main reasons for stalls are branches. When a branch occurs, the pipeline needs to be filled with new instructions, which are probably in a different memory location. Therefore, the processor needs to fetch a new memory location, place the first instruction at the beginning of the pipeline, and then begin working on the instruction. In the meantime, the "execution" phase has to wait for instructions to arrive. To avoid this, some ARM processors have branch prediction hardware, effectively "guessing" the outcome of a conditional jump. The branch predictor then fills in the pipeline with the predicted outcome. If it is correct, a stall is avoided because instructions are already present in the pipeline. Some branch predictors have been reported to be 95 percent correct. More recent branch predictors even manage a 100 percent mark by speculatively fetching both possible execution paths, and discarding one of them once the outcome of the branch is known.

There are several cases where the order of instructions can cause stalls. In the previous example, the result of a memory fetch wasn't required, but what would happen if the instruction immediately afterwards required that result? Pipeline optimization would not be able to counter the stall, and the pipeline might stall for a significant amount of time. The answer to this is "instruction scheduling," which rearranges the order of instructions to avoid stalls. If a memory fetch might stall a pipeline, a compiler may place the instruction earlier, thus giving the pipeline a little more time.

Another technique used on some processors is known as out-of-order execution. Instead of the compiler rearranging instructions, the ARM core can sometimes rearrange instructions itself.

Tightly Coupled Memory

Cache can greatly increase speed, but it also adds problems. Sometimes, you need data to be stored in memory that isn't cacheable to be certain of the contents. Sometimes, you also want data to be "always available" and to have the speed of something in cache but without using up all the system cache. When reading data, if you have a cache hit, the data is immediately available, but if you have a cache miss, that data must be read from the system memory, often slowing down the system, in some cases considerably. You want critical interrupt handler code to be "always available," interrupt stacks, or mathematical data if the calculations require vast amounts of raw data.

Tightly Coupled Memory (TCM) is available on some processors. When available, TCM exists in parallel to the L1 caches and is extremely fast (typically one or two cycles' access time). The TCM is consequently not cacheable, leaving the cache free for other instructions and data.

TCM is like internal RAM, only configurable. By setting registers in the CP15, you can select separate instruction-side and data-side memory, either instruction or data-side memory, or complete deactivation of the TCM. It can be placed anywhere in the address map, as long as it is suitably aligned.

Coprocessors

ARM processors have an elegant way to extend their instruction set. ARM processors have support for coprocessors; secondary units that can handle instructions while the processor continues doing work.

The coprocessor space is divided into 16 coprocessors, numbered 0 to 15. Coprocessor 15 (CP15) is reserved for control functions, used mainly for managing caches and configuring the MMU. CP14 is reserved for debug, and CP 10 and 11 are reserved for NEON and VFP.

For classic processors, when a processor encounters an unknown instruction, it offers that instruction to any coprocessor present. Each coprocessor decodes the instruction to see if it can handle the instruction and signals back to the processor. If a coprocessor accepts the instruction, it takes the instruction and executes it using its own registers. If no coprocessor can handle the instruction, the processor initiates an undefined instruction exception. This is an elegant solution because some software enables "soft" coprocessors. If a coprocessor is not present, the instruction is caught during an exception and executed in software. Although the result is naturally slower than if the coprocessor was present, it does mean that the same code can be run, regardless of the availability of a specific coprocessor.

This system no longer exists; Cortex processors do not have a coprocessor interface, and instead, the instructions have been implemented into the core pipeline. Coprocessor instructions still exist and documents will still talk about the CP15 or other coprocessors; however, in order to simplify the core, the older coprocessor structure has been removed, but the instructions became valid ARM instructions. The coprocessor interface bus has 224 signals in it, so simplifying the coprocessor design was an important step to making processors simpler and faster.

CP15: The System Coprocessor

CP15 is a coprocessor interface developed by ARM and present on almost all processors except for the Cortex-M range.

The CP15's role is to handle system configuration: data cache, tightly coupled memory, MMU/MPU, and system performance monitoring. They are configured using the MRC/MCR instructions and can be accessed only in privileged modes. The registers are processor-specific; refer to your manual for more detailed information.

CP14: The Debug Coprocessor

The CP14 provides status information about the state of the debug system, configuration of certain aspects of the debug system, vector catching, and breakpoint and watchpoint configuration.

UNDERSTANDING THE DIFFERENT CONCEPTS

Before using an ARM processor, you need to know a few concepts. These concepts are the basis of ARM systems; some are related to the embedded systems world; others are purely ARM.

What Is an Exception?

Microprocessors can respond to an asynchronous event with a context switch. Typically, an external hardware device activates a specific input line. A serial driver might create an interrupt to tell the CPU that data is ready to be read in, or maybe a timer that sends signals periodically. It is the hardware's way of saying, "I have something I need done." This makes the processor do something that is called a *context switch*; the processor stops what it was doing and responds to the interrupt. Imagine working at your desk, when the phone rings. This forces you into a context switch. You make a mental note of what you were doing, you acknowledge that the phone is ringing, and now you are free to choose what to do next. You could answer it, and what you were doing before has to wait. You could send the call to someone else or even ignore the call. Whatever you choose, you return to your previous task where you left off. For a processor, it is the same thing. When an interrupt arrives, you initiate a context switch. Registers can change, the current status is updated, and the current memory address is saved so that you can return later.

During its life cycle, a processor runs a program. Anything that disturbs that operation is called an *exception*. A software or hardware interrupt, a data abort, and an illegal instruction change the normal execution of a processor and are all exceptions. Even a reset is called an exception. When an exception occurs, the PC is placed onto the vector table at the corresponding entry, ready to execute a series of instructions before returning to what the processor was doing before (except for the reset exception). Several exceptions are available with different priorities.

Reset

A Reset exception has the highest priority because this is an external action that will put the processor in Reset state. When a CPU is powered on, it is considered to be in a Reset state. From here, you probably need to initialize all the hardware. When starting in Reset state, the core is in Supervisor mode, with all interrupts disabled.

Data Abort

A Data Abort happens when a data memory read or write fails. This can be for several reasons, but mostly it occurs when reading from or writing to an invalid address. When a Data Abort happens, the CPU is put into Abort mode, IRQ is disabled, FIQ remains unchanged, and r14 contains the address of the aborted instruction, plus 8.

IRQ Interrupt

An IRQ interrupt occurs when an external peripheral sets the IRQ pin. It is used for peripherals to indicate that they are awaiting service and need the CPU to do something. Some examples are an input device indicating that the user has entered data, a network controller indicating that data has arrived, or possibly a communication device indicating that it is awaiting data. Frequently, IRQs are also used by a timer, periodically sending an interrupt every few milliseconds, or microseconds. This is known as a *tick*.

FIQ Interrupt

An FIQ is a special type of interrupt designed to be extremely fast. It is mainly for real-time routines that need to be handled quickly. It has a higher priority than an IRQ. When entering FIQ mode, the processor disables IRQ and FIQ, effectively making the code uninterruptable (except by a data abort or reset event) until you manually reactivate the interrupts. These are designed to be fast, very fast, meaning that they are normally coded directly in assembly language. Also, FIQ is located at the end of the vector table, so it is possible (and common) to start the routine right there, instead of branching, saving a few instructions.

Prefetch Abort

The Prefetch Abort exception occurs when the processor attempts to execute code at an invalid memory address. This could happen for several reasons: The memory location might be protected and memory management has specifically denied access to this memory, or maybe the memory itself is not mapped (if no peripherals are available at that address).

SVC

A Supervisor Call (SVC) is a special software instruction that generates an exception. It is often used by programs running inside an operating system when requesting access to protected data. A non-privileged application can request a privileged operation or access to specific system resources. An SVC has a number embedded inside, and an SVC handler can get the number through one of two methods, depending on the core. Most processors embed the SVC number inside the instruction, and some Cortex-M processors will push the SVC number to the stack.

Undefined Instruction

An Undefined Instruction occurs when the ARM core reads an instruction from memory, and the recovered data does not correspond to an instruction that the ARM core can execute. Either the memory read does not contain instructions, or it is indeed an instruction that the ARM core cannot handle. Some Classic processors used this technique for floating point instructions; if the processor could execute the instruction, it would use hardware-accelerated routines, but if the processor did not support hardware floating point, an exception would occur and the processor would use software floating-point.

Handling Different Exceptions

Exceptions exist not only to warn the processor, but also to perform different actions. When handling an interrupt exception, you need to do some work before returning to the main application, but when handling a Data abort, you might think that all is lost. This isn't always the case, and the exception actually exists to avoid everything grinding to a halt. Every Linux developer has, sooner or later, been confronted with the dreaded Segmentation Fault. A *segfault* is, generally, an attempt to access a memory address that the program does not have the right to access, or memory that the CPU cannot physically access. The exception is "trapped"; the operating system takes control and stabilizes the system. This sometimes means that the offending program is terminated, but more often it is just the program's way of telling the operating system that it requires more resources. An application may overflow its stack, in which case the operating system can choose to allocate it some more, or if an application runs off the end of the current code page, the operating system will load and map the next page.

When the operating system finishes handling the exception, it returns control to the application, and the system keeps going.

When an exception occurs, the core copies the CPSR into SPSR_<mode> and then sets the appropriate CPSR bits. It then disables interrupt flags if this is appropriate, stores the "return address" into LR_<mode>, and then sets the PC to the vector address. Note that if the CPU is in Thumb state, it may be returned to ARM state. Most Classic processors could only handle exceptions in ARM state, but the ARM1156 and all Cortex processors can be configured to handle exceptions in ARM or in Thumb state.

To return from an exception, the exception handler must first restore the CPSR from SPSR_<mode> and then restore the PC from LR_<mode>.

Modes of Operation

An ARM core has up to eight modes of operation. Most applications run in User mode, and the application cannot change modes, other than by causing an exception to occur. The modes other than User mode are known as *privileged modes*. They have full access to system resources and can change modes freely. Five of them are known as *exception modes*; they are entered when specific exceptions occur. Each of them has some additional registers to avoid corrupting User mode state when the exception occurs. They are FIQ, IRQ, Supervisor, Abort, and Undefined mode. Some cores also have a further mode — Monitor mode — that enables debugging a system without stopping the core entirely.

User Mode

Normally a program runs in User mode. In this mode, the memory is protected (if the CPU has an MMU or an MPU). This is the standard mode for applications, and indeed, most applications can run entirely in User mode. The only way a program running in User mode can change modes directly is to initiate an SVC. External events (such as interrupts) can also change modes.

System Mode

System mode is a mode that can be entered only via an instruction that specifically writes to the mode bits of the CPSR. System mode uses the User mode registers and is used to run tasks that require privileged access to memory and coprocessors, without limitation on which exceptions can occur during the task. It is often used for handling nested exceptions, and also by operating systems to avoid problems with nested SVC calls.

Supervisor Mode

Supervisor mode is a privileged mode that is entered whenever the CPU is reset or when a svc instruction is executed. Kernels will start in Supervisor mode, configuring devices that require a privileged state, before running applications that do not require privileges. Some bare metal systems run almost entirely in Supervisor mode.

Abort Mode

Abort mode is a privileged mode that is entered whenever a Prefetch Abort or Data Abort exception occurs. This means that the processor could not access some memory for whatever reason.

Undefined Mode

Undefined mode is a privileged mode that is entered whenever an Undefined Instruction exception occurs. This normally happens when the ARM core is looking for instructions in the wrong place (corrupted PC), or if the memory itself is corrupted. It can also happen if the ARM core does not support a specific instruction, for example when executing a VFP instruction on a core where VFP was not available. The undefined instruction was trapped and then executed in software, therefore emulating VFP.

Undefined mode can also occur on coprocessor faults — the coprocessor is present but not enabled; it is configured for privileged access, but access is attempted in User mode; or it rejected an instruction.

IRQ Mode

IRQ mode is a privileged mode entered whenever the processor accepts an IRQ interrupt.

FIQ Mode

FIQ mode is a privileged mode entered whenever the processor handles an FIQ interrupt. In this mode, registers `r8` to `r12` are banked, meaning that they are available for use without having to save their contents. Upon returning to the previous mode, the banked registers are restored to their original state.

Having private registers reduces the need for register saving and minimizes the overhead of context switching.

Hyp Mode

Hyp mode is a hypervisor mode introduced in ARMv7-A for the Cortex-A15 processor (and later) for providing hardware virtualization support.

Monitor Mode

Monitor mode is a special mode used for debugging, but with the advantage of not stopping the core entirely. The major advantage is the possibility for other modes to be called — in monitor mode, the core can be interrogated by the debugger but still respond to critical interrupt routines.

Vector Table

A vector table is a part of reserved memory where the processor looks for information when it enters a specific mode. The classic model is used in pre-Cortex chips and current Cortex-A/R chips. In it, the memory at 0 contains several exception handlers. A typical vector table looks something like this:

```
00000000    LDR    PC,  =Reset
00000004    LDR    PC,  =Undef
00000008    LDR    PC,  =SVC
0000000C    LDR    PC,  =PrefAbort
00000010    LDR    PC,  =DataAbort
00000014    NOP
00000018    LDR    PC,  =IRQ
0000001C    LDR    PC,  =FIQ
```

Upon entering an exception, the corresponding instruction is executed. Typically, in this part of the code, there will be jump instructions, with the possible exception of the FIQ exception. Because FIQ is at the end of the table, it is possible to put instructions here, avoiding the need for a jump and speeding up execution.

There is also an option called *high vectors*. Available on all ARM processors from ARM720T onwards, this option allows the vector table to be placed at `0xffff0000`, and can be configured by software control to relocate the table at any time.

The table is usually called a vector table, but that isn't always true. The vector table can contain one ARM instruction per entry, so they are generally jump instructions. However, it can also contain one 32-bit Thumb instruction, or two 16-bit Thumb instructions.

On Cortex-M chips, this is different. The vector table actually does contain vectors and not instructions. The first entries in a typical vector table on a Cortex-M chip might look something like this:

```
__Vectors    DCD    __initial_sp          ; Top of Stack
             DCD    Reset_Handler         ; Reset Handler
             DCD    NMI_Handler           ; NMI Handler
             DCD    HardFault_Handler     ; Hard Fault Handler
             DCD    MemManage_Handler     ; MPU Fault Handler
             DCD    BusFault_Handler      ; Bus Fault Handler
             DCD    UsageFault_Handler    ; Usage Fault Handler
```

This means that a Cortex-M can address the entire memory space, not just the memory space limited by branch commands.

Memory Management

Memory management is done through the Memory Management Unit (MMU), which enables you to control virtual-to-physical memory address mapping, enabling the processor to transparently access different parts of the system memory. An address generated by an ARM processor is called a *virtual address*. The MMU then maps this address to a physical address, enabling the processor to have access to the memory. The memory might be mapped "flat," in which the virtual address is equal to the physical address.

Another function of the MMU is to define and police memory access permissions. This control specifies whether a program has access to a specified memory zone, and also if that zone is read-only or read-write. When access to the memory zone is not permitted, a memory abort is performed by the processor. This can be essential for protecting code because a privileged application should not read system memory, and especially not modify it. It also enables several applications to run in the same virtual memory space. This requires a little more explanation.

The operating system allocates a certain amount of processor time for each running application. Before switching to the application, the operating system sets up the MMU for that particular application. The application happily runs until it is interrupted by the operating system, and during this time, it believes that it is running at a certain memory location. However, with the mapping of virtual addresses and physical addresses, a program might think it is running at, for example, 0x4000, whereas the operating system has allocated it at 0x8000 in physical memory. When the operating system interrupts the application to enable some processor time to another application, it again reconfigures the MMU. Another program is then run, again thinking that it is running at 0x4000, but the operating system might have allocated it at 0x9000, and so on. It also means that one application cannot access the memory location of another application.

There are many uses for this that have been used throughout computer history. It can be used to relocate the system kernel and has been done on most large operating systems. It can also be used to access more than the physically available memory, by carefully switching memory and writing some memory to disk, flash, or some other form of mass storage.

ARM systems also have a distinct use for memory management. ARM CPUs boot from memory location 0x00000000 (or 0xffff0000 if high vectors are enabled), but this presents a problem. 0x00000000 must be located in ROM on first boot, but it is often useful, if not required, to change the vector table later, meaning that it must be located in RAM. In this case, MMUs can be used to remap the memory; to place the boot ROM elsewhere in memory, and to map fast memory to the position of the vector table. This is illustrated in Figure 3-4.

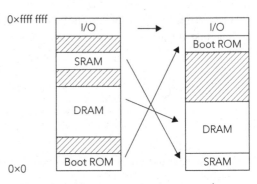

FIGURE 3-4: Memory remapping example

What Is Virtual Memory?

Every address generated by the processor is a virtual address. When the MMU is not enabled, either in reset state or because it was never configured, the memory is flat mapped between virtual and physical. When the MMU is configured and enabled, the processor requests are "translated" by the MMU without the processor actually knowing about the modification. The CPU might think that it is retrieving memory from the DDR2 chip at location 0x2080f080, but the MMU might have changed the request to 0x9080f080.

How Does the MMU Work?

The MMU needs information about the different translations, and to do that, it needs a set of translation tables. This is a zone in memory that contains information about the translations, separated into different sizes.

ARM MMUs support entries in the translation tables that can represent a 1 MB Section, a 64 KB Large page, a 4 KB Small page, or a 1 KB tiny page.

The first part of the table is known as the first-level table. It divides the full 4 GB address space into 4096 1 MB Sections, the largest size available. At the least, an MMU page table should contain these 4096 Section descriptors.

Each entry is called a first-level descriptor and can be one of four different items:

➤   A 1 MB Section translation entry, mapping a 1 MB region to a 1 MB physical region

➤   An entry to a second-level table for more precision

➤   Part of a 16 Mb Supersection

➤   A fault entry that's a 1 MB Section of unreadable data

Each of the 4096 entries describes memory access for a 1 MB Section. Of course, sometimes it is necessary to have a much smaller zone, for example, to have a 1 KB zone at the end of the stack to cause an exception if the stack grows too much, instead of potentially overwriting code or data. That is why a first-level descriptor can point to another memory location, containing a second-level table.

All this data is stored in system memory, but the MMU contains a small cache, the Translation Lookaside Buffer (TLB). When the MMU receives a memory request, it first looks in the TLB and resorts to reading in descriptors only from the tables in main memory if no match is found in the TLB. Reading from main memory often has an impact on performance, so fast access to some translations can become critical. A real-time system may need to access data in a specific region quickly but not often. In the normal case, when a TLB entry is not used, it is replaced by another line that is used often. To react as quickly as possible, therefore, some TLB entries can be locked, meaning that they will always be present and never replaced.

PRESENTING DIFFERENT TECHNOLOGIES

The term *technology* refers to technological advances integrated as default over time. For example, when ARM introduced the Thumb technology, it was an option for the ARM7 processor (used in the ARM7TDMI). Thumb is now included by default in the ARMv5T architecture and all later versions.

JTAG Debug (D)

The Joint Test Action Group (JTAG) was an industry group formed in 1985 and whose aim was to develop a method to test circuit boards after manufacture. At that time, multilayer printed circuit boards were becoming the norm, and testing was extremely complicated because most pathways were not available to probes. JTAG promised to be a way to test a circuit board to detect faulty connections.

In 1990, Intel released the 80486, with integrated JTAG support, which led to the industry quickly adopting the technology. Although JTAG was originally designed just to test a card, new uses were studied, especially debugging. JTAG can access memory and is frequently used to flash firmware. Coupled with the EmbeddedICE debugging attribute, it provides a powerful interface.

Enhanced DSP (E)

As ARM-powered devices were used for more and more digital media applications, it was necessary to boost the ARM instruction set by adding DSP instructions, as well as SIMD instructions.

Digital signal processing (DSP) is the mathematical manipulation of information to modify or improve it in some way. The goal of DSP is usually to measure, filter, and/or compress/decompress real-world analog signals. For example, DSP is used for music players, not only converting a compressed digital file into analog music, but beforehand by converting an analog sound, recorded in a studio, into a digital format. Typical applications are audio compression, digital image processing, speech processing, or general digital communications. The use of SIMD instructions can lead to increased performance of up to 75 percent.

DSP can be done on just about any processor, but the routines are extremely repetitive and time-consuming. By adding specialized instructions, more calculations can be done with less processing power. Some of the early mp3 players used ARM7EJ-S, with enhanced DSP instructions. The DSP instructions enabled mp3 decoding at low speeds with little battery usage, ideal for mobile devices. ARM released a highly optimized mp3 software library, but enhanced DSP works for almost all digital information signals. The DIGIC processor is Canon's processor for its line of digital cameras. The Canon EOS 5D Mark III is a professional 22 megapixel camera, and by using a DIGIC 5, it can take 6 photos a second, apply noise reduction routines, save each image in raw output, and also convert it into JPEG, while keeping enough processor power available to keep the camera's functions running, notably the auto-focus based on the analysis of 63 points.

On Cortex-A class processors, this has been enhanced with NEON, optionally present on Cortex-A processors.

Vector Floating Point (F)

Vector Floating Point was introduced enabling hardware support for half-, single-, and double-precision floating points. It was called Vector Floating Point because it was developed primarily for vector operations used in motion control systems or automotive control applications.

Originally developed as VFPv1, it was rapidly replaced by VFPv2 for ARMv5TE, ARMv5TEJ, and ARMv6 architectures. VFPv3 is optionally available in ARMv7-A and ARMv7-R architectures, using either the ARM instruction set or Thumb and ThumbEE. A synthesizable version was made available, the VFP9-S, as a soft coprocessor for the ARM9E family.

EmbeddedICE (I)

EmbeddedICE is a powerful debug environment, and cores supporting the EmbeddedICE technology have a macrocell included inside the ARM core for enhanced debugging.

The EmbeddedICE macrocell contains two real-time watchpoint units that can halt the execution of instructions by the core. The watchpoint units can be programmed to break under certain conditions, when values match the address bus, the data bus, or various signals. The watchpoints units can also be programmed to activate on data access (watchpoint) or instruction fetches (breakpoint).

Jazelle (J)

The Jazelle DBX (Direct Bytecode eXecution) was a technique that enabled Java bytecode to be executed directly on an ARM processor. With the advances in processor technology, it was no longer required to have specific Java bytecode acceleration, and this technology is now deprecated.

The first implementation of this technology was in the ARMv5TEJ architecture, with the first processor being the ARM 926EJ-S. At the time, ARM processors dominated the mobile phone sector, as it still does today. Mobile phones were becoming more and more advanced, and users were demanding more and more features. New programs and games could be installed onto a mobile phone, enhancing the user experience. These applications were mainly written in Java ME, a special form of Java designed for embedded systems.

Long Multiply (M)

M variants of ARM cores contain extended multiplication hardware. This provides three enhancements over the previous methods:

➤ An 8-bit Booth's Algorithm was used, meaning that multiplications were carried out faster, a maximum of 5 cycles.

➤ The early termination method was improved, meaning that some multiplications could finish faster under specific conditions.

➤ 64-bit multiplication from two 32-bit operands was made possible by putting the result into a pair of registers.

This technology was made standard for ARM cores using architecture ARMv4 and above, and ARM9 introduced a faster 2-cycle multiplier.

Thumb (T)

Thumb is a second instruction set generated by re-encoding a subset of the ARM instruction set in 16-bit format. Because it is an extension of ARM, it was logical to call it Thumb.

Thumb introduced 16-bit codes, increasing code density. On some systems, the memory was 16-bits wide, so it made sense to use 16-bit instructions. Reducing instructions to 16 bit also meant making sacrifices, so only branch instructions can be conditional, and only registers r0 to r7 are available to most instructions. The first processor to include Thumb was the ARM7TDMI. This chip went on to power devices like the Apple iPod, the Nintendo Game Boy Advance, and most of Nokia's mobile phone range at the time. All ARM9 processors and above include Thumb by default.

Thumb-2 technology was introduced in the ARM1156T2-S core and extends the limited 16-bit instruction set by adding 32-bit instructions. Thumb with Thumb-2 is a "complete" instruction set in the sense that it is possible to access all machine features, including exception handling, without recourse to the ARM instruction set.

Synthesizable (S)

ARM licenses their IP, and it is normally delivered in a hard-macro format. Some are synthesizable cores and are delivered to clients in source code form. Synthesizable cores can be flashed onto an FPGA component, and users can add their peripherals to the ARM core before flashing and testing. This can be extremely useful for prototyping and to create small series of processors, since some manufacturers provide FPGA chips with an embedded ARM core and enough programmable logic to add a large range of peripherals. Changes can be tested, and when the logic development is complete, the FPGA chips can be flashed with a final configuration — a custom design without buying an ARM license.

Soft-cores enable greater flexibility but often come at the price of speed. Soft-cores are normally clocked at a slower speed than hard-core variants but have significant advantages.

Today, an ASIC may integrate an entire processor, RAM, ROM, and several peripherals all on one chip and are all user definable. ARM synthesizable cores allow companies to make optimized ARM cores based on the design goal of the company. The core can be optimized for power consumption, performance, cache size — almost all processor parameters can be customized. The flexibility provided by this solution can be seen in the huge ARM ecosystem, where a large number of products exist with different characteristics, but all based on the ARM core.

Synthesizable cores started with the ARM7TDMI-S and exist for some ARM9, ARM10, ARM11, and Cortex cores. Today, almost all ARM cores are delivered in synthesizable forms to ARM licensees.

TrustZone

TrustZone is a security technology implemented by ARM on the ARM1176JZ-S and now an integral part of every Cortex-A class processor.

TrustZone is an approach to security by creating a second environment protected from the main operating system. Trusted applications run in a Trusted Execution Environment and are isolated by hardware. Designed for mobile applications, TrustZone enables users to run unsafe code, while protecting the core functionality.

For example, mobile telephone manufacturers often require this sort of functionality. On a mobile phone, it is quite possible to have two operating systems that run simultaneously. One of them is the "main" operating system, the system that is visually present on the screen, and enables you to download and install programs from the Internet. This environment is not secure; it is possible to download malware despite best intentions. A second operating system, this time a real-time OS, is responsible for the hardware side of the telephone, the modem. Both systems are separated for several reasons: partly because of the operating system (for example, Android can't be compiled for every modem on the market); and secondly for security, the operating system must not have access to core systems. Mobile telephone manufacturers don't like it when you flash a new version of the operating system or have access to factory settings. This is one of the fields where this technology can be useful.

NEON

NEON is ARM's wide Single Instruction Multiple Data (SIMD) instruction set. Historically, computers have always been running one single task at a time. An application may require millions of calculations, and each calculation will be done one at a time. In normal circumstances, this works fine. When working on multimedia files, this proved to be slow and in need of some optimization. Now say, for example, you want to turn a graphics image into a black-and-white image. You might look at each pixel, take the red, green, and blue components, take the weighted average, and then write back the data. For a 320×256 pixel image, you would have to do this 81,920 times. That isn't too bad. When working on a Full HD image, you are working on a 1920×1080 pixel image, meaning 2 million calculations. This is beginning to become huge. A 22-megapixel camera will output files in the range of 5760×3840 — 22 megapixels, so 22 million calculations. Suddenly, this becomes painfully slow. By using NEON instructions, operations can be done on multiple values packed into registers in a single cycle, allowing for higher performance.

big.LITTLE

ARM big.LITTLE processing is ARM's answer to mobile devices' energy consumption. Today's always-on mobile devices are difficult to predict, sometimes requiring little processing power and sometimes requiring enormous amounts of power. Take the example of a tablet with an estimated 8 hours of battery life. On standby, even if the screen is off, the device is still running in the background, connecting to Wi-Fi every so often to fetch e-mails, allowing some programs to run in the background, and especially, running an alarm clock that will go off in 10 minutes to wake you up. And it does. The screen turns on, an alarm sounds, and the device says good morning the best it can. Up until now, you haven't done anything actually CPU-intensive; a low-powered CPU could do the job just fine. One hour later, you are on a flight on the way to your vacation destination, and to kill time, you start playing a game. Now things start to change. The CPU is being used intensively, and power consumption goes up. The processor adapts by increasing the clock rate, and you get the most out of your tablet. One hour later, you still aren't past the last level, but they start serving drinks, so you put your tablet down. The operating system detects that you no longer need as much processing power as you did before, and it scales down the frequency, therefore using less power. The problem with this is simple: More powerful processors use more energy, no matter what the clock frequency is. Even when doing "nothing," there is still more silicon to power, and each clock cycle does more and more things, costing energy. Running your application on a Cortex-A7 will cost less energy than a Cortex A-15, meaning more battery life, but the Cortex-A15 is more powerful than a Cortex-A7, meaning better applications. The ideal solution would be to have a Cortex-A15 that has the battery life of a Cortex-A7, but that isn't possible. It is, however, possible to have a Cortex-A15 and a Cortex-A7 in the same chip. Enter ARM's big.LITTLE technology.

ARM's big.LITTLE works on the principle that both processors are architecturally identical. Because both processors have the same architecture, they can also have the same applications that can, if needed, switch from one processor to another. Processes switch between the two processors, depending on what is needed and depending on instructions issued by the kernel. When using background applications, applications are run on the low-powered CPU, and when the system is under load, the processes are run on the faster CPU. ARM estimates that by using this technology, substantial energy savings can be achieved. In ARM's tests, web browsing used 50 percent less power, and background tasks, such as mp3 playing, used 70 percent less energy. All this is achieved transparently for applications; software changes are made only in the operating system's kernel scheduler. Software doesn't even need to know if it is running on a big.LITTLE enabled processor.

SUMMARY

In this chapter, I have explained the different subsystems of an ARM processor, and provided an explanation of the different options available on select processors. I have presented how the processor starts, what the vector table is, and how it is used for exceptions, I have explained the different registers and which ones are reserved, before presenting some service registers, and finally, basic memory management.

In the next chapter, I will give a brief introduction to assembly language, with an explanation of what it is used for and how it is still essential to know assembly for embedded systems. I will also go through an example assembly program, but please don't run away! Assembly isn't that difficult, and it can even be fun.

4

ARM Assembly Language

WHAT'S IN THIS CHAPTER?

➤ Introduction to ARM assembly

➤ Use of assembly

➤ Understanding condition codes

➤ Understanding addressing modes

➤ Understanding your first ARM assembly program

Assembly language is the most basic programming language available for any processor. It is a collection of commands, or instructions, that the processor can execute. A program is a list of instructions in a specific order telling the computer what to do. Just like a calculator, you can tell a processor to take a number, to multiply it by 2, and to give you the answer. However, you need to supply some more information; you need to tell the processor where to get the number and what to do with it afterward.

INTRODUCTION TO ASSEMBLY LANGUAGE

A processor runs machine code, and machine code can be specific from one processor to another. Machine code written for a 6502 cannot, and will not, run on a 68000. Machine code is a list of numbers that make no sense whatsoever to (most) humans. To make the programmer's life a little more bearable, Assembly language was invented. Assembly language consists of words and numbers, and although it isn't as easy to understand as the English language, it is much easier to understand than reading numbers or punch cards.

Assembly language enables programmers to write computer programs, telling the processor exactly what it must do.

TALKING TO A COMPUTER

Talking to a computer isn't as easy as you would think. Hollywood has made a good job of making you think that computers are highly intelligent, but they aren't. A computer can follow instructions, no matter how badly written they are. To write good instructions, you need to know exactly how a computer works. You learned about the memory and about input and output, but now here's a little more about the processor and what it contains.

All processors use registers, internal memory used for specific reasons. ARM processors have 16 registers, named r0 to r15. But what exactly is a register?

A register is, put simply, a memory location that can contain one number. Remember when you were at school, and you had a written test in front of you. "How much is 5 times 3?" Instinctively, today, you would write down 15. The habit over the years makes you forget about what actually goes on, but try to think of it through a child's perspective. This is an operation that he does not immediately know the answer to, so he takes it step by step. Take the first number, 5, and put it into your memory. Then take the next number, 3, and put that into your memory, too. Then do the operation. Now that you have the answer, write that down onto the paper. This is illustrated in Figure 4-1.

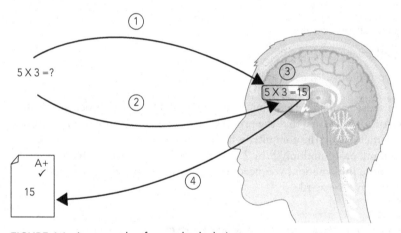

FIGURE 4-1: An example of mental calculation

A processor does the same thing. An ARM processor cannot do mathematical operations straight to and from memory, only registers. In this example, take the number 5 and load it into a register, let's say r0. Now, take the number 3, and load it into r1. Next, issue an instruction to multiply the value stored in r0 by the value stored in r1, and put the result in r2. Finally, write the value stored in r2 into the system memory. This is illustrated in Figure 4-2.

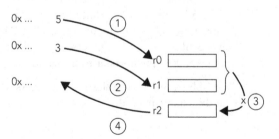

FIGURE 4-2: A calculation on an ARM processor

The question remains: Why do you need registers? Couldn't you do your operations directly into memory? The reason is simple, speed. By designing this functionality into the processor, it also makes the processor simpler, and reduces the amount of transistors required. This is one of the key factors in Reduced Instruction Set Computer processors.

WHY LEARN ASSEMBLY?

Assembly has been around since, quite literally, the beginning of processors. It is the lowest-level instruction set that a processor can use, and each processor has its own instruction set. Initially, everyone had to write computer programs in assembly. In today's world you have a choice of more than 100 programming languages, each with its strong points and weak points. Most low-level development today is done in C, a language that can be easily ported from one processor to another. It is easier to read than assembly and has many advantages over assembly. There is also another reason — portability. As seen previously, an assembly program written for one type of processor will not function for another type. Not all processors have the same instructions, or the same way of handling data. It is the C compiler's job to convert the C files into machine code for the correct processor. This might not seem important, since you may already know exactly what processor you will be using, but the C compiler knows about some of the optional features of the processor and can create optimized programs. Also, an external library might be designed to be used on a wide variety of processors, not just one specific processor.

So why would anyone need to learn assembly? Although languages such as C might present huge advantages, what you see is most certainly not what you get. It doesn't matter what language you choose — C, Python, Java, etc. — in the end, the only language a processor can use is assembly. When writing a program in C, the code is eventually compiled into assembly language. Although most programmers might not be concerned by assembly, embedded engineers will, sooner or later, be confronted by assembly code.

Embedded systems have two constraints that might not be as important for larger computer systems: speed, and size. Embedded systems often have to be as fast as possible and are usually heavily limited in terms of memory.

Speed

The Airbus A320 relies on a 68000 processor for the ELAC, the Elevator and Aileron Control. The 68000 was introduced in 1979, and although it is considered to be an "old" processor, it is also one of the most reliable. It is for this reason that it is used in mission-critical systems, but it comes at a price. It is not one of the fastest processors available, so all instructions must be carefully written and optimized to make sure that the chip runs as fast as possible.

This brings a question, one that sometimes surprises newcomers. Doesn't the compiler always create the most optimized code possible? The answer is no. They normally do a good job, but once in a while, they surprise you, or they won't quite understand exactly what it is you want to do. They can never be any better than you are. Imagine a shopping list. You have friends visiting, and you want to cook something for them, such as Chicken Basquaise. So, you start your list; you need a pound of tomatoes, a chicken (or six chicken breasts), four red peppers, three onions, some white wine, some thyme, and some basmati rice. And off you go with your recipe list. The list contains everything you need. (Although you might add a few more ingredients here and there.) You have several choices as to what to do. You can get the ingredients as they appear on the list; start with the tomatoes, then get the chicken, and then go back to where the tomatoes were to get the peppers. Depending on the size of the supermarket, you can lose a lot of time. If you plan ahead, you could have at least grouped everything together. So this time, get the tomatoes, the red peppers, and the onions because they are in the same place. You don't need to backtrack to get something that was close to you. You have just optimized. The result is exactly the same, but it is quicker. But can you do anything else? Yes, you can; you can go even further. In the supermarket close by, there are two entries. Thinking cleverly about this, start with the tomatoes because they are close to the south entry. A few feet later, you can find the red peppers. From there, get the chicken. Going right, two lanes later, you find the white wine. Then continue your list getting the ingredients in the order that they appear while making your way to the north entry. Making the list would probably take much longer, but you now have the optimal list, one that takes you the shortest time possible. How much time would you spend on your shopping list? And how much time would you save with your new optimized path? Well, that depends. You won't spend an hour making a list if it saves only 8 minutes in the supermarket. If it can save 5 minutes, you will probably take 2 minutes to group the ingredients together. But what would happen if you had lots of friends and invited them over every weekend? Assuming that your friends wouldn't mind eating only Basquaise chicken, you could theoretically save 8 minutes each time, about 50 times a year? That 2-hour shopping list would have saved you a total of 6 hours in the supermarket.

Although this example is ridiculous, it serves a point. On an embedded system, there are parts of the program that you will run thousands, if not millions of times. A few milliseconds here and there could save you a lot of time later. It could also mean using a cheaper chip because you might not need the expensive 40MHz version since you were clever and managed to optimize everything so that the 20-MHz version would work.

Code from C and C++ can be compiled into machine language, and although the compilers normally do a good job, sometimes you have to write heavily optimized routines in assembly, or correct what the compiler is outputting. Also, some start-up routines cannot be written in C; to activate memory controllers or cache systems, you have to write some assembly code.

Rear Admiral Grace Hopper was one of the first programmers of the Harvard Mark I computer, an electro-mechanical computer built in 1944. She became obsessed with well-written code and often lectured on the subject. She became famous for her representation of a microsecond and a nanosecond, producing lengths of wire corresponding to the maximum distance that light could travel in that amount of time. When talking about a nanosecond, she produced a series of wires that were 11.8 inches long (29.97 cm). In comparison, she produced a wire corresponding to the maximum distance traveled by light in one microsecond, a total of 984 feet long (just under 300 meters). Producing a wire that long, she went on to say: "Here's a microsecond. Nine hundred and eighty-four feet. I sometimes think we ought to hang one over every programmer's desk, or around their neck, so they know what they're throwing away when they throw away a microsecond."

Size

A while ago, I was working on a bootloader for a mobile phone. A bootloader is the first piece of code that is run on an embedded system; its job was to test to see if a program existed on the telephone. If such a program existed, there were cryptography checks to make sure that this was an official program. If the tests failed, or if no program was present, it put itself into a special mode, enabling a technician to download a new firmware via USB. To do that, we had to initialize the DDR memory, activate the different caches available on our CPU (in this case, an ARM926EJ-S), and activate the MMU. We also had to protect the bootloader; its job was to flash a new firmware but not give access to protected systems (the baseband, or confidential user information). We had to do all this in 16 Kb of NAND flash memories. Of course, in the beginning, there were huge ambitions; we could add a nice logo, a smooth menu interface, a diagnostics check, and so on. The list went on. When we released our initial binary, we were four times over the size limit. With a little optimization, we were three times over the limit. By getting rid of the fancy image, and the fancy menu, we were at 32 Kb. We started optimizing our C code, getting rid of a few functions here and there, and we came up with a binary just above 17 Kb. Several people tried to modify the C code, but we just couldn't get it below 16 Kb; we had to dig deeper, so we looked at the assembly code.

We soon realized that there were a few things that we could do, but we would shave off only a few bytes here and there. By changing how the program jumped to different functions, by modifying a few loops, and by repeating the process, we slowly made our way down to 16 Kb. In the end, we not only made the 16 Kb, but we also reduced the code further, allowing a few routines to be added.

Code compilers normally do a good job, but they aren't perfect. Sometimes they need a little bit of help from the developer.

Fun!

Writing in assembly can even be fun. No, seriously! In 1984, a new game called *Core War* was developed. It simulated the inside of a small computer. Two programs are inserted at random locations into the virtual memory, and in turn, each program executes one instruction. The aim of the game was to overwrite the other program and to control the machine.

In *Core War*, a dedicated language was used, called Redcode. However, it was rapidly "ported" to other systems, including ARM-based systems, as a fun way to learn programming. Battles were waged for entire evenings, with people testing their code. It wasn't that simple. Code couldn't be too large; otherwise, it might be damaged by the adversary. Different strategies were developed, and soon several "classes" became known, some often highly specialized in defeating another specific class. It was also an excellent way of teaching people what would happen if code was badly written.

Compilers Aren't Perfect

From time to time, you will be faced with a situation in which your product does not function as it should, but for some reason the code looks perfectly good.

On one occasion, I was confronted by a problem on an embedded system. We needed to read in a number from a sensor and to do a few calculations on that number to output a chart. There were three ways we could access the information, but one of them wouldn't work. We got a completely incoherent value, every time. The other two worked fine, so we knew that the sensor was working correctly, but these two ways were not available everywhere in our code. In one particular place, we had no choice but to use the third way. It didn't take us long to use a debugger, a Lauterbach Trace32. We were confident that we could find the problem immediately, using step by step, but this just confused us more. The code was perfect, everything looked fine, but on one particular instruction, the output was meaningless. We had no choice but to dig deeper and look at the assembly code. It didn't take us long to realize that there was an alignment problem; instead of reading in one 32-bit integer from memory, the processor had to read in 4 bytes and do a quick calculation on all 4 to create a 32-bit integer, but the compiler failed to do this correctly, resulting in a corrupt value. Realigning the data fixed the problem immediately.

On another occasion, a basic routine didn't work as we wanted it to. We needed to loop 16 times and do a calculation each time. For some reason, we never managed to. The code was simple:

```
for (i = 0; i < 16; i++)
    DoAction();
```

Except it didn't work as intended. We checked: i was an integer, correctly defined. It worked before and afterward. Bringing up the assembly listing, we saw that it did indeed loop, but the variable was never initialized; the value of i was never set to 0. To this day, we use the same code, but just before, we set i to zero, and there is a comment explaining that the line must never be removed.

Understanding Computer Science through Assembly

Computers are a mystery to most people and embedded systems even more so. When talking to engineers, most understand the system, some understand what happens on lower layers, but today, relatively few understand what actually happens deep inside the mainboard. A good way to learn about what happens deep inside a CPU is to learn assembly. With Assembly language, you are at the lowest level possible and can understand what happens when you run a program.

Shouldn't You Just Write in Assembly?

Sooner or later, everyone asks, "Shouldn't I just write in Assembly? It's fast! It's lightweight!" Yes, but don't. There are very, very few projects that are written in assembly. Your time is valuable; *don't start in assembly.* Writing in C is much faster, and the compilers normally do an excellent job. If they don't, or if you need a routine that is highly optimized, carry on writing the code in C, and then look at what the compiler generates. You can save time doing this, and even if the end result is not 100 percent what you expect, the compiler probably does all the structuring that you want.

Writing in assembly does not automatically mean fast and elegant code, on the contrary. Just like with any language, it all depends on the quality of what you write; it is possible to make something in assembly that is slower than in C. Assembly is useful to know; you may face it several times in a single project, but with years of development, higher-level languages do make more sense.

Most experts agree; start by completing a project before looking to optimize it. Numerous tools exist to analyze code, and see what portions are called, and which portions take the most time to execute. It is always possible to return to some code and try to optimize, but working with highly optimized code from the start can be a nightmare. When you know where your CPU spends most of its time, then you can replace some parts with assembly.

USES OF ASSEMBLY

Few projects will be written entirely in assembly; using higher-level languages such as C just makes sense. They are quicker to develop and easier to maintain, and compilers do a good job in translating C to assembly. So, what exactly are the uses of assembly?

There are several reasons why assembly is still used, from bootloading the first steps of a project all the way to debugging a finished project.

Writing Bootloaders

You've almost certainly seen a lot of programs written in C, but the first instructions of a bootloader are generally written in assembly. Some routines, like setting up the vector tables, cache, and interrupt handling cannot easily be done in C. Also, some bootloaders need highly specialized code, either for size or speed, where assembly is needed.

Much of the processor's low-level configuration cannot be done in C; changing registers in a coprocessor requires assembly, and it cannot be done by writing memory. The first instructions of the Linux kernel are in assembly for this reason.

Reverse Engineering

Reverse engineering has been used from the beginning of the computer era, for good and for bad reasons. Sometimes it is necessary to see how a peripheral is initialized, and only the assembly code is available. Many drivers have been created this way, supporting devices made by companies that no longer exist, where no source code is available.

The Gaming Industry, Building a Better Mousetrap

As soon as the first computers became reasonably small, games have been available. People have always been fascinated with computer games, and today it is one of the biggest industries. The first medium for games was the good old cassette; an analog media that the new generation will probably never know. A standard tape player could be plugged into a computer to load programs directly. After a few minutes of watching colored bars on a screen, you were ready to play! And ever since the first games, software piracy has existed.

Copying tapes was ridiculously easy. High-end tape players could simply copy the audio from one tape to another, possibly degrading quality, but still allowing almost anyone to play a copy.

Game developers fought back. New systems were invented; questions were asked during the game. Upon reaching the doors to the city, a guard would ask, "What is the second word of the third paragraph on page 20 of your game manual?" Giving a wrong answer would mean never allowing you into the city, effectively stopping your game. Although it was possible to photocopy a manual, it did make things considerably more difficult for software pirates and also for people who actually did own the game.

Disk protection was also added. By directly modifying data on a disk's surface, a game could easily detect if the disk was an original. The disk copy program from the operating system would refuse to copy a sector that it thought to be in error, stopping disk copying. Again, systems were made that enabled disk copying, but it stopped most cases.

Hardware dongles were considered to be the "ultimate" protection. An application would look at the hardware on the computer, most often on the serial port, and ask a question. The dongle would provide an answer, and the program was effectively authenticated. Copying a dongle was very, very complicated. Most often, custom hardware chips were used, and the cost of creating a copy vastly outweighed the cost of a software license.

Software pirates changed their strategy. Instead of using hardware to make copies, they turned to software. Buried deep inside the application was a few lines of code of particular interest. Somewhere in the code, the application would look at something particular, receive an answer, compare that answer, and then either continue if the answer was correct, or stop if the answer was wrong. It didn't matter what language the program was initially written in; it all came down to assembly. By reading the assembly code, and finding out where the program looked for this particular piece of information, pirates could either force the answer to always be correct, or skip the question completely. Although this might sound easy, a program can be millions of lines of code long, and the portion that checks for copy protection might be as little as 10 lines. Also, the original code might have comments explaining what the developer was doing, or variables with useful and meaningful names, but not in assembly. There were certain techniques for helping pirates; serial ports mostly use the same address, so it was possible to analyze code looking for a specific address and then find out which of the results looked like the copy protection.

Software developers fought back. Copy protection was added into several parts of the code, making reverse engineering more difficult. Secondary routines checked to see if the primary routines hadn't been changed. False copy protection routines were added as a lure. Techniques became more and more sophisticated, but still someone came up with something to disable the copy protection features. Some do it for Internet fame, some do it to play the latest games, but some do it simply as a challenge.

Optimization

Most compilers do a good job at taking C files and converting them to assembly instructions. With a few command-line options, compilers can be told to optimize for speed or for size (or a mixture of both), but there are times when a compiler cannot correctly do its job and delivers functional code, but far from optimized.

ARM's weakness is division. More recent Cortex-A cores can do integer division, but previous cores had to do division in software — something that could take a lot of cycles to complete. When a function does one division, it isn't always necessary to optimize, but when a function does repeated calculations, sometimes several thousand times, it is often worthwhile to spend a little bit of extra time to see what can be done. Maybe a routine will divide only by 10, in which case a new function can be created, with tailor-made assembly instructions to get the job done as fast as possible.

ARM ASSEMBLY LANGUAGE

The ARM Assembly language is a well-designed language that, despite first impressions, can actually be easy to read. Where possible, it has been designed so that it can be easily read by a human, for example:

```
ADD r0, r1, r2
```

This instruction can look a little frightening at first, but it is easy. ADD is the shorthand for a mathematical addition. The three subsequent registers define the operation, but in what order? Well, a human would write the operation as r0 = r1 + r2, and that is exactly what is written here; ADD result = value 1 + value 2. The processor adds the value contained inside r1 and the value contained inside r2, and puts the result into r0.

Layout

An assembly program source file is a text file and consists of a sequence of statements, one per line. Each statement has the following format:

```
label:      instruction      ;comment
```

Each of the components is optional.

> **Label** — A convenient way to refer to a memory location. The label can be used for branch instructions. The name can consist of alphanumeric characters, the underscore, and the dollar sign.

> **Comment** — All characters after an @ are considered comments and are there only to make the source code clearer.

> **Instruction** — Either an ARM instruction or an assembler directive

```
    .text
start:
    MOV r1, #20 ;Puts the value 20 into register r1
    MOV r2, #22 ;Puts the value 22 into register r2    ADD r0, r1, r2 ;Adds r1 and
        r2, r0 now contains 42
end:
    b end ;Infinite loop, always jump back to "end"
```

Instruction Format

This is the standard layout used in ARM assembly:

```
<op>{cond}{flags} Rd, Rn, Operand2
```

For example, the following code is used to add two registers together:

```
ADD R0, R1, R2
```

> <op> — Three-letter mnemonic, called the operand

> {cond} — Optional two-letter condition code

> {flags} — Optional additional flag

> Rd — Destination register

> Rn — First register

> Operand2 — Second register or second operand

Condition Codes

You can add a two-letter condition code to the end of the mnemonic, allowing the instruction to be executed under certain conditions. For example, you can jump to some other code if the answer is equal to zero and continue otherwise. In the same way, you can branch to some new code if there is an overflow. This is mainly used when branching but can sometimes be used for other instructions. For example, you can tell the processor to load a register with a particular value if and only if a certain condition has been met. You see the command MOV later on, but put simply, MOV changes the value of a register. You can specify that you want the register to be changed, with a MOV command. However, you can also specify that you want the register to be changed if and only if the carry bit was set, with MOVCS, or if a previous compare was lower or the same, with MOVLS.

Condition codes look at the N, Z, C, and V flags on the CPSR (the CPSR is presented in Chapter 3). These flags can be updated with arithmetic and logical operations.

AL — Always

An instruction with this suffix is always executed. The majority of instructions are nonconditional; therefore AL is not required and may be omitted (and indeed should be omitted). For example, ADD and ADDAL are identical; they are both run unconditionally.

NV — Never

The opposite of AL, instructions with NV are never executed. Instructions with this condition are ignored. This code is now deprecated and shouldn't be used. It originally provided an analog for the AL condition code but was rarely used.

EQ — Equal

The instruction is executed if the result flag Z is set. If the Z flag is cleared, this instruction is ignored:

```
MOV r0, #42 ;Write the value 42 into the register r0
MOV r1, #41 ;Write the value 41 into the register r1
CMP r0, r1 ;Compare the registers r0 and r1, update CPSR register
BEQ label ;This command will not be run, since Z = 0
MOV r1, #42 ;Write the value 42 into the register r1
CMP r0, r1 ;Compare r0 and r1, update the CPSR
BEQ label ;This command will be run, since Z = 1
```

NE — Not Equal

The opposite of EQ, this instruction is executed if the Z flag is cleared. If the Z flag is set, this instruction is ignored:

```
MOV r0, #42 ;Write the value 42 into the register r0
MOV r1, #42 ;Write the value 42 into the register r1
CMP r0, r1 ;Compare the registers r0 and r1, update CPSR register
BNE label ;This command will not be run, since Z = 1
MOV r1, #41 ;Write the value 42 into the register r1
CMP r0, r1 ;Compare r0 and r1, update the CPSR
BNE label ;This command will be run, since Z = 0
```

VS — Overflow Set

This condition is true if the Overflow (V) bit is set, resulting in a mathematical operation that was bigger than the signed container (for example, adding together two 32-bit signed numbers that result in a 33-bit signed result).

VC — Overflow Clear

This condition is true if the Overflow (V) bit is clear. It is the opposite of VS and triggers only if the result of a mathematical operation was small enough to be held in its container. (For example, adding together two 32-bit signed numbers together resulted in a signed number that could be placed into a 32-bit signed container without data loss.)

MI — Minus

This condition is true if the Negative (N) bit is set:

```
MOV r0, #40
MOV r1, #42
SUBS r2, r0, r1 ; 40 - 42, the result is negative
BMI destination
; this portion of code is never executed
```

PL — Plus

This condition is true if the Negative (N) bit is cleared. This happens when a mathematical operation results in a positive number, but also when the result is zero. (Zero is considered positive.)

CS — Carry Set

The Carry Set flag is set when an operation on an unsigned 32-bit overflows the 32-bit boundary.

CC — Carry Clear

The instruction is executed if the Carry Flag (C) is cleared.

HI — Higher

The instruction is executed if the Carry Flag (C) bit is set and if the result is not Zero (Z).

LS — Lower or Same

The instruction is executed if the Carry Flag (C) bit is cleared or if the result is Zero (Z).

GE — Greater Than or Equal

Greater than or equal works on signed numbers and is executed if the Negative (N) bit is the same as the Overflow (V) bit.

LT — Less Than

Less than works on signed numbers and is executed if the Negative (N) bit is different from the Overflow (V) bit.

GT — Greater Than

Greater than works on signed numbers and is equivalent to GE (Greater Than or Equal) and is executed if the Negative (N) bit is the same as the Overflow (V) bit, but also only if the Zero (Z) flag is not set.

LE — Less Than or Equal

Like LT (Less Than), this condition is executed if the Negative (N) bit is different from the Overflow (V) bit, or if the Zero (Z) flag is set.

Comparison of the Different Conditions

Table 4.1 lists the different condition codes and shows exactly which condition flags are used.

TABLE 4.1: Condition Codes

CODE	MEANING	FLAGS
EQ	Equal equals zero	Z
NE	Not equal	!Z
VS	Overflow	V
VC	No overflow	!V
MI	Minus/negative	N
PL	Plus/positive or zero	!N
CS	Carry set/unsigned higher or same	C
CC	Carry clear/unsigned lower	!C
HI	Unsigned higher	C and !Z
LS	Unsigned lower or same	!C or Z
GE	Signed greater than or equal	N == V
LT	Signed less than	N != V
GT	Signed greater than	!Z and (N == V)
LE	Signed less than or equal	Z or (N != V)
AL	Always (default)	Any

Updating Condition Flags

By default, data processing instructions do not update the condition flags. Instructions update the condition flag only when the S flag is set (ADDS, SBCS, and so on). The exception to this rule is comparison operations, which automatically update the condition flags without the need to specify S.

Consider this code:

```
MOV r0, #0x8000000F
MOV r1, r0, LSL #1
```

In the first instruction, you can put the value 0x8000000F into the register r0. In the second instruction, you can move that value to r1, after having performed a left shift by 1 bit. This operation is shown in Figure 4-3.

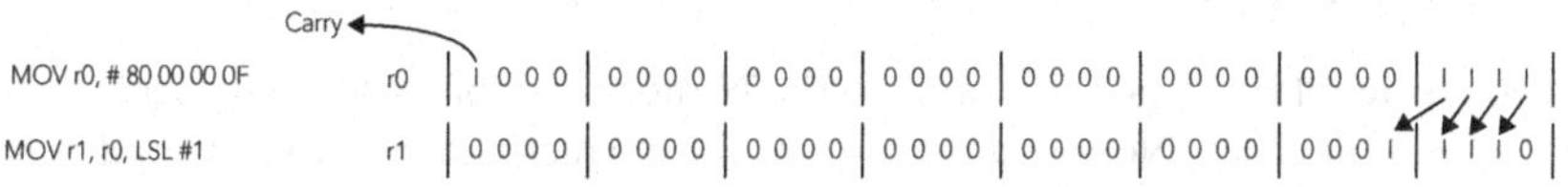

FIGURE 4-3: Result of a barrel shift

By performing a left shift, the value held in r0 was read in, and then its value was changed by the barrel shifter to 0x1E. Bit 31 was shifted left, effectively leaving the scope of a 32-bit number and was discarded. Bits 4, 3, 2, and 1 were shifted to bits 5, 4, 3, and 2, and a new bit 1 was inserted, or "padded" as a 0, as specified by the LSL instruction. You didn't ask for a status update, so you didn't get one. The condition flags in the CPSR remain unchanged. Now look at what would have happened if you had specified the S flag:

```
MOV r0, 0x8000000F
MOVS r1, r0, LSL #1
```

Just like before, you insert the value 0x8000000F into r0 and then use the barrel shifter. Just like before, bit 31 leaves the 32-bit scope. Because you are currently working in unsigned 32-bit numbers, the result is considered to be a Carry; the C flag of the CPSR is updated.

By performing manual updates to the CPSR condition flags, you can now execute conditional instructions. You can also execute several conditional instructions if you take care not to modify the CPSR again. After this calculation, you could, for example, have branch instructions depending on several factors. Was your value zero? This is equivalent to a BEQ. No, your result was not equal to zero, so this would not result in a branch. Maybe afterward you would do some quick calculations, and so long as you don't specify the S flag (or you don't execute a compare operation), the CPSR condition flags remain unchanged. However, on the next line, you could have a Branch if Carry Set, or BCS, and this time you would branch. Because the CPSR hasn't been modified since your last MOVS, you can still use the results many lines of code later. This is one of the strong points of ARM; a single calculation can be tested several times.

Now look at a more complete example:

```
MVN r0, #0
MOV r1, #1
ADDS r2, r0, r1
```

The first instruction, MVN, is a special instruction that moves a negated number to the specified register. By writing the inverse of 0, you are actually writing 0xFFFFFFFF to the register. The reasons for this will be explained later. For now, don't worry about the instruction; just remember that r0 contains 0xFFFFFFFF.

The second instruction moves the value 1 into r1.

The final instruction is an ADD instruction; it simply ADDs the content of r0 and r1, and puts the result into r2. By specifying S, you can specify that you want to update the CPSR condition flags. Now add 0xFFFFFFFF and 0x1, resulting in 0x100000000. A 32-bit register cannot contain this number; you have gone further than is possible. The logical addition result is held in r2; the result is 0x0.

The result is 0, which is considered to be positive, and so the N (negative) bit is set to 0. Because the result is exactly 0, the Z (zero) bit is set. Now you need to set the correct values for the C and V bits, and this is where things get tricky.

If you are talking about unsigned 32-bit numbers, then the result exceeded 32 bits, so you lost some data. Therefore the C (carry) bit is set.

If you are talking about signed 32-bit numbers, then you essentially did a −1 + 1 operation, and the result is zero. So even though the answer exceeded the 32-bit boundary, the answer did not overflow (meaning the answer did not exceed a signed 32-bit value), and therefore the V (oVerflow) flag is not set.

It is essential to know exactly what sort of result you are expecting. Carry and Overflow do not show the same thing, and the condition codes you specify need to be precise.

Addressing Modes

In ARM assembly, you invariably need to fetch data from one place and put data in another. Your system could just take a set of predefined numbers and do some calculation on them, but that would have severely limited use. Instead, a typical system is constantly fetching data from memory, or from external components (a pressure sensor, a keyboard, or a touch screen, for example).

In assembly, you have several ways of specifying where you want your data to come from. Don't worry too much about the actual instructions yet, more detail will be given in Chapter 7, "Assembly Instructions," but for now, concentrate on two instructions. MOV moves data from one register to another, and LDR loads data from a specific place in memory to a register.

One of the most common things that you can do is to put a value into a register. You can do this with an immediate value. An immediate value is an integer but only one of a certain type. For this example, use a simple value, one that is an immediate value. To specify an immediate value, put a hash sign in front of the number, like this:

```
MOV r1, #42
```

In this case, tell the processor to put the value 42 into r1.

In some cases, you want to move data from one register to another. This is a simple case and can be specified like this:

```
MOV r1, r0
```

This command "moves" the contents of r0 into r1. Converted to C, this is the equivalent of r1 = (int)r0. Technically it is a copy and not a move because the source is preserved, but you look at that more closely later in the chapter. By specifying two registers, you simply copy the value from one to another. However, in some cases, you want to do something called a shift. Shift operations are done by the barrel shifter; more information is available in Chapter 7, "Assembly Instructions." A shift takes a binary number and "shifts" the bits to the left or to the right.

Shifting is a quick way to multiply or divide by powers of 2 or sometimes to read in only a portion of a number. It takes the binary value and "pushes" the numbers in one direction or another, increasing or decreasing by a power of two. This is illustrated in Figure 4-4, where 0100 in binary (4 in decimal) is shifted left, becoming 1000 in binary, or 8 in decimal.

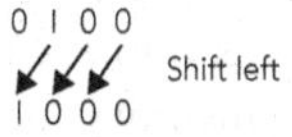

FIGURE 4-4:
Binary shift left

To MOV a register after performing a shift, use the LSL or LSR operand.

```
MOV r1, r0, lsl #2
```

Like the previous instruction, this command takes the value in r0, and puts it into r1; however before doing that, it performs a left shift of the number by 2 bits. In C, this translate to r1 = (int)(r1 << 2). It is also possible to shift a number to the right:

```
MOV r1, r0, lsr #4
```

This is the power of ARM assembly, and one of the reasons why ARM systems are so powerful. Now have a close look at what you have done. You have read in a value from a register, performed a shift, and then put the result into another register. This was all done in one instruction.

LSL and LSR are not the only instructions that you can use; for a complete list, please see the "Barrel Shifter" section in Chapter 7, "Assembly Instructions."

What happens if you don't know exactly how much you need to shift? ARM assembly again comes to the rescue; you can specify the contents of a register to perform your shift:

```
MOV r1, r0, lsr r2
```

By specifying a register for your shift, r0 can be shifted by the value contained in r2.

So now you know how to specify registers and how to put arbitrary values into registers, but it doesn't stop there. However, MOV can put values only from registers or from immediate values into registers, so for the rest of this section, you will have to use another instruction, LDR. LDR reads data from the system memory and puts the result into a register:

```
LDR r1, [r0]
```

By putting r0 in square brackets, you tell the compiler that you want to get the value of the memory address stored in r0. For example, r0 might contain 0x101E4000, which is the GPIO1 interface on an ARM Versatile board. Executing this instruction can make the processor look at the memory pointed by r0 and put the result into r1. This is illustrated in Figure 4-5.

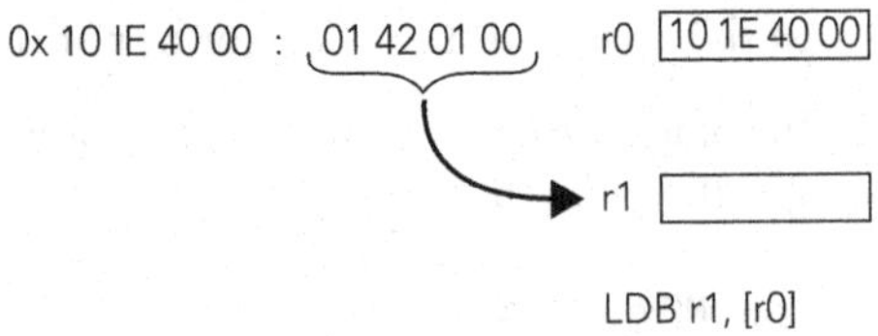

FIGURE 4-5: Loading a register from pointer

To get the memory contents stored at the address in r0 with an offset, add a number, for example:

```
LDR r1, [r0, #4]
```

This works in the same way as your previous example, except now the processor fetches the memory location r0 + 4, or in C, r1 = *(r0 + 1) because you read in 32 bits. This is illustrated in Figure 4-6.

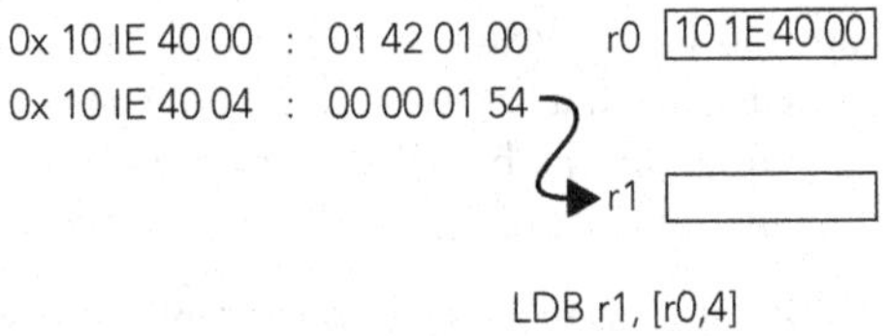

FIGURE 4-6: Loading a register from pointer with offset

Of course, just like before, you can also specify an offset not only as an immediate value, but also as the contents of a register:

```
LDR r1, [r0, r2]
```

This instruction fetches the memory location r0, plus the offset r2. Shifts can also be used directly in the instruction, like this:

```
LDR r1, [r0, r2, lsl #2]
```

This loads r1 with the memory located at r0, plus the value in r2, divided by 2. The equivalent in C is r1 = *(r0 + ((r2 << 2) /4)). This gives you the possibility to read, for example, a string of characters from memory, using r0 as the base address and r2 as an offset. Of course, after that, you would have to increase the offset register, but there are ways of doing that automatically:

```
LDR r1, [r0], #4
```

Just like in a previous example, this instruction takes the data held in the memory location pointed by r0 and places it in r1. However, the immediate value 4 is then added to r0. Consider this example:

```
MOV r0, #200    ; Put 200 into r0
LDR r1, [r0], #4    ; Reads in memory location 200, then r0 = 204
LDR r1, [r0], #4    ; Reads in memory location 204, then r0 = 208
```

This is known as post-index addressing because you have your index, and after having used it, you increment the value. Pre-index addressing works on the same principle and is designated by an exclamation mark:

```
LDR r1, [r0, #4]!
```

This increases r0 by 4 before fetching the memory. Let's look at another example:

```
MOV r0, #200    ; Put 200 into r0
LDR r1, [r0, #4]!    ; r0 = 204, then reads in memory location
LDR r1, [r0, #4]!    ; r0 = 208, then reads in memory location
```

ARM ASSEMBLY PRIMER

Like any programming language, Assembly can be a little confusing when starting, and like just about any programming language, there are different dialects, or different ways of writing the same thing. The current standard is known as Unified Assembler Language (UAL) and is a common syntax for both ARM and Thumb (which is discussed in Chapter 7, "Assembly Instructions").

Loading and Storing

Essential to any calculation, data must first be loaded into one or several registers before you use it. ARM cores use a load/store architecture, meaning that the processor cannot change data directly in system memory; all values for an operand need to be loaded from memory and be present in registers to be used by instructions.

There are only two basic instructions used to load and store data: LDR loads a register, and STR saves a register.

Setting Values

Frequently, you need to update a register with a particular value, not something located in memory. This is useful when comparing data. Is the value of the register r0 equal to 42? You can also use it when writing specific data into a device register; for example, place the data 0x27F39320 into the DDR-II control register to activate system memory.

Branching

Branching is the power of any processor; the capacity of running segments of code depend on a result. It is a break in the sequential flow of instructions that the processor executes.

There are two types of branches possible: relative and absolute. A relative branch calculates the destination based on the value of the PC. Relative branches can be in the range of +/– 32 M (24 bits x 4 bytes) for ARM, and +/– 4 M for Thumb. Because branch instructions are PC-relative, the code generated is known as relocatable; it can be inserted and run at any address.

Absolute branching works differently. Absolute branches always jump to the specified address and are not limited to the +/– 32 M barrier. They use a full 32-bit register, so this value needs to be entered before, costing cycles, but the advantage is that you can access the full 32-bit address range.

Conditional branching is the basis of every system. A computer is not a computer if it cannot be told to do one thing or another, depending on a previous result. Understanding branching is vitally important.

Branching can be done by linking, thereby saving the next instruction address, allowing the program to return to the exact same location after executing a subroutine. Branching can also be done without saving the link register, which is often used during loop instructions.

All processors can branch, but ARM systems take this a step further. ARM cores can execute either ARM assembly instructions, or Thumb instructions, and switching between the two is as easy as issuing a branch and exchange instruction.

All the jump instructions are detailed later in Chapter 7, "Assembly Instructions."

Mathematics

Because every value inside a processor is a number, everything that is done to that number is in some way mathematical. A graphical user interface consists of lines and rectangles, and resizing windows often involves manipulating numbers. Listening to digital music often involves heavy and repetitive mathematics. ARM cores contain a complete instruction set that can handle just about any calculation required for low-end microcontrollers all the way to advanced application processors.

Assembly instructions attempt to be readable; MUL is short for multiplication, SUB subtracts, and SBC subtracts with carry, and in all cases, the variables are in human-readable format.

Understanding an Example Program

Now look at an example program, without having had a look at all the instructions available. This is a mystery routine, and all that is known is that it accepts a single parameter: r0.

```
sum
        MOV r1,#0
sum_loop
        ADD r1,r1,r0
        SUBS r0,r0,#1
        BNE sum_loop
sum_rtn
        MOV r0,r1
        MOV pc,lr
```

At a glance, this is an easy routine, but it doesn't make much sense. Now break that down into several sections:

```
sum
        MOV r1,#0
```

This portion of code "moves" the value 0 into r1. Presumably, you use r1 during a calculation, and this is just to set the parameter. In C code, it would be the equivalent of int x = 0.

```
sum_loop
        ADD r1,r1,r0 ; set sum = sum+n
        SUBS r0,r0,#1 ; set n = n-1
        BNE sum_loop
```

The first instruction adds together the values held in `r1` and `r0` and puts the result in `r0`. The second line is a subtract instruction, `SUB`, but because the S is present at the end of the instruction, it also updates the condition flags of the CPSR. The instruction takes the value 1 from the value held in `r0` and puts the result back into `r0`. So, `r0` = `r0` - 1, or, in C, `r0--`. The third instruction is a branch operation, making the execution "jump" to a specific location, but only if the NE condition is met. So, this instruction jumps back to the beginning of the code if `r0` is not equal to zero.

So, `r0` holds a value, and `r1` equals `r1` plus the value held in `r0`. Then, subtract 1 from `r0`, and repeat the process while `r0` isn't equal to 1. If you started off with the value 5, the operation would have been $5 + 4 + 3 + 2 + 1$, before continuing. In other words, this routine takes a number n and returns the result of $1 + 2 + 3 + ... + n$:

```
sum_rtn
      MOV r0,r1
      MOV pc,lr
```

So, what happens here? In the first instruction, the register `r1` is "moved" into `r0`. In the second instruction, the Link Register is "moved" into the Program Counter, but why? ARM functions return their result in `r0` so that is why the temporary register, `r1`, must be first copied into `r0`; otherwise the result would be lost. As for the Link Register, it is a way for returning from a Branch with Link, or a specific way of calling a subroutine. This program was a subroutine, and now it returns back to the main program after completing its task.

Congratulations; you have just survived your first ARM assembly program!

SUMMARY

In this chapter, I have given a brief introduction to ARM Assembly, its uses and applications, and a brief introduction to some of the instructions and options that make ARM assembly unique. You have considered the different condition codes that make most ARM instructions conditional, and I explained what makes this so powerful. I have also shown an example program in assembly, and you've seen that it isn't too difficult to understand assembly.

In the next chapter, I will give a few example applications, from the simplest emulated program to two real-world programs using evaluation boards.

5

First Steps

WHAT'S IN THIS CHAPTER?

➤ Setting up a cross-compile environment

➤ Your first ARM program

➤ Running an ARM program in a simulator

➤ Presenting some evaluation boards

➤ Running a program on an evaluation board

WROX.COM CODE DOWNLOADS FOR THIS CHAPTER

The wrox.com code downloads for this chapter are found at www.wrox.com/go/
profembeddedarmdev on the Download Code tab. The code for this chapter is divided into the
following major examples:

➤ hw-code.zip

➤ hw2-code.zip

The time has come to start working. The first task consists of installing everything needed
to compile for an ARM processor. By default, a development computer can compile code for
itself; for example, a Linux i7 PC can compile code that runs on an x86 Linux system. You
probably need something different; a cross compiler. A cross compiler is a compiler that can
create executable code for a platform other than the one on which the compiler is run. My
personal development machine is an i7, so to compile code for an ARM system, I needed to
install a cross compiler.

Sourcery CodeBench Lite is a free cross compiler available from its website. Download the Embedded Application Binary Interface (EABI) version, and install it on your development PC. The Lite versions are available at http://www.mentor.com/embedded-software/sourcery-tools/ sourcery-codebench/evaluations/.

Sourcery CodeBench Lite comes with a multitude of programs; most starting with arm-eabi. Don't be frightened by all the programs; you will use a few, but not all of them. It also comes with a complete documentation explaining their use.

For the first steps, you will be compiling code for an ARM926EJ-S, which used to be a reference for embedded ARM platforms. You could, of course, have chosen just about any ARM core available, but the ARM9 core is a good choice for the tools available, since qemu has support for an entire board, called the Versatile. Newer projects should not use Classic ARM processors; they should use the newer Cortex processors. However, the Versatile board is an excellent resource for learning. The previous Versatile board has been superseded by the newer Versatile Express boards.

You can also compile these examples for other processors.

HELLO WORLD!

Traditionally, the first program anyone writes in a new language or on a new computer is *Hello, world!*, which is a program that outputs "Hello, world" onto a display device. Because it is typically one of the simplest programs possible in most programming languages, it is by tradition often used to illustrate to beginners the most basic syntax of a programming language, or to verify that a language or system is operating correctly. In embedded systems, this is sometimes tricky because you do not necessarily have a display, but there are other means. You can write out your text onto a serial port, but remember that when a system first starts, there are no drivers. To write any text onto a serial port, you must first initialize the device and create a driver, which is out of the scope of this book.

This example creates a barebones system using the absolute minimum. This system will not require any interrupt handlers or cache management, and therefore it will not be used. It is a basic program that you can add to later. The basic C routine looks like the following and is called hw-entry.c (code file: hw-code.zip):

```
int entry(void)
{
    return 0;
}
```

The routine isn't called "main" by choice because when writing a program using "main," you can presume that most of the hardware is initialized, which is not the case here. Some hardware might be initialized in assembly, but other components will be initialized in C. This is one possible use of the entry function, an entry point from assembly to C.

Now compile that, like you would with any C routine. You need to cross compile your program; by using traditional tools, you can build a binary that would work on your current development platform: probably an x86. You want to compile your routine for an ARM processor and specifically an ARM926EJ-S.

```
arm-none-eabi-gcc -c -mcpu=arm926ej-s entry.c -o entry.o
```

This command compiles `entry.c` into `entry.o`, using ARM instructions. You aren't done here — far from it. As explained previously, this is not a program that will be run inside an operating system, but this is a program run directly onto a processor with nothing else running. It is a bare metal application, meaning that you need to set everything up in assembly.

Of course, your C routine will be called from assembly, and before running your routine, you need to set some things up, notably the vector table. This is what the assembly file, called `hw-startup.s` (code file: `hw-code.zip`), will look like:

```
.section INTERRUPT_VECTOR, "x"
.global _Reset
_Reset:
   B Reset_Handler /* Reset */
   B . /* Undefined */
   B . /* SWI */
   B . /* Prefetch Abort */
   B . /* Data Abort */
   B . /* reserved */
   B . /* IRQ */
   B . /* FIQ */

Reset_Handler:
   LDR sp, =stack_top
   BL entry
   B .
```

Specify that the section is called `INTERRUPT_VECTOR`, and that it contains executable code. The vector table is called `_Reset`; you need this later to specify exactly where you want this code. Because you need the vector table to be at location `0x0`, you can specify that later.

The vector table contains jump instructions, and in this case, you have specified only one. The function `Reset_Handler` will be called whenever a Reset exception occurs. All other exception vectors point to themselves; you don't need them yet. Even if you aren't using them, it is always good practice to write the entire table. The reset handler sets up only the stack pointer and then calls your C routine. When the C routine returns, the final branch instruction branches to itself, putting the processor into a state of limbo.

Now assemble the assembly file.

```
arm-none-eabi-as -mcpu=arm926ej-s hw-startup.s -o hw-startup.o
```

Again, you aren't quite finished. You now have compiled parts of your program, but when creating a bare metal program, there are other things you need to specify. You need to tell your linker where everything will go in memory. Of course, your vector table has to go to a specific memory address, and to do that, you need to create an LD file. The LD file, or linker file, is a text file containing the memory architecture. You can specify where certain parts of the code are to be placed. You can reserve space and then set another memory location. That is exactly what you need to do. Put the reset vector at `0x0`, reserve 4 kilobytes of memory for the .data section, the .bss section. and the stack. Finally, it then initializes the stack pointer. This is the content of the file `hw-boot.ld`.

```
ENTRY(_Reset)
SECTIONS
{
  . = 0x0;
  .text : {
  hw-startup.o (INTERRUPT_VECTOR)
  *(.text)
  }
  .data : { *(.data) }
  .bss : { *(.bss COMMON) }
  . = ALIGN(8);
  . = . + 0x1000; /* 4kB of stack memory */
  stack_top = .;
}
```

Now that you have created your file, you can tell your linker to mix all those files together.

```
arm-none-eabi-ld -T hw-boot.ld hw-entry.o hw-startup.o -o hw-boot.elf
```

This goes and creates an ELF file, but you aren't finished yet. You go more into ELF in the next section, but in short, ELF contains much more than simple binary; it contains memory positions, possible debug names, and sections. When you run a Linux binary, you are actually loading an ELF into RAM, where the header contains important information about how to load the binary, where to place it, how much memory you will require, and so on. A bare metal system has no such requirements because you will be specifying everything. Also, you do not yet have an operating system that could parse the information; you need a real binary. To obtain a binary from an ELF file, you need to use objcopy. And specify that you want a binary output, with the −O option. This command strips all the ELF information and leaves you with the bare minimum, exactly what you need for your system.

```
arm-none-eabi-objcopy -O binary hw-boot.elf hw-boot.bin
```

This creates a file for you: boot.bin. Congratulations, you have just created your first ARM executable! And not just any program; this is a program that correctly sets up a vector table and an entry point. This is the basis for every embedded application on ARM. The next step will be to initialize hardware or to run an application, but first it is time to see exactly what has been done.

Each source file has been "compiled," that is to say it has been transformed into an object file. A linker combines one or more object files into an executable file, optionally reading in a file that defines memory locations. Finally, objcopy "strips" the ELF headers, converting the program into a binary file that can be run directly on the processor. This is illustrated in Figure 5-1.

All of these source files are available in the ZIP file called hw-code.zip.

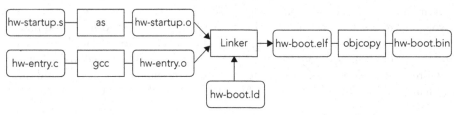

FIGURE 5-1: Compiling and Linking

TAKING THE WORLD APART

So what exactly have you done? The compiler and linker have done their magic and created a file, but it is difficult to know exactly what they have done. What you have actually done is created an ELF file. An ELF file, short for Executable and Linkable Format, is a file that contains more than just the bare metal program. It also contains debugging information, and you can use this to peek inside.

Now check to see what you have built. By "dumping" the information held in the ELF file, you can verify what you have done. The application readelf is a program available on most development systems, and CodeSourcery supplies a version if none are available on your system. ARM also supplies a series of excellent tools, and their version is called fromelf.

The -A option prints out architecture specific details.

```
readelf -A hw-boot.elf
Attribute Section: aeabi
File Attributes
  Tag_CPU_name: "ARM926EJ-S"
  Tag_CPU_arch: v5TEJ
  Tag_ARM_ISA_use: Yes
  Tag_THUMB_ISA_use: Thumb-1
  Tag_ABI_PCS_wchar_t: 4
  Tag_ABI_FP_denormal: Needed
  Tag_ABI_FP_exceptions: Needed
  Tag_ABI_FP_number_model: IEEE 754
  Tag_ABI_align_needed: 8-byte
  Tag_ABI_enum_size: small
```

The Tag_CPU_name field tells you that this ELF file has been compiled for an ARM926EJ-S processor, exactly what you wanted. The following information also tells you exactly why it was important to specify the processor — and not just try to compile for a generic ARM. This is important for optimizations, and it also lets the compiler verify that everything you write is supported on this processor. The Tag_CPU_arch is v5TEJ. This means the target processor is a v5 architecture. "T" means that this processor supports the Thumb instruction set; "E" means that this processor contains Enhanced DSP instructions; and "J" means that the processor also supports Jazelle DBX. For more information, see the ARM Naming Convention section in Chapter 1.

The vector table needs to be at the address 0x0, so look at the binary that you just created. By "dumping" your ELF file, you can disassemble the file and take a closer look. This is where objdump comes in. The command from the CodeSourcery suite is called arm-none-eabi-objdump. Specify that you want to disassemble with the -d option.

This is what my output looks like this:

```
hw- boot.elf:     file format elf32-littlearm

Disassembly of section .text:

00000000 <_Reset>:
   0:   ea000006        b       20 <Reset_Handler>
   4:   eafffffe        b       4 <_Reset+0x4>
   8:   eafffffe        b       8 <_Reset+0x8>
```

```
    c:    eafffffe       b       c <_Reset+0xc>
   10:    eafffffe       b       10 <_Reset+0x10>
   14:    eafffffe       b       14 <_Reset+0x14>
   18:    eafffffe       b       18 <_Reset+0x18>
   1c:    eafffffe       b       1c <_Reset+0x1c>

00000020 <Reset_Handler>:
   20:    e59fd004       ldr     sp, [pc, #4]     ; 2c <Reset_Handler+0xc>
   24:    eb000001       bl      30 <entry>
   28:    eafffffe       b       28 <Reset_Handler+0x8>
   2c:    00001050       .word   0x00001050

00000030 <entry>:
   30:    e52db004       push    {fp}                ; (str fp, [sp, #-4]!)
   34:    e28db000       add     fp, sp, #0
   38:    e3a03000       mov     r3, #0
   3c:    e1a00003       mov     r0, r3
   40:    e28bd000       add     sp, fp, #0
   44:    e8bd0800       ldmfd   sp!, {fp}
   48:    e12fff1e       bx      lr
```

In this example, you can clearly see that the vector table has been placed at 0x00000000, called _Reset. Now look at the first line.

```
    0:    ea000006       b       20 <Reset_Handler>
```

This is the instruction at address 0x0. ea000006 is the hexadecimal dump; it is what you would find if you took a hex dump of the memory. Fortunately, you don't have to decode that by hand; the disassembler does it for you. The instruction is B, or branch. It branches to the address 0x20, which as you can see later in the code, is the address of Reset_Handler. To help you, the disassembler also writes the name of the address, or the closest name possible with an offset. For the next instruction, the Undefined Instruction vector, the branch address is Reset_Handler + 0x4, which in this case is 0x4.

So, the table has been set up, but there is one problem. How do you put this on to your system? And what happens when you turn the power off and then back on? It would be extremely complicated to be forced to manually reflash your device every time you turn on your TV or telephone, but the chances are that they use ARM processors, so the same boot sequence applies. Well, that all depends on your system.

Normally, the first few kilobytes of memory are located in read-only memory, or ROM. Sometimes, this is programmable ROM, sometimes not; it all depends on your needs. So when your system starts, it reads in the vector table from ROM and then probably runs some code from the ROM. This is known as a bootloader, and its job is to make sure that your main application (or system) can boot. Your application, or firmware, might be on another type of ROM, or maybe even on an external SD. The bootloader will do everything necessary to load that code into memory before executing it.

Bootloaders sometimes have a second function, known as recovery. In the case of a bad software update, the bootloader might detect a faulty firmware, or at least be forced into a special mode to reflash the firmware. This is often the case with mobiles phones; in the case of a faulty upgrade, the mobile telephone will no longer boot. By pressing a special (often hidden) key sequence, the firmware opens a serial connection and waits for a new firmware.

HELLO WORLD, FOR REAL THIS TIME!

Unless you have an ARM system ready, the previous example will be difficult to use. Fortunately, there are alternatives. However, they do have drawbacks. Qemu is an excellent open source program that emulates several systems, including several ARM systems. However, it is mainly used for running kernels, not fully embedded systems. When running qemu with the –kernel option, qemu loads a binary but places it at position `0x10000`, not `0x0`. The vector table still exists, but you cannot load a binary image into `0x0`.

On a normal computer system, the kernel is loaded fairly "late." On a desktop or laptop computer system, when you first turn it on, some implementation of BIOS runs. The BIOS checks basic configuration: system memory, sets some timers, initializes PCI express devices, and so on. The list of things to do is rather long. When that is done, it then looks for a suitable boot medium. It might be a hard drive, a USB disk, a CD-ROM, to name but a few. If it finds valid code, it loads that code into memory before executing it. This code, often called a bootloader, is responsible for low-level checks and initialization before running a kernel. On PC systems, GRUB2 and LILO are examples of boot loaders. For embedded systems, U-Boot is well known.

Qemu has its own bootloader, one that you cannot change. It does most of the hardware initialization and then expects you to supply a kernel, one that will be loaded into address `0x10000`. From here on, you have two options. One is to simply ignore the vector table and load the binary straight into `0x10000`. The other is to keep the vector table but to load it into `0x10000`. Because the first entry of the vector table is a jump instruction, this should be transparent.

Qemu can emulate several systems, including the Versatile Platform Baseboard. The Versatile/PB is a complete system, based on an ARM926EJ-S core and also includes four UART ports. You can use this functionality to test a binary and to finally see your Hello, world!

From the Versatile/PB documentation, you can see the UART0 address is `0x101f1000`. Qemu can be run with an option to display the output of UART0 directly as a terminal. The Qemu implementation of the Versatile/PB system automatically initializes some of the hardware, including the serial port. However, not all systems will do this, and indeed it is good practice to fully initialize hardware before attempting to use it. Your code will be minimal, but only for this system. For a real embedded system, you would need more code to initialize the baud rate, set some registers, and also to check that the output buffer is not full. On this simplified system, you don't need to, and you will take advantage of that.

The `hw2-entry.c` file looks like this (code file: `hw2-code.zip`):

```
volatile unsigned char * const UART0_PTR = (unsigned char *)0x101f1000;

void print_uart0(const char *string)
{
    while (*string != '\0')
    {
        *UART0_PTR = *string;
```

```
            string++;
        }
    }

    int entry(void)
    {
        print_uart0("Hello, world!\n");
        return 0;
    }
```

You have added two things here. First, the address of your serial port register used to send data. Second, you have added a routine that outputs your string to a serial device, character by character. Yes, UART devices are that simple. That's why they are so often used for debugging. Modern PCs might be trying to get rid of "legacy" components such as serial ports, but embedded systems laboratories are full of them.

Now compile your C file. Use the ARM version of GCC.

```
arm-none-eabi-gcc -g -c -mcpu=arm926ej-s hw2-entry.c -o hw2-entry.o
```

By using the ARM GCC compiler, you can compile your C program into ARM assembly code.

Also, because your start address will be 0x10000, and because you will not be putting your binary directly into the vector table, you will not use a vector table. You change your assembly file to call your C routine directly. You can always add to that later, changing the vector table as needed. This brings a question; because you don't need a vector table, why do you go through all the effort of creating a memory map? Why can't you just compile a file and let the system load it? There are several reasons. When you create a program for an operating system, for example Linux, Windows, or MacOS, you don't need to specify the memory location of the application. This is because the compiler looks for a specific function, main, and automatically compiles a program to start at a specific address. The operating system handles all the tasks involved: virtual memory, clearing memory space, and loading a program into a specific address before handing control over to the new program. However, on a bare metal system, there is no operating system present capable of doing the work; you have to do it. Because you know that Qemu expects a binary file present at 0x10000, you have to specify to your program that it will start at that address.

There is another reason for this. When the processor executes a jump instruction, you are telling the processor to change the PC to a specific address. Although you can use relative addresses, it is often much easier just to specify a specific memory location. If you compiled your program for a different memory address, on your first jump, the PC would have an incorrect value, and the rest of the program would be unpredictable.

In the meantime, start with a basic file. This is what your qemuboot.ld file will look like:

```
ENTRY(_MyApp)
SECTIONS
{
  . = 0x10000;
  .startup . : { startup.o(.text) }
  .text : { *(.text) }
  .data : { *(.data) }
  .bss : { *(.bss COMMON) }
```

```
    . = ALIGN(8);
    . = . + 0x1000; /* 4kB of stack memory */
    stack_top = .;
}
```

By using this file, you place the contents of `startup.o` at memory location `0x10000`, where Qemu will be waiting for a binary file. After your program, you will reserve some space for the .data section, the .bss section, and some stack space.

Now for the `startup.s` file:

```
.global _MyApp
_MyApp:
LDR sp, =stack_top
BL entry
B .
```

Assemble this with an ARM assembler.

```
arm-none-eabi-as -g -mcpu=arm926ej-s startup.s -o startup.o
```

Now that you have assembled your code, you need to link the two files together using the memory map.

```
arm-none-eabi-ld -T qemuboot.ld entry.o startup.o -o qemuboot.elf
```

Just as before, this creates an ELF file, but you need to strip the ELF contents.

```
arm-none-eabi-objcopy -O binary qemuboot.elf qemuboot.bin
```

For the final part: You have compiled your bare metal program, and now you can run it inside Qemu. Configure Qemu to use the Versatile board, and ignore any graphics. All you want is the serial output.

```
qemu-system-arm -M versatilepb -nographic -kernel qemuboot.bin
```

There may be some warnings about different hardware problems that you can ignore. Qemu doesn't emulate only a simple ARM board; you can run entire operating systems on it, complete with sound and video. According to your system, there might be different warnings about initializing sound systems. You can ignore these.

If all goes well, Qemu displays your "Hello, world!" on the screen.

SOFTWARE IMPLEMENTATION

Depending on the ARM core, some will implement hardware units for certain functions, others will rely on software. For example: division. In any project, sooner or later, the code will have to divide. The only problem is that some previous ARM cores cannot perform hardware division.

Consider the following simple helper routine:

```
int mydiv(int a, int b)
{
  return a/b;
}
```

This is an extremely simple routine, and it isn't something that is normally coded, but it serves as an example. The compiler doesn't know what a and b will be, so it will have to create a routine that can divide any signed integer. To compile it, you can use the following:

```
arm-none-eabi-gcc -c -mcpu=arm926ej-s ./div.c
arm-none-eabi-objdump -S div.o
```

This is the output on my development computer:

```
Disassembly of section .text:

00000000 <intdiv>:
   0:   e92d4800        push    {fp, lr}
   4:   e28db004        add     fp, sp, #4
   8:   e24dd008        sub     sp, sp, #8
   c:   e50b0008        str     r0, [fp, #-8]
  10:   e50b100c        str     r1, [fp, #-12]
  14:   e51b0008        ldr     r0, [fp, #-8]
  18:   e51b100c        ldr     r1, [fp, #-12]
  1c:   ebfffffe        bl      0 <__aeabi_idiv>
  20:   e1a03000        mov     r3, r0
  24:   e1a00003        mov     r0, r3
  28:   e24bd004        sub     sp, fp, #4
  2c:   e8bd8800        pop     {fp, pc}
```

The compiler did indeed compile the code, but not quite as expected. What is this mysterious __aeabi_idiv? It isn't part of the project; it is a helper class available in the GNU Compiler Collection and also from ARM directly for users of the ARM compiler. Even though this code isn't a complete project, and it will print out a warning, it is still compilable. Well, almost.

```
arm-none-eabi-ld div.o -o div.elf
arm-none-eabi-ld: warning: cannot find entry symbol _start; defaulting to 00008000
div.o: In function 'intdiv':
div.c:(.text+0x1c): undefined reference to '__aeabi_idiv'
```

The first warning is normal. This isn't a project; you don't have an entry point. The compiler is doing the best it can, but it can't do everything. The second warning is slightly more worrying. The compiler can't find the function '__aeabi_idiv' and therefore cannot continue. The problem is, you didn't want a function called '__aeabi_idiv', you just wanted to make a simple division. The short answer is, you can't. This particular ARM core does not support hardware division.

This is where libraries come in. Because this core cannot natively divide, it makes use of software libraries. More recent cores do support hardware division, and a library call would have been replaced by a simple SDIV assembly instruction. For example, compile the same code for a Cortex-A15:

```
arm-none-eabi-gcc -c -mcpu=cortex-a15 ./div.c
arm-none-eabi-objdump -S div.o
00000000 <intdiv>:
   0:   e52db004        push    {fp}            ; (str fp, [sp, #-4]!)
   4:   e28db000        add     fp, sp, #0
   8:   e24dd00c        sub     sp, sp, #12
   c:   e50b0008        str     r0, [fp, #-8]
  10:   e50b100c        str     r1, [fp, #-12]
  14:   e51b2008        ldr     r2, [fp, #-8]
  18:   e51b300c        ldr     r3, [fp, #-12]
```

```
1c:   e713f312        sdiv    r3, r2, r3
20:   e1a00003        mov     r0, r3
24:   e28bd000        add     sp, fp, #0
28:   e8bd0800        ldmfd   sp!, {fp}
2c:   e12fff1e        bx      lr
```

MEMORY MAPPING

Upon RESET, an ARM core automatically deactivates the MMU, if present. Any memory fetches will directly fetch that portion of memory. That might sound strange, but there are cases in which this isn't practical.

More advanced processors come with a specific bootloader, a small application that runs on RESET. The bootloaders generally come directly from the manufacturer and cannot be modified or deactivated. They normally enable basic tasks, like uploading a new binary in case of flash corruption or security checks to see if a valid binary is present before executing it.

For example, the reset vectors are often placed in ROM, not in RAM. Also, from a hardware point of view, RAM is not always located in the same place. A system may require placing the DDR2 controller at 0x90000000, but your software actually wants memory to start at 0x20000000. On some systems, there may be two DDR2 chips, and their memory locations might not be adjacent. To simplify this, the MMU must be configured.

The Memory Management Unit (MMU) is embedded into some ARM cores, and its primary job is to translate virtual memory to physical memory. Physical memory is what is actually physically present on the memory bus, and virtual memory is what the processor sees. When accessing memory, the processor requests a certain memory access. This access is sent to the MMU, which analyzes the request. The processor has requested memory at 0x2000F080, thinking that it is talking to DDR memory, but what it actually wants is the memory location at 0x9000F080, so give that to it instead. The processor has no idea of the change that has been done; as far as it is concerned, it has fetched the memory at 0x2000F080. Figure 5-2 shows the MMU on an ARM system. The ARM processor makes a request for a memory address, and the MMU receives the request, looks at the Translation Table, and if required, translates the memory address. The result is fed straight back to the processor.

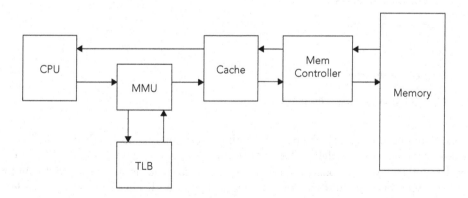

FIGURE 5-2: MMU and memory requests

MMUs do not map only memory; they can also police access rights. An MMU can be programmed to refuse access to a certain portion of memory and can configure which portions of memory are cached.

Without going into too much detail about the different uses for virtual memory, one of the most common starting memory maps is the flat map, where virtual memory is the same as physical memory. It is a good starting point; it enables setting up memory access rights and cache.

The first thing to do is to know where to put the translation tables. A translation table is a zone in physical memory that contains the different translations. A translation table contains translation entries, and for this example, the only entry that will be used is the L1 entry.

To load the address, you need to program the CP15.

```
LDR r0, tlb_l1_base
MCR p15, 0, r0, c2, c0, 0
```

The variable `tlb_l1_base` can be defined as follows:

```
tlb_l1_base:
    .word 0x00008000
```

By writing this, you define `tlb_l1_base` as a 32-bit value. The instruction `mcr` is short for Move to Coprocessor from ARM Register. Coprocessor instructions cannot use variables or fixed values; they can transfer only to and from ARM registers.

The first part has been done; the MMU now knows where the page data will be stored, but of course, the page data still has to be populated. That will be the next part of the program.

The Translation Table is full of Translation Entries, and as said earlier, for simplicity, I will use only L1 tables. The mapping will be flat; virtual memory = physical memory. Because L1 entries define 1 megabyte of memory, and because ARM processors can access 4096 megabytes of memory, you need 4096 section entries. Table 5.1 defines a section entry.

TABLE 5.1: Section Entry Layout

BITS	DESCRIPTION
31:20	Section base address
11:10	Access permissions
8:5	Domain
3:2	Cacheable/Bufferable
1:0	0b10 for section page table entry

Undefined bits should be left as zero. The part that will interest you the most is the Section base address. For flat mapping, you will define that 0x000xxxxx will map to 0x000xxxxx, all the way to 0xfffxxxxx that will map to 0xfffxxxxx. So that is exactly what your loop is going to do. As for the other bits, the Access permissions will be 0x11; meaning that both supervisor and user code can access the memory.

```
        LDR r0,=tlb_l1_base
        MOVT r1, #0x0000
        MOVW r1, #0x0C02 ; Full access, domain 0, no cache, page table entry
        MOV r2, #4095 ; The number of entries to do, minus one
mmuloop:
        STR r1, [r0] ; Store the contents of r1 into the translation table
        ADD r0, #4 ; Next entry
        ADD r1, #0x00100000 ; Next page
        SUBS r2, #1
        BNE mmuloop
done:
```

This small program starts by loading the address of the translation table into r0. The first page table entry is loaded into r1, and kept, because all pages will use the same parameters for now. Then, r2 is loaded with the value 4096, or the amount of entries to load into the translation table.

The mmuloop section is easy to understand. First, the value held in r1 is saved into the memory location pointed to by the value in r0 — the first table entry. The register r0 is then incremented by 4 because section entries are 32 bits long. It now contains the next address in the table. The register r1 is then incremented by 0x00100000, or the size of a section. Finally, r2 is decreased by 1, and the routine loops if the value of r2 is not equal to zero. If it is equal to zero, then the program continues.

The MMU now knows about the base address, and the table has been populated, but there is still one more thing left to do — activate the MMU. The following code does just that:

```
        MRC p15, 0, r0, c1, c0, 0
        ORR r0, r0, #0x1
        MCR p15, 0, r0, c1, c0, 0
```

Just like the previous coprocessor example, this small portion of code updates the MMU registers, but it first reads from the coprocessor. MRC will read a coprocessor register into an ARM register. Next, a logical OR is performed, setting the first bit to one. Then, the updated register is put back into the coprocessor.

Congratulations, the MMU is now activated!

REAL WORLD EXAMPLES

Theory can be fun, but the real fun is in trying applications on real-world systems. Some people are often frightened about purchasing an ARM system, mainly because of the price. Indeed, some high-end evaluation boards can be expensive, but they are often used for specific tasks: prototyping a next-gen telephone, or for testing multicore environments. Most people don't know that a complete ARM system can be purchased for less than $50, together with all the tools needed to start a project.

This section presents three evaluation boards: Silicon Labs' STK3800 and STK3200, and Atmel's SAM D20 Xplained Pro.

Silicon Labs STK3800

ARM cores are not born equal. Because ARM licenses the technology, customers are allowed a certain degree of liberty, greatly enhancing the ARM ecosystem. Some clients modify the core to integrate more or less cache, others to be faster. Silicon Labs specializes in low-power devices and creates some of the most energy-efficient Cortex-M chips available on the market.

The Cortex-M series has always been well known for its exceptionally low power usage, but there are some cases in which a Cortex-M will consume just a little bit more energy, especially in high temperature environments. Silicon Labs has spent a lot of time and energy perfecting an already impressive design, and the result is the Gecko series.

Silicon Labs' line of Gecko chips also come with exceptionally well-designed evaluation boards, equipped with numerous sensors that enable the end user to experiment freely. When the time has come to do a little more experimentation with external components, the board is equipped with solder points so that users can incorporate their own inputs and outputs. Also of note, these boards have a built-in hardware debugger, allowing developers to debug, to flash, and to profile code.

The Wonder Gecko STK3800 board integrates a Cortex-M4 with a Floating Point Unit (FPU), and two user buttons, one light sensor, one metal detector, a full-size LCD screen with numerous information displays, and something that is not found often on boards, a touch-sensitive sensor. All this comes with all the cables needed to function, two USB ports (one for debugging and one available as I/O), as well as a CD containing some interesting applications to flash test programs and to also show real-time power consumption. The board is shown in Figure 5-3.

FIGURE 5-3: Silicon Lab's STK3800 Evaluation Board

To show just a fraction of what this board can do, I'll create a desk clock. The STK3800 board comes with a battery connector, allowing the board to be powered by a single CR2032 battery. Therefore, the board can be mobile, and the battery lasts longer than you'd first think. When the battery does run out, the EFM32 has yet another trick up its sleeve; the STK3800 has a super capacitor that can not only keep critical sections of the processor powered, but it also allows the board to keep RTC time; in this application it can keep time for up to 8 hours.

The clock will be event-driven, meaning that the Wonder Gecko will spend most of its time sleeping, therefore saving energy. The Wonder Gecko will wake up and respond to interrupts, but which ones exactly? I'll create a program that shows only hours and minutes, so in theory that means only one interrupt a minute, but what about screen animation? The LCD display comes with a circular widget, something that would be ideal to tell the user that the system is still working. Again, the Wonder Gecko series has another trick; the LCD controller can actually do basic animations without help from the MCU.

The entire program will be separated into several stages: first, basic system initialization. For debugging, the application also initializes trace output. This can be removed later in the production stage.

After the basics have been set up, the application needs to do further configuration; core frequency, the LCD controller, and the real-time clock all need to be set up. After that is done, the GPIO will be configured for interrupts.

After all the initialization and configuration is done, it is time to run the real code; the clock itself.

Initialization

Initialization is a work that can frighten a lot of people. In theory, it means low-level system configuration: setting up the cache, preparing any system devices before entering your application. Remember that Cortex-M chips are designed to be "simple," both architecturally and for developers. Cortex-M programs can be designed entirely in C, but Silicon Labs makes it even easier. The time has come to initialize the processor.

```
/* Chip errata */
CHIP_Init();
```

And that's it. No, really. Due to some differences between chips, Silicon Labs created the CHIP_Init() function to set all the reset registers to the latest version of documentation. This keeps things nice and simple. Now that the chip itself is initialized, the power and code profiler can optionally be activated.

```
/* Enable the profiler */
BSP_TraceProfilerSetup();
```

Now, values can be read from the debug port, indicating power usage, a listing of which interrupts cause a change of state and the time they took. Next, you ensure that the core frequency has been updated.

```
/* Ensure core frequency has been updated */
SystemCoreClockUpdate();
```

For a clock application, you must initialize the LCD display.

```
/* Initialize LCD display with no voltage boost */
SegmentLCD_Init(false);
```

With four simple lines in C, the EFM32 is set up and ready to go.

Configuration

You want to save as much energy as possible, and for that, the processor must spend most of its time in a low power state. Instead of looping continuously, you will program the RTC to wake the processor every minute to update the LCD screen. After the processor awakens, you update a few variables and then go back to sleep. First, you need to configure the RTC.

```
1   void rtc_setup(void)
2   {
3       RTC_Init_TypeDef rtcInit = RTC_INIT_DEFAULT;
4       CMU_ClockEnable(cmuClock_CORELE, true);
5       CMU_ClockSelectSet(cmuClock_LFA, cmuSelect_LFXO);
6       CMU_ClockDivSet(cmuClock_RTC, cmuClkDiv_32);
7       CMU_ClockEnable(cmuClock_RTC, true);
8       rtcInit.enable = false;
9       rtcInit.debugRun = false;
10      rtcInit.comp0top = true;
11      RTC_Init(&rtcInit);
12      /* Schedule an interrupt every minute */
13      RTC_CompareSet(0, ((RTC_FREQ / 32 ) * 60 ) - 1;
14      /* Enable Interrupts */
15      NVIC_EnableIRQ(RTC_IRQn);
16      RTC_IntEnable(RTC_IEN_COMP0);
17      /* Enable the RTC */
18      RTC_Enable(true);
19  }
```

This merits a little bit of explanation. First, on line 3, you create a default RTC structure. Then, the Clock Management Unit is set to use a clock divider of 32, to save power, before activating the CMU.

Now you are ready to configure the RTC. Set it so that it is not enabled by default, and also so that it is halted on debug, making it easier for you if you need to run the application step by step.

The `RTC_CompareSet` instruction on line 13 is where a comparison register is set up. You will set it up for exactly 60 seconds, so every minute it will trigger an interrupt, which is what is configured in the next lines. Finally, when everything is set up, the RTC is enabled.

In just a few lines of code, the RTC and the CMU have been configured, and your application is almost ready. When an interrupt triggers, it will call a function called `RTC_IRQHandler`. This is what the source will look like:

```
1   void RTC_IRQHandler(void)
2   {
3       RTC_IntClear(RTC_IFC_COMP0); /* Clear the interrupt source */
4       minutes++; /* Increment minutes by one */
5       if (minutes > 59)
6       {
7           minutes = 0;
8           hours++;
9           if (hours > 23)
10          {
11              hours = 0;
12          }
13      }
14  }
```

When an interrupt occurs, first, you need to clear the interrupt source. Then the `minutes` variable is incremented, incrementing the hours as needed.

Main Application

The main application will be incredibly simple. A small loop will keep running in a `while(1)` structure, update the LCD screen, and then return to sleep mode.

```
while(1)
{
    SegmentLCD_Number(hours * 100 + minutes);
    EMU_EnterEM2(true);
}
```

The `SegmentLCD_Number` routine simply updates the LCD screen with the requested number; in this case, the time. Then, the processor is put into Energy Mode 2.

EFM32 chips have five energy modes, from 0 to 4. In Mode 2, the ARM core is powered down, and certain low power devices are still powered, including the LCD display and the RTC. Energy Modes 3 and 4 provide even more energy conservation but disable the RTC, which would need external support. Energy Mode 0 is normal operation, and this is the state to which the processor returns when an interrupt occurs.

Because the processor is put into sleep mode as soon as the LCD is updated, the LCD update routine is run only once per minute, meaning the processor spends almost all its time sleeping, conserving energy.

If the result is so energy efficient, just how long would that last? Well, Silicon Labs has a solution for that, too. They provide an application that inputs data from the different states. You will be spending approximately 1 minute in EM2, and just to be on the safe side, you can say that you will be spending 1 millisecond in EM0. In reality, the few routines present execute much faster than that, but it is always worth considering the worst-case scenario. If your clients have to change batteries every 2 weeks, they are not going to like your product. Running this in the Silicon Labs energyAware Battery software indicates that the problem is actually going to be the opposite; you had better make battery replacement easy, not because it is going to last just a few weeks, but because it will last for years on a simple CR2032 battery. My simulator predicts that my setup will last for more than 8 years, so our clients will probably have lost the instructions by then.

What Now?

Silicon Labs provides a more complete version of this clock as an example program. My version has no way of setting the current time, but that is easy to accomplish using the two push buttons on the evaluation board. Using the same techniques, by listening to an interrupt on the GPIO, the processor can increment hours and minutes.

The clock application is a basic application, and lots of functionality can be added. For example, the LCD isn't back lit, and the STK3800 comes with a light sensor; why not turn the LCD screen off when the light falls below a certain level? Maybe even add an alarm clock feature. It wouldn't take much to add a simple buzzer onto the board, but with a little bit of tweaking, it is also possible to set up the board to turn on a coffee machine, by enabling another GPIO.

Silicon Labs STK3200

The Wonder Gecko is a Cortex-M4 with an FPU, but for a clock application, this is often too powerful. While the Wonder Gecko is very energy efficient, there is an even better solution. The

Cortex-M0+ is ARM's most energy efficient microcontroller, and Silicon Labs has developed the Zero Gecko, based on the Cortex-M0+.

The STK3200 evaluation board is similar to the STK3800 board mentioned previously, but the major difference is that this board does not have a segment LCD. Instead, it has a Memory LCD screen, allowing for graphics while remaining very energy efficient. The 128 x 128 display is crisp and fast, and would be an excellent choice of screen for a smart watch. The STK-3200 is shown in Figure 5-4.

FIGURE 5-4: Silicon Lab's STK3200 Evaluation Board

Of course, the board still has input devices; it has two push buttons and two touch-sensitive buttons, and has the same extension header as the STK3800. It has a USB input for debugging, and also a CR2032 battery slot.

In this application, you will again be making a clock. Since the STK3200 has a 128 x 128 Memory LCD, you will be using that to display an analogue clock. It will have an hour hand, a minute hand, and also a second hand. Once again, you will be using the power saving modes available on the Zero Gecko, to keep the application running as long as possible on battery power.

Initialization

Initializing the Zero Gecko is exactly the same as the Wonder Gecko. One single function does the entire low-level initialization.

```
CHIP_Init();
```

This function sets up the clocks and some of the low-level drivers, setting up registers to a stable state. Once the initialization state is done, you can move on to configuration.

Configuration

Next, the GPIO must be configured. There are four buttons on the STK3800 — two push buttons, and two touch-sensitive pads. For this application, you will only be using the push buttons. PB1 will be configured to advance time by one minute, PB0 to advance time by one hour. The two buttons are connected to the GPIO, which must be configured. Like the previous clock application, the CPU will spend most of its time sleeping, so the buttons must be configured to create an interrupt.

The documentation states that for the STK3200 board, PB0 is connected to PC8, and PB1 is connected to PC9. Before configuring these inputs, the GPIO clock needs to be configured so that the GPIO can react to inputs. Then, each pin is configured as an input, and configured to issue an interrupt when triggered. Finally, IRQs are enabled.

```
1   static void GpioSetup(void)
2   {
3       /* Enable GPIO clock */
4       CMU_ClockEnable(cmuClock_GPIO, true);
5
6       /* Configure PC8 as input and enable interrupt  */
7       GPIO_PinModeSet(gpioPortC, 8, gpioModeInputPull, 1);
8       GPIO_IntConfig(gpioPortC, 8, false, true, true);
9
10      NVIC_ClearPendingIRQ(GPIO_EVEN_IRQn);
11      NVIC_EnableIRQ(GPIO_EVEN_IRQn);
12
13      /* Configure PC9 as input and enable interrupt */
14      GPIO_PinModeSet(gpioPortC, 9, gpioModeInputPull, 1);
15      GPIO_IntConfig( gpioPortC, 9, false, true, true);
16
17      NVIC_ClearPendingIRQ(GPIO_ODD_IRQn);
18      NVIC_EnableIRQ(GPIO_ODD_IRQn);
19  }
```

The STK3200 does not have a segment LCD display, but rather a Memory LCD. Configuration is done differently, but once again, software abstraction makes it extremely easy to do. Rather than specifically configuring a device, you initialize the display driver, which correctly configures the device that is present on that microcontroller.

```
DISPLAY_Init();
```

From here on, you can use instructions to write geometric shapes and text directly onto the display.

There is one more thing required before you are ready to start. In the previous example, the system spent most of its time in low power mode, using the RTC to wake up the device every minute to refresh the time. This application will be similar, but since this evaluation board has an impressive Memory LCD screen, you will be writing an application that shows analog time, and with a second hand. Therefore, the RTC has to be configured, but this time, instead of waking the system every minute, the RTC will be programmed to wake the system every second. The STK3800 had an intelligent Segment LCD controller that could perform basic animations on its own, but that isn't possible on a Memory LCD. Instead, every second, the screen will be updated with a graphical second hand.

First things first; programming the RTC. The RTC configuration looks very much like the configuration for the STK3800, the only differences being the interrupt configuration and the divider. Since the RTC is counting a relatively small lapse of time, there is no need for a divider. The code will look like this:

```
1  void RtcInit(void)
2  {
3      RTC_Init_TypeDef rtcInit = RTC_INIT_DEFAULT;
4      /* Enable LE domain registers */
5      CMU_ClockEnable(cmuClock_CORELE, true);
6      /* Enable LFXO as LFACLK in CMU. This will also start LFXO */
7      CMU_ClockSelectSet(cmuClock_LFA, cmuSelect_LFXO);
8      /* Enable RTC clock */
9      CMU_ClockEnable(cmuClock_RTC, true);
10     /* Initialize RTC */
11     rtcInit.enable   = false;  /* Do not start RTC after initialization */
12     rtcInit.debugRun = false;  /* Halt RTC when debugging. */
13     rtcInit.comp0Top = true;   /* Wrap around on COMP0 match. */
14     RTC_Init(&rtcInit);
15     /* Interrupt at specified frequency. */
16     RTC_CompareSet(0, (CMU_ClockFreqGet(cmuClock_RTC) / RTC_FREQUENCY) - 1);
17     /* Enable interrupt */
18     NVIC_EnableIRQ(RTC_IRQn);
19     RTC_IntEnable(RTC_IEN_COMP0);
20     /* Start counter */
21     RTC_Enable(true);
22 }
```

On line 3, the RTC structure is created, and it is filled in on lines 11 to 13. Finally, the RTC is initialized on line 14, but not enabled (line 11). At line 16, the interrupt is set to every second, and interrupts are enabled on lines 18 and 19. Finally, the RTC is enabled, and the function returns.

Main Application

First, the application will need to know the current time. It will use a structure that only needs to be used inside the main function:

```
struct tm *time = localtime((time_t const*)&curTime);
```

A routine will need to be created that sets the graphics background and prints the background image. To save space and time, you could create an entire background image in Flash — a constant table 128 bits by 128 bits. To copy this table to the framebuffer, a simple command is used:

```
status = GLIB_drawBitmap(&glibContext,
                         0, 0, BACKGROUND_WIDTH, BACKGROUND_HEIGHT,
                         (uint8_t*)background);
```

This routine will start in one corner (0, 0), and finish in the opposite corner (BACKGROUND_WIDTH, BACKGROUND_HEIGHT), and fill in the image with the table found at background. For this example, the background width and height are set to the resolution of the Memory LCD:

```
#define BACKGROUND_WIDTH   (128)
#define BACKGROUND_HEIGHT  (128)
```

The interesting part of Memory LCD screens is that only the pixels that need updating are actually updated. Each pixel has its own one-bit memory, providing an always-on image, and using very little current. Memory LCD screens are fast enough to display animations, and the Cortex-M0+ has fast I/O capability that is more than able to keep up with animations. Therefore, displaying the background before displaying the hands is an acceptable solution. Only the pixels that have changed since the last screen refresh are updated (where the hands used to be), so there is no screen tearing.

Once the background has been transferred to the Memory LCD memory, it is time for a little bit of arithmetic. The "hands" are digital — a graphical line from the center of the screen to the exterior of a circle, depending on the time. This will be done with some trigonometry. You will be calculating the sine and cosine of the current time to produce coordinates for lines. This brings up a question: This processor will be calculating sines and cosines; wouldn't a Cortex-M4 with an FPU be a better choice? The answer is no. While it is true that a Cortex-M4 with an FPU would have better precision and be faster, the Cortex-M0+ is more than capable. Firstly, even though you will be calculating trigonometry, there is no need for lots of precision. The result of a calculation will be used to display a line, and then immediately be discarded. In the very worst case, a lack of precision means that a hand might be off by one pixel, something that the end user will never notice. The application does not need that much precision. Secondly, what the application requires is a low-powered processor. The Cortex-M4F might be slightly faster for this type of calculation, but the processor will only be calculating a few sines and cosines per second before returning to a low-power mode. The Cortex-M0+ is the best candidate for this situation.

First, the minute hand. The minute hand will be a line, starting from the center of the clock, and it will have a length of 45 pixels. Imagine a circle, the center of which is the middle of the Memory LCD, and with a radius of 45 pixels. The minute hand will be a line from the center to a point on this circle, depending on the amount of minutes. You need to define a few variables before starting.

```
#define BACKGROUND_WIDTH    (128)
#define BACKGROUND_HEIGHT   (128)
#define CENTER_X        (BACKGROUND_WIDTH/2)
#define CENTER_Y        (BACKGROUND_HEIGHT/2)
#define MIN_START   0
#define MIN_END     45
```

Now, you will need to create a function to calculate the start and end of the line. For the minute hand, the line will start at the center, so this is easy, only the end coordinates will be calculated.

```
void MinuteHandDraw(int minute)
{
  double a = (double)minute / 30.0 * PI;

  GLIB_drawLine(&glibContext,
                CENTER_X,  /* start x */
                CENTER_Y,  /* start y */
                CENTER_X + (int)(MIN_END * sin(a)),   /* end x   */
                CENTER_Y - (int)(MIN_END * cos(a)));  /* end y   */
}
```

This function calculates the end coordinates, and then performs the drawing via the function GLIB_drawLine. Now you will do the hour hand. The hour hand will be a little different from the minute hand. The angle will be calculated as a mixture of the hours and the minutes. Hour hands are also shorter, so make this one 30 pixels long.

```
#define HOUR_START   0
#define HOUR_END    30
```

Now, create an `HourHandDraw` function.

```
void HourHandDraw(int hour, int minute)
{
    int position = hour * 5 + minute / 12;
    double a = (double)position / 30.0 * PI;

    GLIB_drawLine(&glibContext,
            CENTER_X,   /* start x */
            CENTER_Y,   /* start y */
            CENTER_X + (int)(HOUR_END * sin(a)),    /* end x   */
            CENTER_Y - (int)(HOUR_END * cos(a)));   /* end y   */
}
```

The code is almost identical to the previous function, except that a slight adjustment is made for the current amount of minutes. As the minute hand advances towards 12, the hour hand will also slowly advance towards the next hour, just like a real clock.

If you require very low power operation, it is possible to stop here and to program the RTC to create an interrupt every minute. That way the screen will be updated by the microcontroller every minute. However, for this application, the requirement is to have a second hand, and the RTC has already been programmed to interrupt every second.

The second hand is slightly shorter, but also, for aesthetics, it will not start at the center, but slightly off, at a radius of 10 pixels.

```
#define SEC_START   10
#define SEC_END     35
```

Since the beginning coordinate will not start at the center of the screen, you must calculate both the start and the finish coordinates.

```
void SecondHandDraw(int second)
{
    double a = (double)second / 30.0 * PI;

    GLIB_drawLine(&glibContext,
            CENTER_X + (int)(SEC_START * sin(a)),   /* start x */
            CENTER_Y - (int)(SEC_START * cos(a)),   /* start y */
            CENTER_X + (int)(SEC_END * sin(a)),     /* end x   */
            CENTER_Y - (int)(SEC_END * cos(a)));    /* end y   */
}
```

You can now display the background image and the three hands of the clock. All that remains to be done is to create a main loop.

```
void main(void)
{
    while(1)
    {
        time = localtime((time_t const*)&curTime);
        GLIB_drawBitmap(&glibContext,
                    0, 0, BACKGROUND_WIDTH, BACKGROUND_HEIGHT,
```

```
                                        (uint8_t*)background);
                  HourHandDraw(time->tm_hour % 12, t->tm_min);
                  MinuteHandDraw(time->tm_min);
                  SecondHandDraw(time->tm_sec);

                  /* Enter low-power mode */
                  EMU_EnterEM2(false);
            }
      }
```

The main loop simply gets the current time before updating the background image and displaying the three hands. Finally, the microcontroller is put into low-power mode, stopping program execution but retaining RAM. The microcontroller will stay in that state until it receives an interrupt, continuing program execution.

What Now?

Silicon Labs provides a more complete version of this application with their evaluation kit. It only briefly shows some of the functions, but the complete version has support, not only for an analog clock, but also a digital interface and functions for setting the time.

Using the same principle, it would be interesting to create a stopwatch and some other functions found commonly on wristwatches; showing the current date, for example. Once again, the STK3200 has excellent I/O capacity, and this card can be programmed to activate GPIOs depending on the time, for example a buzzer, useful for an alarm clock function.

Atmel D20 Xplained Pro

Atmel was founded in 1984, and ever since then, it has been close to hobbyists and makers, while also being a world-class supplier of next-gen logic circuits.

In 1995, Atmel did something unique; it developed a processor with integrated flash memory: a Flash Micro. It was based on the Intel 8051 and was a huge success with the simplified programming mechanism; the processor itself was programmed and no longer required external ROM.

In 1996, Atmel developed the AVR, an 8-bit RISC microcontroller that was also a Flash Micro. All other microcontrollers at the time used PROM or EEPROM, making modifications difficult, sometimes even impossible. Although the integrated flash memory was comparable to Atmel's version of the Intel 8051, the design itself was radically different. The AVR was designed to be used with high-level programming languages such as C and was an efficient RISC core.

The AVR line was an instant hit and was loved by electronics enthusiasts everywhere. Some amazing projects have been created, but they were still 8-bit microcontrollers. Recently, Atmel developed AVR microcontrollers based on 32-bit cores, but also created a new line of products, using an ARM Cortex-M core, delivering a unique combination of power efficiency, flexibility, and performance. However, Atmel hasn't simply taken an ARM core and put its logo on it; the Peripheral Event System is something that was loved by AVR enthusiasts and enables peripherals to interact with each other without using CPU resources. This technology is still available in Atmel's AVR line, in both Atmel's 8- and 32-bit versions, and Atmel has also created something very similar for their ARM-powered line of devices.

Atmel's D20 microcontroller line is based on a Cortex-M0+ core and comes with an evaluation board, the SAM D20 Xplained Pro (see Figure 5-5). Although other boards may have different sensors or LCD screens, the D20 Xplained Pro has one user button and one LED. It doesn't have an LCD screen, and it doesn't have a light sensor, but what it does have is three extension headers; all three are the same electronically.

FIGURE 5-5: Atmel's SAM D20 Evaluation Board

The Xplained Pro series isn't just based on the SAM D20; other processors use the same interfaces. Atmel therefore also created an interesting line of external peripherals, or "wings" as they are sometimes called. The I/O1 board provides a light sensor, temperature sensor, and micro-SD reader. The OLED1 board provides a 128 x 32 OLED display, as well as three buttons and three LEDs. The QT1 board contains touch sensors used with Atmel's Peripheral Touch Controller. If none of these boards contains what you need, the PROTO1 board provides a bread-boarding area where you can use your own components. All of these boards use a common connector — the Xplained Pro header.

Atmel Studio integrates Atmel Software Framework (ASF), a large library with thousands of project examples and code extracts.

All of these boards are supported by Atmel's SDK, and ASF provides primitives and examples for each of the different components. You won't spend any time developing your own drivers for these devices; Atmel Studio allows you to import the modules you require directly into your application.

Test Application

The SAM D20 Xplained Pro board does not have some of the peripherals found on other boards, like a segment LCD, for example. That does not stop it from being able to test simple applications. It does have a user LED, and a user button. Using these two devices, it is very easy to create a test application. In just a few lines of code, it is possible to create an application that turns the LED on if the button is pressed, or turns it off otherwise. The application will look like this:

```
int main(void)
{
    system_init();

    while(1)
    {
        if (port_pin_get_input_level(BUTTON_0_PIN) == BUTTON_0_ACTIVE)
        {
            port_pin_set_output_level(LED_0_PIN, LED_0_ACTIVE)
        }
        else
        {
            port_pin_set_output_level(LED_0_PIN, !LED_0_ACTIVE)
        }
    }
}
```

The function system_init() quickly sets up the board. Then the application loops, and scans the state of the user button, BUTTON_0. If BUTTON_0 is active, the LED output is set to high; otherwise, it is set to low. This is the default program that is generated when creating a new project, and is an excellent way to test that the board is functioning.

With the click of a button, Atmel Studio compiles the project. All project dependencies are compiled, and a binary is generated. Another click later, and the binary is flashed onto the Xplained Pro board. The SAM D20 comes with a hardware debugger built directly onto the board, and Atmel Studio makes the most of this to automatically flash an application and to perform debug operations.

Weather Station

As stated previously, Atmel also makes a large set of extension boards, notably the I/O1 board and the OLED1 board. The I/O1 board has a temperature sensor, and the OLED1 board has a 128 x 32 OLED display. With these two boards, it is possible to create a digital thermometer, reading the temperature from one board and displaying it on the other. The temperature will be precise to one tenth of a degree.

Atmel provides a training document for the SAM D20 series, to get to know the processor as well as Atmel's development environment — Atmel Studio. This document shows how to set up Atmel Studio 6, which is beyond the scope of this book. In this section, I will concentrate on the code, not Atmel Studio. Atmel has excellent documentation that comes with Xplained Pro boards; please consult that documentation for information on how to use their interface.

Initialization

The SAM D20 requires some initialization before being able to run an application. This includes setting up the system clocks and some hardware configuration, but thanks to Atmel's SDK, this is a simple task. When creating a blank project, several files are generated. One of them, conf_clocks.h, contains default clock settings, and can be used without any modification. As seen in the previous example, a single line of code is sufficient:

```
system_init();
```

This function takes the information in conf_clocks.h and performs low-level system initialization. Once this is done, you are now ready to perform configuration.

Configuring the Temperature Sensor

Atmel produces a wing that is perfect for this application, the I/O1. The I/O1 is a relatively small circuit board, but packed with peripherals. It contains a light sensor, temperature sensor, an SD card reader, and even a free GPIO connector. The I/O1 board is shown in Figure 5-6.

The temperature sensor on the I/O1 wing is an Atmel AT30TSE758, a lightweight component which is interfaced with I2C. Atmel provides a driver for this component, and including the driver is as simple as importing an ASF driver from Atmel Studio. This imports a new file, `conf_at30tse75x.h`, containing the driver configuration options. Most of Atmel's drivers exist in two formats: polled, or callback. For this application, all operations will be polled.

FIGURE 5-6: Atmel's I/O1 Wing

Once the driver has been imported, all of the necessary calls are added to the project. Initializing the temperature sensor is as easy as calling a single function:

```
at30tse_init();
```

For this application, a sensor resolution of 12 bits will be used. This can be set with another function, `at30tse_write_config_register`. To keep all the configuration routines together, a new routine will be created:

```
static void temp_sensor_setup(void)
{
    /* Init and enable temperature sensor */
    at30tse_init();

    /* Set 12-bit resolution */
    at30tse_write_config_register(
        AT30TSE_CONFIG_RES(AT30TSE_CONFIG_RES_12_bit));
}
```

Reading from the temperature sensor is once again a simple command; `at30tse_read_temperature` returns a double, containing temperature information. However, before reading the temperature, you must configure the output device on which the temperature will be written.

Configuring the OLED Display

Atmel's OLED1 wing contains a bright 128 x 32 OLED display, three buttons and three LEDs, and also connects to an Xplained Pro extension header. It is illustrated in Figure 5-7. This is an excellent way of viewing the current temperature.

Once again, adding the OLED display to your project is as simple as importing a driver. An entire library has been created, not only to access the display, but also graphical functions for writing text and for graphical primitives. In order to import the driver, you must add the "GFX Monochrome - System Font" service. This not only imports the display driver, but also the communication method (SPI), graphical primitives, and the framebuffer device. Adding this ASF adds two header files:

```
conf_ssd1306.h and conf_sysfont.h.
```

FIGURE 5-7: Atmel's OLED1 Wing

Once again, a C function is required to initiate the graphics device. This is done in a single statement:

```
gfx_mono_init();
```

Putting It All Together

The two components used on this project have been imported, and one configuration routine has been created, for the temperature sensor. The graphics device only requires one line, so there is no need to create a function.

What is needed now is to add the device configuration. Add the configuration to the main function. Also, add a variable to hold the temperature value. The main function will look like this:

```
int main(void)
{

    double temp_result;

    /* Low-level initialization */
    system_init();

    /* Setup the graphics */
```

```
gfx_mono_init();

/* Setup the temperature sensor */
temp_sensor_setup();
/* Get a first reading */
temp_result = at30tse_read_temperature();

}
```

The application is beginning to take shape, but it doesn't yet tell the user what the temperature is. Luckily, the OLED can be used as a terminal device; printing text is as simple as `snprintf`.

There are three things that must be declared before continuing. First, the maximum size of a string to be printed out — 20 should be more than enough.

```
#define APP_STRING_LENGTH 20
```

Secondly, the application must know where to print the text, in XY coordinates.

```
#define APP_POSITION_X 0
#define APP_POSITION_Y 0
```

Now, add a variable to hold the text.

```
char temp_string[APP_STRING_LENGTH];
```

This application needs to convert the temperature data into a string that can be displayed, and to do that the standard library must be imported.

```
#include <stdio.h>
```

Now, time to display the temperature. The temperature is held in the variable `temp_result`, which has been defined as a double. The standard library does not support many floating-point conversions due to size constraints, and especially the `%f` formatting specifier is not included. Therefore a bit of calculation is required.

➤ For the decimal number, casting `temp_result` to `int` will discard the fractional part.

➤ For the fractional part, the first digit after the decimal point will be used. To obtain this, `temp_result` will be multiplied by 10, before casting to an `int` to remove the remaining fraction. Finally, taking the `modulo 10` will obtain the digit in the ones' place.

This can be expressed by the following instructions:

```
snprintf(temp_string,
    APP_STRING_LENGTH,
    "Temp: %d.%dC\n",
    (int)temp_result",
    ((int)(temp_result * 10)) % 10);

gfx_mono_draw_string(temp_string,
    APP_POSITION_X, APP_POSITION_Y, &sysfont);
```

Now all that remains to be done is to add a loop, continuously read the temperature, and print the result. The final application will look like this:

```c
#include <stdio.h>

#define APP_POSITION_X 0
#define APP_POSITION_Y 0
#define APP_STRING_LENGTH 20

int main(void)
{
    double temp_result;
    char temp_string[APP_STRING_LENGTH];

    /* Low-level initialization */
    system_init();

    /* Setup the graphics */
    gfx_mono_init();

    /* Setup the temperature sensor */
    temp_sensor_setup();

    /* Keep looping */
    while (true)
    {
        /* Get a first reading */
        temp_result = at30tse_read_temperature();

        /* Print the temperature */
        snprintf(temp_string,
            APP_STRING_LENGTH,
            "Temp: %d.%dC\n",
            (int)temp_result",
            ((int)(temp_result * 10)) % 10);

        gfx_mono_draw_string(temp_string,
            APP_POSITION_X, APP_POSITION_Y, &sysfont);

    }

}
```

What Now?

With only a few lines of code, and without having knowledge of the electronic components on the wings, you have created a fully functional application. It is, of course, possible to add to this application. On the same wing as the temperature sensor is a light sensor and also an SD card reader. It is possible to create an application that not only records the temperature, but also the light levels, and to store them on an SD card. An entire Xplained Pro header is still available, so it is perfectly possible to add even more components; you could place a barometer or possibly a tachometer for measuring wind speed. With a small battery (Atmel also provides a battery case, the ATBATTERY-CASE-4AAA), this weather station could sit in a garden for weeks and record the weather for statistical data. You could even add a low-power Bluetooth device to automatically upload data when you connect, so you don't have to take out the SD card. With the SAM D20 Xplained Pro board and accessories, anything is possible.

CASE STUDY: U-BOOT

When a computer is turned on, most people think that the first program to run is the operating system. When turning on a computer, you are greeted by a Windows logo, a MacOS background, or a Linux penguin. Most people tend to be unaware of the BIOS, which is actually a program in itself. Linux users who dual boot often see another application: either LILO or GRUB during the boot process. These two applications are known as boot loaders; their job is to provide the processor with a kernel to load. When they have loaded a kernel into RAM, they give full control to the kernel and are subsequently deleted from memory.

U-Boot from Denx Software is a well-known bootloader for embedded systems. Not only is it used extensively on development boards for its ease of use, it is also open source and can therefore be used to study bootloader operation and low-level programming.

U-Boot doesn't just load a kernel into memory, it does far more. It can open a serial port and accept commands. It can use serial protocols to upload new binaries; it can output board and flash information; and it can also load kernels from specific locations, including from an Ethernet adapter. U-Boot has an impressive list of commands, which can be augmented with some development.

Inside the examples folder are a few programs that show you the power of this application. For example, the `hello_world.c` program can be compiled and copied to the target system using serial:

```
=> loads
## Ready for S-Record download ...
~>examples/hello_world.srec
1 2 3 4 5 6 7 8 9 10 11 ...
[file transfer complete]
[connected]
## Start Addr = 0x00040004

=> go 40004 Hello World! This is a test.
## Starting application at 0x00040004 ...
Hello World
argc = 7
argv[0] = "40004"
argv[1] = "Hello"
argv[2] = "World!"
argv[3] = "This"
argv[4] = "is"
argv[5] = "a"
argv[6] = "test."
argv[7] = ""
Hit any key to exit ...

## Application terminated, rc = 0x0
```

U-Boot can be used on almost any system because it supports most processor families, including ARM processors. It natively supports some filesystems, including common filesystems such as FAT and EXT2, as well as embedded filesystems such as JFFS2.

It is common to see development boards running U-Boot for flexibility and to have a suite of test applications written for U-Boot. With this bootloader, engineers can simulate events that are hard to reproduce; a program might corrupt specific areas of NAND flash to see how a backup partition reacts, or hardware might be set to a specific state before system boot. Some applications are also geared toward performance, running benchmarking applications independently of hardware to know the true throughput of a device bus, for example, and then comparing it to what is achieved running an operating system.

MACHINE STUDY: RASPBERRY PI

In 1981, Acorn released the BBC Micro, a computer system designed to be used in schools. Acorn designed a processor that was spun out into ARM, and in 2012, those processors were again back in schools with the Raspberry Pi, a credit-card sized single-board computer designed by the Raspberry Pi Foundation based on an ARM core: an ARM1176JZF-S.

The original intention of the Raspberry Pi Foundation was to create a computer for schools, perfect for teaching computer literacy. The low-cost design makes it easy to buy one computer per child, and with no internal hard drive, it is rugged and is not easy to break. Also of interest, because all the firmware resides on the SD card, it is almost impossible to get a Raspberry Pi into a state in which it cannot boot. There is no BIOS to flash, and there is no way of corrupting the bootloader image. This makes it perfect for learning ARM programming.

The Raspberry Pi boots from an SD card, so switching operating systems is as simple as swapping SD cards. Several operating systems are available: Debian and Arch Linux distributions are available, and a Fedora remix is also available. Also of interest is RISC OS, an operating system originally designed by Acorn and bundled with all Acorn Archimedes machines.

Although the Raspberry Pi was originally designed for schools, it has made a huge impact on the Maker community, a community of electronics and programming enthusiasts that dream of new contraptions, or simply identify a need and create a solution, and multiple projects have been created for this small-factor computer. It has been used for robotics systems, home automation, security, and just about anywhere that a user has identified a need. It is an excellent tool to learn about ARM systems, and a great way of having fun. When you have finished writing ARM binaries, you can swap the SD card and relax while playing a special version of *Minecraft* for the Raspberry Pi, or watching your favorite film directly on your television through some excellent video programs.

The Raspberry Pi is an entire computer system; it has video capabilities, USB, Ethernet, and enough system resources to run a full Linux system, so why is this considered to be embedded? Well, that all depends on your definition of embedded. It is a small factor computer, with everything on-board, and compared to a desktop computer, it has limited resources. What is interesting about this system is its versatility; by studying the boot procedure, it is possible to have a full Linux system, or to create a bare metal application, without all the fuss of flashing via specialized tools. The Raspberry Pi is an excellent low-cost starter platform.

Boot Procedure

The Raspberry Pi has an interesting boot procedure. On power on, the ARM core is held in a reset state, while the GPU takes control of the system. The GPU has some internal firmware that is responsible for the first boot steps, including reading from the first partition of the SD card. For the Raspberry Pi to boot, the first partition must be formatted to FAT32 and must contain several files.

bootcode.bin

This is the first file to be loaded from the SD card by the GPU. It is loaded into the L2 cache, and its role is to enable the SDRAM memory and to configure a few system settings. It then loads the next bootloader stage.

loader.bin

This file contains the binary routines necessary to load and execute ELF binaries, and looks for start.elf on the SD card.

start.elf

This is the final bootloader stage and where the magic starts. This file can load a file called kernel.img and place it at memory location 0x8000 (from the ARM core's point of view). The start.elf file can also use an external file called config.txt that contains different parameters to fine-tune the ARM core (overclocking and overvoltage, for example). After kernel.img has been loaded into system memory, start.elf releases the reset state on the ARM core and gives it control.

kernel.img

This file is an ARM executable file, more often than not a Linux kernel. This can also be a bare metal application that you can design.

Compiling Programs for the Raspberry Pi

The interesting thing about the Raspberry Pi is that it comes with a complete Linux distribution and is fast enough to have its own compiler to compile binaries for itself. If you have another computer next to it, it is also possible to test out a cross-compiler environment, for both Linux binaries or for barebones applications because the Raspberry Pi can do both.

As seen previously, the GCC compiler needs to know a little bit more about the target processor before compiling. The Raspberry Pi uses an ARM1176JSF-S, which is an ARMv6 core, and has an FPU. So, the GCC command-line options should look like this:

```
-Ofast -mfpu=vfp -mfloat-abi=hard -march=armv6zk -mtune=arm1176jzf-s
```

In all the previous examples, you had to configure the vector table, but because start.elf places the binary at 0x8000, you don't have to do that. Of course, if you need interrupts or if you want to handle exceptions, then you will have to configure that, but for basic barebones applications, you can ignore that.

Now try a simple program.

```
void main(void)
{
    while(1)
    {

    }
}
```

Save this as `kernel.c`. This program doesn't do anything, but it serves to show how the compilation works. So now compile that application.

```
arm-none-eabi-gcc -O2 -mfpu=vfp -mfloat-abi=hard -march=armv6zk \
    -mtune=arm1176jzf-s -nostartfiles kernel.c -o kernel.elf
```

The `-nostartfiles` option tells the compiler to avoid all the code used to start programs in an operating system environment; it especially avoids adding `exit()` functions, something that you do not need here. The binary is compiled as an ELF, so it needs to be transformed into a binary before you proceed.

```
arm-none-eabi-objcopy kernel.elf -O binary kernel.img
```

You can output this program to the filename `kernel.img` because that is what is expected on the SD card. Now that everything is compiled, you can copy `kernel.img` to your SD card along with the other files (provided by the Raspberry Pi Foundation, available on its website), and you are good to go. More information can be found at `http://www.raspberrypi.org/downloads`.

What's Next?

This simple program does nothing except put the processor into an infinite loop, but the Raspberry Pi also has other output devices. There is a serial port for writing a possible "Hello, World!" line. It has a GPIO header, and expansion boards are available, so you can create electronic projects to automate your home (example projects of a door lock are available), but there is also an HDMI output if you want to create graphic output and maybe even animation.

SUMMARY

This chapter gives a few example programs and techniques on both emulated and real-world boards. They have been in a mixture of assembly and C, some require specific hardware initialization, and some are close to systems programming. Now that you have followed these examples, you have two desktop clocks and a weather station, all made using readily available boards and programming tools.

The next chapter will present the Thumb extension, a versatile language created for high-density applications and microcontroller profiles. You will see the different instructions, and how to generate efficient Thumb code.

Thumb Instruction Set

WHAT'S IN THIS CHAPTER?

➤ Presenting Thumb

➤ What is Thumb used for?

➤ What cores run Thumb?

➤ What are the advantages of Thumb?

➤ How to switch between ARM and Thumb

➤ Writing for Thumb

Many of the most popular 32-bit processors for mobile devices use Reduced Instruction Set Computer (RISC) technology. Unlike Complete Instruction Set Computer processors (CISC), Reduced Instruction Set Computer engines generally execute each instruction in a single cycle, often resulting in faster program execution using the same clock speed.

Increased performance, however, comes at a price: a RISC processor typically needs more memory than a CISC does to store the same program. To achieve the same results as a single CISC instruction, RISC engines often require two, three, or more simpler instructions. For most embedded devices, memory constraints are more important than execution speed, so reducing code size is important.

In 1995, ARM released the Thumb instruction set, used for the first time on the ARM7TDMI core. Thumb instructions are denser than their ARM counterparts, being 16-bits long in the original Thumb extension. All Thumb instructions map directly to ARM instructions, but to save space, the instructions were simplified.

Thumb was introduced not only for the denser code, but also for devices that did not have full 32-bit wide memory access. One of the first devices to use Thumb, the Game Boy Advance, had little memory that was accessible in 32-bits; most of the memory was 16-bits wide. Accessing a 32-bit instruction meant accessing the first 16-bits and then waiting for the next 16-bits, which was very slow. By using Thumb, the Game Boy Advance could keep the game instructions to 16-bits long and avoid the slowdown of accessing 32-bits.

Although using Thumb codes is often slightly slower to the ARM counterpart due to simplification, accessing 16-bit memory meant that the ARM7TDMI outperformed full 32-bit processors with 16-bit wide data channels.

Performance, energy efficiency, and memory footprint are the most important considerations for designers of embedded systems, and Thumb effectively addresses each requirement, making it perfect for mobile applications.

Thumb-2 technology was introduced in the ARM1156T2-S core in 2003. It extended the original Thumb instruction set by including 32-bit instructions, therefore making the instruction set variable-length. This addition made Thumb-2 on average 26 percent denser than the ARM instruction set, while providing a 25 percent performance boost over original Thumb code.

ThumbEE was introduced in 2005 and was marketed as Jazelle Runtime Compilation Target (RCT). By making small changes to the Thumb-2 instruction set, it was designed to target languages such as Python, Java, and Perl. ARM deprecated the use of ThumbEE with revision C of its ARMv7 architecture. ThumbEE was an addition to, not a replacement of, Thumb-2. New cores continue to support Thumb-2.

Of course, reducing a 32-bit instruction to 16-bits means making sacrifices, and 16-bit Thumb opcodes have less functionality. The condition codes were removed for everything except branching. Also, most of the opcodes can no longer access all the registers, but only the lower half. However, because Thumb instructions are mapped to ARM instructions in hardware, the result is an execution speed that is identical to ARM execution speed. However, only accessing one-half of the registers implies some slowdowns.

Because Thumb is designed as a target for C compilers, it is not designed to be used directly; rather, developers should use a higher language such as C. You must understand the principles behind the instruction set to write optimized code, but unlike the ARM ISA, almost all optimization should be done directly in C.

THUMB

Thumb was released in 1995 in the ARM7TDMI, one of the most versatile ARM cores produced. Most application code written in C can be compiled directly in Thumb; however, some driver code may need to be written in ARM code. For the Game Boy Advance, lower memory was 32-bit, in which ARM instructions could be run without degrading performance, and all the driver code was located in this portion of memory. The upper memory was 16-bits wide, and this is where Thumb code was located: the game code. The problem was how to switch between the two.

Originally created for the ARM7TDMI, Thumb is a "state," and developers can switch between ARM state and Thumb state. In ARM state, executing a Thumb instruction results in an undefined instruction exception. The processor needs to be told that the following instructions are Thumb, and the best place for that is the Branch instruction.

The original Thumb ISA by itself isn't enough for all core components of a bare-bones system. Although perfectly suited for applications, it does not have all the required instructions to handle a complete system. (For example, it has no way of interacting with a coprocessor.)

THUMB-2 TECHNOLOGY

Thumb-2 technology is a major enhancement to the already popular Thumb extension. It provides 32-bit instructions that can be intermixed with the existing 16-bit instructions, making the Thumb extension variable length. The ARM core automatically detects the length of the next instruction and fetches the entire instruction.

By adding 32-bit instructions, almost all the ARM ISA functionality is now covered and adds DSP functionality. Because Cortex-M processors support only the Thumb ISA and cannot use the ARM ISA, Thumb-2 added major functionality, including the possibility of performing advanced calculation on a microcontroller architecture.

Thumb-2 didn't only introduce 32-bit instructions; there are also new 16-bit instructions, adding enhanced energy efficiency and making the instruction set closer to C. Thumb-2 also makes it possible to create an entire system, not just an application, using only the Thumb ISA.

HOW THUMB IS EXECUTED

The question that most people ask is, "Why does the ARM core have two separate instruction sets?" In reality, it has only one; Thumb can be considered shorthand for the ARM instruction set. Thumb was originally developed by looking at the most-used ARM instructions and creating 16-bit counterparts. Therefore, the Thumb instruction ADD r0, #1 is automatically "translated" in hardware to the ARM instruction ADDS r0, r0, #1, incurring no penalty to execution time. This is illustrated in Figure 6-1.

Originally, the ARM7TDMI had separate decompressor logic, but with the ARM9TDMI onwards, this was integrated into the pipeline's decoder logic. This is illustrated in Figure 6-2. Its function remains the same — all Thumb instructions are mapped to an ARM instruction, only the logic has been moved to the pipeline to simplify the processor's design and to increase efficiency.

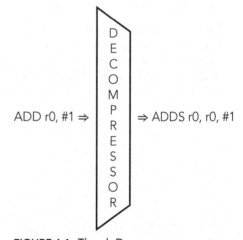

FIGURE 6-1: Thumb Decompressor

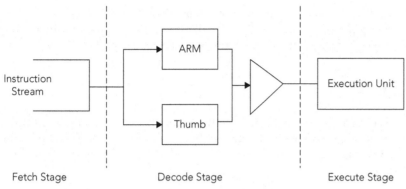

FIGURE 6-2: 3-stage pipeline with Thumb decoder

ADVANTAGES OF USING THUMB

There are two major advantages to using Thumb ISA over ARM ISA. Thumb instructions are 16-bits wide, and Thumb-2 adds a mixture of 16 bit and 32 bits. Because more instructions can be written per word of memory, Thumb is *denser*. This is useful for systems with limited memory; although writing in Thumb sometimes means a few more instructions, the end result is often 40 percent denser than code written for the ARM ISA, meaning less memory requirements.

Another major advantage of using Thumb is also due to the instruction size. Since Thumb instructions are denser, the cache can contain more Thumb instructions than ARM instructions, so Thumb applications often cache better than their ARM equivalent.

Take, for instance, a simple division program. This program takes a number in r0 and divides it by the number provided in r1. It returns the quotient in r0 and the remainder in r1. In this unoptimized code, it simply subtracts r1 from r0 as many times as possible and returns the amount of times it can do so. In ARM, such a routine could be written like this:

```
        MOV r3, #0
loop
        SUBS r0, r0, r1
        ADDGE r3, r3, #1
        BGE loop
        ADD r2, r0, r1
        MOV r0, r3
        MOV r1, r2
```

This code is 7 instructions long, and each instruction is 4 bytes long, so the code is 28 bytes long. This is a short subroutine, but it is a perfect example to show how Thumb can take up less space. In Thumb, taking into account the various subtleties of the instruction set, this could be written:

```
        MOV r3, #0
loop
        ADD r3, #1
        SUB r0, r1
        BGE loop
```

```
SUB r3, #1
ADD r2, r0, r1
MOV r0, r3
MOV r1, r2
```

There are more instructions in Thumb, and developers that are used to the ARM instruction set might be surprised at the way in which this code was written. The changes between Thumb and ARM are explained later in this chapter, in the section "Introduction to Thumb."

This routine in Thumb is 8 instructions long, but because each instruction is only 2 bytes long, that means that the entire code is only 16 bytes long, whereas the ARM code was 28 bytes long.

One of the worries about using Thumb ISA is that Thumb is slower than ARM. Although it is sometimes slightly slower than ARM code, it isn't for the reasons that you might first think. Thumb code is often slightly longer than ARM code, so more cycles might be necessary to obtain the same result. Also, fewer registers are readily available, which might impact some routines. However, the benefits outweigh the inconvenience. Since the code is denser, it uses less memory, meaning an embedded system can contain less memory, making them more cost efficient and power efficient. More instructions can fit into the same cache size, meaning that Thumb applications can out-perform ARM equivalent programs. To prove Thumb's power, an entire family of ARM cores, the Cortex-M, relies solely on Thumb code to obtain powerful microcontrollers with incredibly low power consumption.

Thumb was also designed with rapid development in mind. Thumb was developed as a compiler target, meaning that all development can be done in a higher language such as C. Although Cortex-A and Cortex-R cores need at least some development in assembler for boot code, Cortex-M cores that use only the Thumb ISA can be developed entirely in C.

CORES USING THUMB

The Thumb ISA was introduced in the ARM7TDMI design. All ARM9 and later chips support the Thumb instruction set.

Thumb-2 technology was introduced in the ARM1156T2-S and extends the Thumb ISA. All ARMv7 cores and later include Thumb-2.

The Cortex-A and Cortex-R families, supporting the ARMv7 and later architecture, both support Thumb and Thumb-2. These processors use the ARM ISA but can switch to the Thumb ISA when needed.

Cortex-M processors are a little different. They do not support the ARM ISA and support only the Thumb/Thumb-2 ISA. The Cortex-M3 and Cortex-M4 cores belong to the ARMV7-M and ARMV7E-M architectures, respectively, and support the full subset of Thumb and Thumb-2.

The Cortex-M0, M0+, and M1 belong to the ARMv6-M architecture and have more restrictions. They support the Thumb ISA but do not implement three instructions: CBZ, CBNZ, or IT. They do however support Thumb-2, but only a limited subset: BL, DMB, DSB, ISB, MRS, and MSR. Table 6-1 shows the different instructions supported by the different versions of Cortex-M cores. Instructions are listed according to their availability in Cortex-M cores, as well as the instruction length. All instructions available in one Cortex-M core are always available in later cores. For example, all of the instructions available in the Cortex-M0 core are available in the Cortex-M3.

TABLE 6-1: Cortex-M Core Instructions

M0	M0+	M1	M3	M4	SIZE	INSTRUCTIONS
Yes	Yes	Yes	Yes	Yes	16	ADC, ADD, ADR, AND, ASR, B, BIC, BKPT, BLX, BX, CMN, CMP, CPS, EOR, LDM, LDR, LDRB, LDRH, LDRSB, LDRSH, LSL, LSR, MOV, MUL, MVN, NOP, ORR, POP, PUSH, REV, REV16, REVSH, ROR, RSB, SBC, SEV, STM, STR, STRB, STRH, SUB, SVC, SXTB, SXTH, TST, UXTB, UXTH, WFE, WFI, YIELD
Yes	Yes	Yes	Yes	Yes	32	BL, DMB, DSB, ISB, MRS, MSR
No	No	No	Yes	Yes	16	CBNZ, CBZ, IT
No	No	No	Yes	Yes	32	ADC, ADD, ADR, AND, ASR, B, BFC, BFI, BIC, CDP, CLREX, CLZ, CMN, CMP, DBG, EOR, LDC, LDMA, LDMDB, LDR, LDRB, LDRBT, LDRD, LDREX, LDREXB, LDREXH, LDRH, LDRHT, LDRSB, LDRSBT, LDRSH, LDRSHT, LDRT, MCR, LSL, LSR, MLS, MCRR, MLA, MOV, MOVT, MRC, MRRC, MUL, MVN, NOP, ORN, ORR, PLD, PLDW, PLI, POP, PUSH, RBIT, REV, REV16, REVSH, ROR, RRX, RSB, SBC, SBFX, SDIV, SEV, SMLAL, SMULL, SSAT, STC, STMIA, STMDB, STR, STRB, STRBT, STRD, STREX, STREXB, STREXH, STRH, STRHT, STRT, SUB, SXTB, SXTH, TBB, TBH, TEQ, TST, UBFX, UDIV, UMLAL, UMULL, USAT, UXTB, UXTH, WFE, WFI, YIELD
No	No	No	No	Yes	32	PKH, QADD, QADD16, QADD8, QASX, QDADD, QDSUB, QSAX, QSUB, QSUB16, QSUB8, SADD16, SADD8, SASX, SEL, SHADD16, SHADD8, SHASX, SHSAX, SHSUB16, SHSUB8, SMLABB, SMLABT, SMLATB, SMLATT, SMLAD, SMLALBB, SMLALBT, SMLALTB, SMLALTT, SMLALD, SMLAWB, SMLAWT, SMLSD, SMLSLD, SMMLA, SMMLS, SMMUL, SMUAD, SMULBB, SMULBT, SMULTT, SMULTB, SMULWT, SMULWB, SMUSD, SSAT16, SSAX, SSUB16, SSUB8, SXTAB, SXTAB16, SXTAH, SXTB16, UADD16, UADD8, UASX, UHADD16, UHADD8, UHASX, UHSAX, UHSUB16, UHSUB8, UMAAL, UQADD16, UQADD8, UQASX, UQSAX, UQSUB16, UQSUB8, USAD8, USADA8, USAT16, USAX, USUB16, USUB8, UXTAB, UXTAB16, UXTAH, UXTB16

Some Cortex-M4 cores have an optional Floating Point Unit, allowing for more advanced calculations to be done with hardware optimization.

Due to the differences between the ARMv6-M and ARMv7-M architectures, you must know both Thumb and the Thumb-2 extension. Although you might be tempted to start a new project directly with a Cortex-M4 to have access to the entire Thumb and Thumb-2 ISA, the Cortex-M0+ is still an excellent microcontroller core, in active production, and has advantages over the more recent Cortex-M4 core.

ARM-THUMB INTERWORKING

On processors supporting both the ARM and Thumb ISA, you can switch from one state to another, which is known as *interworking*. Changing state is a simple process that you can do without any penalty compared to a basic branch instruction.

When a Cortex-A/R or Classic ARM core is turned on (when it enters the RESET state), it automatically starts in ARM state. A specific instruction must be issued for the core to switch to Thumb state.

Cortex-M cores are different. Because these cores do not support the ARM ISA, the core is automatically in Thumb state.

With the exception of the Cortex-M, the core must be told to switch to Thumb state; it does not do it automatically. Attempting to execute Thumb instructions while in ARM state most often results in an illegal instruction.

To enter Thumb state from ARM state (or vice versa), use the BX/BLX instruction: Branch and Exchange Instruction (with possible link). ARM processors are natively aligned; they must have instructions on a certain boundary. Typically, the processor looks for instructions aligned on 32 bits, or in the case of Thumb, 16 bits. In either case, the last address bit is not used and should always be 0. Thumb-capable cores make use of this by using the least significant address bit of the branch destination to indicate the instruction set state. By setting the LSB to 1, instead of looking for an impossible address, this tells the core that the next instruction will be a Thumb instruction and that the core should change to Thumb state.

Note that when a non-Cortex-M core handles an exception, the processor is automatically returned to ARM mode, or on select processor, whatever state was configured in the SCTRL register. When returning to the previous code, the CPSR is restored and the state of the processor is contained in the CPSR, returning the processor to its original state.

INTRODUCTION TO THUMB-1

Thumb was created after an analysis of the most-used ARM instructions in compiled C code. To have a complete 16-bit instruction set, several sacrifices were made. Thumb instructions cannot access all registers; they cannot access status or coprocessor registers; and some functionality that might have been done in one instruction in ARM state can take two or three in Thumb state. However, Thumb is not an entirely new language; an ARM core does not have two distinct languages embedded into silicon. Thumb instructions are mapped directly to ARM-state counterparts, expanding 16-bit instructions to 32-bit equivalents.

Writing efficient code for Thumb is a little more challenging, and for those who already know the ARM ISA, Thumb is easy to learn. It isn't a question of what can be done, but rather what can't be done in Thumb. That doesn't mean that Thumb is limited, it means that Thumb is designed differently.

Register Availability

The biggest change is in the register access. When operating in Thumb state, the application encounters a slightly different set of registers. As stated previously, most Thumb instructions can access only r0 to r7 (known as the low registers), not the entire set of registers. However, the SP, LR, and PC registers are still available, as shown in Figure 6-3.

Three instructions enable access to the high registers: MOV, ADD, and CMP. The reason for this is the shortening of instructions from 32 bits. One of 16 registers can be expressed as a 4-bit number, and one register in 8 can be expressed as a 3-bit number; therefore, saving 1 bit. For instructions that require multiple registers as arguments, this saves lots of space.

Removed Instructions

Some instructions had to be removed to create Thumb ISA. Because Thumb was originally designed for application-level code and not system code, no instructions exist to access coprocessors. Swap instructions were removed because they were not used often enough to merit a specific opcode. Reverse subtractions were also removed (RSB and RSC) and of all the different multiplications that exist, only MUL remains.

For those developing full applications on a Cortex-M0+, or other cores belonging to the ARMv6-M specification, these cores support a small subset of the Thumb-2 ISA, including MUL/MLA instructions.

ARM	Thumb
R0	R0
R1	R1
R2	R2
R3	R3
R4	R4
R5	R5
R6	R6
R7	R7
R8	
R9	
R10	
R11	
R12	
R13(SP)	SP
R14(LR)	LR
R15(PC)	PC

FIGURE 6-3: Comparison between ARM and Thumb register availability

No Conditionals

Conditional execution has been removed from almost all instructions; only branch instructions still have condition flags. This makes code more in line with C code; different sections of code are now separated, and the C instruction if (a == b) now becomes a compare instruction and a conditional branch.

Set Flags

With Thumb, almost every operation automatically executes an Update Status Register, effectively adding the S suffix to every instruction. ADD now becomes ADDS, without having to add the S to the end of the opcode. This is a major change from the ARM ISA where the status flags were updated only on request, and multiple conditional instructions could be executed. In Thumb, this is no longer possible because sacrifices had to be made to keep instructions 16-bits long, but it does make the assembly code more in line with C.

No Barrel Shifter

Barrel shift operations can no longer be used directly inside instructions. The barrel shifter still exists, of course, and can still be used, but in Thumb, specific instructions now exist to perform shifts. Thumb therefore introduced some new instructions: ASR, LSL, LSR, and ROR now become instructions instead of operators on operands. What used to be done in a single instruction now takes two; a single shift instruction followed by another instruction.

Some decompilers will still show these instructions even in ARM, since they are Unified Assembly language instructions. However, in its true ARM form, these instructions are MOV instructions with a barrel shift used as a second operand. Unified Assembly Language will be discussed in the next chapter.

Reduced Immediates

With the ARM ISA, most instructions allowed for a second operand, which was either an immediate value or a (shifted) register. In Thumb, this is no longer the case because the instructions have been simplified and now resemble C assignment operators (for example, += and |=).

As with most rules, there are exceptions. ADD, SUB, MOV, and CMP can have both immediate values and second operands, making their usage close to the ARM ISA.

Stack Operations

Stack access has been greatly simplified; where ARM instructions could specify pre- or post-indexing and specify if the stack is ascending or descending, Thumb simplifies this with two simple instructions: PUSH and POP. These instructions, just like all Thumb instructions, are mapped to ARM instructions, and in this case they are mapped to STMDB and LDMIA.They do not specify a register; they assume that the stack pointer is r13 and update the SP automatically.

Stack operations work on the lower registers (r0 to r7) but also on the link register and program counter. The PUSH register list can also include the link register (LR), and POP can include the Program Counter (PC). Using this, you can return from a subroutine with the following sequence:

```
PUSH {r1, lr}
; subroutine
POP {r1, pc}
```

INTRODUCTION TO THUMB-2

Thumb-2 does not replace the original Thumb ISA; it enhances it. Code written in Thumb remains compatible in a Thumb-2 environment.

Thumb-2 adds both 16-bit and 32-bit instructions to the instruction set, making Thumb-2 a variable width instruction set. Some instructions have 16-bit and 32-bit versions, depending on the way they are implemented.

32-bit instructions were added to the Thumb ISA to provide support for exception handling in the Thumb state, as well as access to coprocessors and the addition of DSP instructions. This is a huge advantage to Cortex-M cores, adding processing power to an energy-efficient design. Cortex-M processors belonging to the ARMv7-M architecture support the entire Thumb-2 subset, and the Cortex-M4F also supports Thumb DSP instructions.

Thumb-2 also supports conditional execution, albeit in the form of a new instruction, IT, short for If-Then. Thumb-2 offers the best of both worlds: the performance of ARM and the memory footprint of Thumb.

New Instructions

Thumb-2 introduced a large amount of instructions to make Thumb-2 almost as complete as the ARM ISA and to enable Cortex-M cores to have full access to most of the ARM functionality. The following is a non-exhaustive list of instructions added to Thumb ISA in Thumb-2.

If Then

One of the new instructions is the IT instruction, short for If-Then. Just like the C equivalent, IT conditionally executes one portion of code or another but avoids the need for jumping. The benefit is that this avoids the penalty for taking a branch due to the nature of the pipeline.

The instruction is defined as follows:

```
IT<x><y><z> <cond>
```

The cond variable is any of the condition codes available in the ARM ISA: EQ, GT, LT, NE, and so on.

The variables x, y, and z are optional and are either T (for Then) or E (for Else). Depending on the amount of Ts and Es (including the first T in IT), the processor conditionally executes code. This can sound confusing, so here's an example.

The easiest form is the IT instruction itself:

```
CMP r0, r1 ; r0 == r1?
IT EQ ; was the result EQ?
MOVEQ r0, r4 ; If r0 == r1, execute this instruction
```

This is the most basic form and can execute the MOV instruction if r0 equals r1. Note that inside an IT block, all instructions must have condition codes.

Up to four instructions can be linked to the IT command, in any order. For example, a typical C If/Then section could look like this:

```
CMP r0, r1 ; r0 == r1?
ITE EQ ; was the result EQ?
MOVEQ r0, r4 ; If r0 == r1, execute this instruction
MOVNE r0, r5 ; Else execute this instruction
```

Or for a more complete example, use this:

```
CMP r0, r1 ; r0 == r1?
ITEET EQ ; was the result EQ? Then / Else / Else / Then
MOVEQ r0, r4 ; If r0 == r1, execute this instruction
MOVNE r0, r5 ; Else execute this instruction
SUBNE r0, #1 ; Else execute this instruction too
BEQ label ; If r0 == r1, branch
```

People are often surprised at the instruction layout; you can specify a Then instruction, followed by an Else instruction, and then another Then instruction, something that isn't possible in C. This is actually a clever design from ARM. IT code blocks have restrictions; each instruction inside the IT block must have condition codes. Also, it is not allowed to branch into an IT block unless returning from an exception. Branching from inside an IT block is allowed only if it is the last instruction inside the block, which is the case in this example.

Compare and Branch

Thumb-2 introduced two new branch methods: CBZ and CBNZ. CBZ, short for Compare and Branch if Zero, compares a register with zero, and branches to a label if the comparison EQ is true. CBNZ is the opposite and branches if the comparison NE is true.

CBZ and CBNZ have the advantage of not updating the condition code flags, potentially reducing code size. In ARM, or in Thumb, this portion of code compares a register and breaks if it equals zero:

```
CMP r0, #0
BEQ label
```

In Thumb-2, this is reduced to a single 2-byte instruction (with the difference that it does not update the condition flags).

```
CBZ r0, label
```

In C, this is the equivalent of: if x == 0 { function }.

Bitfield Operations

Bitfield instructions were added to Thumb-2, enabling the copy of portions of a register to another, or clearing and inserting portions of a register. The BFC and BFI instructions enable clearing and inserting data at a variable offset, whereas SBFX and UBFX enable signed and unsigned bitfield extraction.

Coprocessor

System coprocessor instructions can be executed in Thumb, using the MCR and MRC instructions. On Cortex-A/R cores, CP15 instructions can also be executed directly from Thumb-2.

DSP

Thumb-2 also introduced 32-bit Digital signal processing instructions, giving Thumb the calculation power that until now was reserved for ARM code, either enabling Thumb applications to access advanced calculation routines, or enabling more powerful Cortex-M cores. The Thumb-2 DSP instructions were added to the Cortex-M4.

FPU

Floating-point instructions were added to Thumb-2 and are supported by the optional Floating Point Unit in the Cortex-M4. Floating-point operations can now be done directly in hardware by the ARM core, in Thumb state. FPU extensions enable Thumb-2 to be used in intensive calculations such as audio compression and decompression, and automotive applications.

WRITING FOR THUMB

By default, a compiler automatically compiles for the ARM ISA. It needs to be told about the target CPU and what instruction set it will use.

Start with a basic program:

```
int myfunc(int a)
{
    a = a + 7;
    return a / 2;
}
```

This is a basic program that doesn't access any system registers and could be written in both ARM and Thumb. Now, compile this for a Cortex-A8 processor, using default settings:

```
arm-none-eabi-gcc -c -mcpu=cortex-a8 test.c -o testarm.o
```

What exactly has the compiler made of this?

```
arm-none-eabi-objdump -S testarm.o
```

This is just a few lines of output:

```
28:    e1a030c3       asr     r3, r3, #1
2c:    e1a00003       mov     r0, r3
30:    e28bd000       add     sp, fp, #0
34:    e8bd0800       ldmfd   sp!, {fp}
38:    e12fff1e       bx      lr
```

Those five instructions are all 32-bits long, and what is that LDMFD instruction? LDMFD can be used on the Cortex-M3 and Cortex-M4; however, fp is a high register, so this can't be Thumb code. This code has been compiled for the ARM ISA. So how do you compile for Thumb? By telling the compiler:

```
arm-none-eabi-gcc -c -mcpu=cortex-a8 -mthumb test.c -o testthumb.o
```

By specifying the `-mthumb` option in the CodeSourcery compiler, the compiler now knows that it needs to compile in Thumb. Time to have a look at that file:

```
arm-none-eabi-objdump -S testthumb.o
```

Again, these are just a few lines of output:

```
1c:   4618            mov     r0, r3
1e:   f107 070c       add.w   r7, r7, #12
22:   46bd            mov     sp, r7
24:   bc80            pop     {r7}
26:   4770            bx      lr
```

The first thing that can be seen is the instruction length: both 16-bits and 32-bits. After all, the Cortex-A8 supports both Thumb and the Thumb-2 extension, so why not make the most of it?

As for Thumb Interworking, the compiler and linker handle this transparently. Any ARM code calling the `myfunc` subroutine automatically results in a BLX instruction, telling the core to switch to Thumb mode. If called from Thumb code, the compiler makes no changes.

SUMMARY

The Thumb instruction set is designed to be a compiler target, and as such, it is advised to use a higher language, such as C or C++. Some of the changes made in Thumb, compared to ARM systems, make the code different. Porting code from ARM to Thumb at assembly level is often difficult because ARM code relies heavily on conditional execution.

Instructions in the original Thumb extension are 16-bits wide and can be used to reduce the memory footprint of an application and can potentially allow the data bus path to be reduced to 16-bits without a major performance penalty. Thumb-2 is an extension to Thumb, adding both 32-bit instructions and 16-bit instructions, and adding instructions for both DSP and floating-point calculations.

With this background, the chapter showed how to compile source code for the Thumb ISA by telling the compiler to use a specific instruction set.

In the next chapter, I will talk more about ARM Assembly Language, including the Unified Assembly Language that allows developers to write programs for both Thumb and ARM modes. I will talk more about each category of instruction, and give examples for some of the most common instructions.

Assembly Instructions

WHAT'S IN THIS CHAPTER?

➤ Different assembly instructions

➤ Assembly arithmetic

➤ Different branch instructions

➤ Use of assembly instructions

Assembly is just like any other computer language; you must first know the basics: the syntax of the language. After you know how to speak assembly, then comes the interesting part — vocabulary.

ARM cores follow a Reduced Instruction Set Computing (RISC) design philosophy. They have fewer instructions than CISC counterparts, but each individual instruction, being simpler, is also faster. Just like a box of Legos, it is possible to make amazing sculptures with simple pieces. Learning ARM Assembly is the same; after you grasp the power of each simple instruction, it becomes easy to read and write programs.

Because most ARM cores now support two instruction sets, ARM and Thumb, ARM created the Unified Assembler Language (UAL) to write programs for both languages. The following chapter is written in UAL, and as such, the instruction format should be supported by all the modern compilers and environments.

ARM assembly instructions have gone through different versions, as architectures have added more and more instructions. Some cores may have more instructions due to its architecture; for more information, consult the manufacturer's documentation. This documentation will contain the ARM Architecture version. ARM's documentation will list all the instructions available.

MOVEMENT

Movement instructions are used to transfer data into registers, either the data from another register (copying from one register to another), or by loading static data in the form of an immediate value.

The following sections discuss the instructions used for movement.

MOV

```
MOV{<cond>}{S} Rd, Rs
```

MOV (Move) copies data into a register. The source can either be a register or static information. The destination is always a register. When using static data, MOV can only use immediate value.

Contrary to most Thumb instructions, MOV can access low registers and high registers. The ARM implementation can access any register.

To move static data into a register, specify the source after the destination:

```
MOV r0, #42
```

which moves the constant 42 into register r0.

Then use:

```
MOV r1, r2
```

which moves the contents of r2 into r1, leaving r2 untouched.

Use this:

```
MOV r0, r0
```

to move the contents of r0 into r0, equivalent to a NOP (no operation). While alone it has no use, it can be used for padding, to keep data aligned.

MVN

```
MVN{<cond>}{S} Rd, Rs
```

MVN (Move Negated) copies a negated value into a register (destination = NOT(source)). This is useful for storing some numbers that MOV cannot handle, numbers that cannot be expressed as an immediate value, and for bitmaps that are mainly composed of 1s.

For example, due to the nature of immediate values, MOV cannot store 0xFF00FFFF, but this result can be achieved by issuing a MVN command with 0x00FF0000. Because MVN will negate the number, and because 0x00FF0000 can be expressed as an immediate value, it can be achieved in a single instruction.

```
MOV r0, #42
MVN r1, r0
```

This copies an inverse of r0 into r1. r1 now contains −43. 42 in binary is 0000 0000 0010 1010, and the inverse is 1111 1111 1101 0101, or −43 in decimal.

MOVW

MOVW (Move Wide) copies a 16-bit constant into a register while zeroing the top 16 bits of the target register. This is available in ARMv7 cores and higher. MOVW can use any value that can be expressed as a 16-bit number.

MOVW is unavailable in the original Thumb technology and was introduced in the Thumb-2 extension.

When using:

```
MOVW r0, #0x1234
```

r0 now contains the value 0x00001234, no matter what was there before.

MOVT

MOVT (Move Top) copies a 16-bit constant into the top part of a register, leaving the bottom half untouched. This is available on ARMv7 cores and later.

MOVT is unavailable in the original Thumb technology and was introduced in the Thumb-2 extension. In the following example, the first instruction clears the top half of r0, setting the bottom half to 0x0000face. The second instruction sets the top half of the register, leaving the second half untouched. The result will be 0xfeedface.

```
MOVW r0, #0xface
MOVT r0, #0xfeed
```

NEG

When using:

```
NEG{<cond>}{S} Rd, Rs
```

NEG (Negate) takes the value in Rs and performs a multiplication by –1 before placing the result into Rd.

Example: Loading a 32-Bit Constant from the Instruction Stream

This is one of the pitfalls of embedded programming. Say you want r0 to contain 0xdeadbeef. An immediate thought is to use MOV:

```
MOV r0, 0xdeadbeef
```

Technically, this isn't possible. Some assemblers might accept this, but it isn't exactly what *you* are doing, and the assembler will make modifications. If the assembler fails, there will be cryptic messages about what went wrong. But what did go wrong?

Remember, all ARM instructions are 32-bit wide. In these 32 bits, there is the instruction itself, and in the case of MOV, the destination register information and the destination value. Therefore, quite logically, it is not possible to encode an arbitrary 32-bit value in a 32-bit instruction — or at least not always.

When using an *immediate value* for an operation, the processor uses an 8-bit number and a rotation factor. Using this scheme, you can express immediate constants such as 0x000000FF, 0x00000FF0, 0xFF000000, or 0xF000000F. In this case, an 8-bit number, 0xFF, is used and rotated as needed. 0x000001FF is not possible because 0x1FF is not an 8-bit number. 0xF000F000 is not possible either because there is no rotation possible allowing such a number. So you can load a 32-bit integer into a register, as long as it can be expressed as an immediate value in this format. The reason for this is simple. In C, constants tend to be small. When they are not small, they tend to be bitmasks. This system provides a reasonable compromise between constant coverage and encoding space.

When the integer is a complete 32-bit number that cannot be expressed as an immediate value, there are three choices. Either the value is fetched from memory, or it is loaded in two different instructions or in four instructions.

When fetching the values from memory, you need to make sure that the value is in the instruction memory, close to the instruction, as follows:

```
loaddata
    ldr r0, [pc, #0] @ Remember PC is 8 bytes ahead
    bx lr
    .word 0xdeadbeef
```

Because you know where your data is, you can simply tell the CPU to fetch it and to load it using an LDR instruction. Remember that with an ARM pipeline, the PC is always two instructions ahead of your current instruction. The compiler automatically does this for you.

Another solution available on ARMv7 cores and higher is to load the data in two steps. MOVW and MOVT can help to do this, by loading two 16-bit values into a register. These instructions are specially designed to accept a 16-bit argument. MOVW can move a 16-bit constant into a register, implicitly zeroing the top 16 bits of the target register. MOVT can move a 16-bit constant into the top half of a given register without altering the bottom 16 bits. Now moving an arbitrary 32-bit constant is as simple as this:

```
MOVW r0, #0xbeef @ r0 = 0x0000beef
MOVT r0, #0xdead @ r0 = 0xdeadbeef
```

Both of these examples take up the same amount of code. The second approach has the advantage of not requiring a memory read because the values are encoded directly into the instructions.

It can be confusing to have two 16-bit variables. It is much easier to have a single 32-bit variable, exactly what will be loaded into a register. MOVW and MOVT work only with 16-bit values. To simplify this, the GNU assembler enables some flexibility, with the :upper16: and :lower16: prefixes, as shown in this example:

```
.equ label, 0xdeadbeef
MOVW r0, #:lower16:label
MOVT r0, #:upper16:label
```

Now everything becomes more readable and safer.

In the case in which you cannot use ARMv7 code, and you don't want to read the data from RAM, there is a third option, which takes up four instructions. First, you can load part of the register using an immediate value and then repeat an ORR instruction.

```
MOV r0, #0xde000000 @ r0 = 0xde000000
ORR r0, r0, #0x00ad0000 @ r0 = 0xdead0000
ORR r0, r0, #0x0000be00 @ r0 = 0xdeadbe00
ORR r0, r0, #0x000000ef @ r0 = 0xdeadbeef
```

This is not the most memory-efficient but is most often faster than reading the value from RAM.

In some rare cases, you can load a large 32-bit integer into a register in one instruction on the condition that its inverse can be expressed as an immediate. For example, you want to put the value 0xFFFFFAFF into a register, which looks suspiciously like a bit mask. You cannot express this number as an immediate value, so you cannot load it with a simple MOV. You can still use MOV and ORR, or MOVW and MOVT, but in this case, there is another option. The inverse of 0xFFFFFAFF, or NOT(0xFFFFFAFF) is 0x00000500, which can be expressed as an immediate value. Now, you can use Move Not, or MVN, to load your register.

```
MVN r0, #0x500
```

ARITHMETIC

Arithmetic instructions are the basis of any central processing unit (CPU). Arithmetic instructions can do most of the basic mathematical instructions, but there are a few exceptions. ARM cores can add, subtract, and multiply. Some ARM cores do not have hardware division, but there are, of course ways to do that.

All the arithmetic instructions work directly to and from registers only; they cannot read from the main memory or even the cache memory. To make calculations, the data must previously be read into registers.

Arithmetic instructions can work directly on both signed and unsigned numbers because of the two's complement notations.

The following is a discussion of some of the mathematical instructions included on many ARM cores.

ADD

ADD adds together two registers and places the result into a register, such as:

```
ADD{cond}{S} Rd, Rm, Rs
MOV r1, #24
MOV r2, #18
ADD r0, r1, r2
```

This adds Rm and Rs and puts the result into Rd. In this example, r0 now contains 42.

```
ADDS r0, r1, r2
```

This adds r1 and r2 and puts the result into r0. If the result exceeds the register width, it updates the Carry flag in the CPSR. This can be useful on 32-bit CPUs to add 64-bit numbers together using ADC.

ADC

ADC (Add with carry) adds two numbers together and also uses the carry flag. For example, if you want to add two 64-bit numbers on a 32-bit CPU, you would do the following. r2 and r3 contain the first number; r4 and r5 contain the second number. You can put the result in r0 and r1.

```
ADDS r0, r2, r4 ; Adds the low words, update status
ADCS r1, r3, r5 ; Add the high words, using carry, update status
```

This example first adds the low words, storing the result in r0, and updates the status. If the end result is larger than 32-bits, the carry flag is set. When you ADC the result, you add both r3 and r5, and also add the carry bit if previously set. If the carry bit is not set, this command is equivalent to ADD. However, the first command is always ADD because you don't want a previous carry bit to interfere. Also, remember to update the status register.

SUB

SUB subtracts one number from another, placing the result in a register.

```
SUB{cond}{S} Rd, Rm, Rs
```

For example:

```
SUB r0, r1, #42
```

This instruction takes the value in r1, and subtracts the value in the second operand (in this example, 42) and places the result in r0.

SBC

SBC (Subtract with carry) is like the SUB instruction. SBC subtracts two numbers, but if the carry flag is set, it further reduces the result by one. Using a mixture between SUB and SBC, you can perform 64-bit calculations:

```
SUBS r0, r0, r2 ; Subtract the lower words, setting carry bit if needed
SBC r1, r1, r3 ; Subtract upper words, using borrow
```

RSB

RSB (Reverse subtract) is like SUB; RSB subtracts the value of two registers but reverses the order of the operation. This can be useful with the barrel shifter, effectively allowing the barrel shifter to be used on the first operand during subtraction. For example:

```
MOV r2, #42
MOV r3, #84
SUB r0, r2, r3 ; r0 = r2 - r3
RSB r1, r2, r3 ; r1 = r3 - r2
```

In this example, the SUB instruction takes the value in r2, subtracts the value in r3, and puts the result into r0. Using the same variables, RSB takes the value in r3, and subtracts the value in r2 before placing the result into r1. It can save instructions when the barrel shifter is required, for example:

```
MOV r2, #42
MOV r3, #84
MOV r4, r2, LSL #1 ; Multiply r2 by two
SUB r0, r4, r3 ; r0 = (r2 * 2) - r3
```

In this example, r2 needs to be multiplied by two before continuing. Then the subtract instruction takes r4 (which is r2 multiplied by two), and subtracts the value of r3, before placing the result in r0. This can be written in another way using RSB:

```
MOV r2, #42
MOV r3, #84
RSB r1, r2, r3, LSL #1 ; r1 = (r3 * 2) - r2
```

It can also be used for quick multiplications by some values that are not powers of two:

```
RSB r0, r1, r1, LSL #4 ; r0 = (r1 << 4) - r1 = r1 * 15
```

RSC

RSC (Reverse subtract with carry) is like RSB. It inverses the order of operation, but because it uses carry, it can further reduce the result by one if the Carry bit is set.

Example: Basic Math

When using basic math, you frequently see fairly large calculations on a single line of code. This is an example of a common function in C:

```
r0 = (r1 + r2) - r3;
```

The same can be written in assembly as follows:

```
ADD r0, r1, r2 ; compute a + b
SUB r0, r0, r3 ; Complete Computation of x
```

It is also useful to understand how Arithmetic functions work, since they are one of the keys to optimization. As stated previously, it is often quicker to rotate a number when multiplying or dividing by a power of two. When multiplying or dividing by a number that is a power of two plus or minus one, arithmetic can provide an optimized solution, as shown in the following example:

```
ADD r0, r1, r1, LSL #3 ; r0 = r1 + (r1 * 8) = r1 * 9
RSB r0, r1, r1, LSL #4 ; r0 = (r1 * 16) - r1 = r1 * 15
```

SATURATING ARITHMETIC

Normal mathematical operations are prone to overflow. If the result of a mathematical operation is bigger than the container, then overflow will occur, sometimes with surprising results. For example, the largest number possible in an unsigned byte is 255. When adding 128 and 128 together, the result is 256, or in binary 1 0000 0000. Put into a byte, this result is zero. An overflow has occurred, and precision has been lost. More surprising, the result gives no indication that the number was large.

Saturating arithmetic is a version of arithmetic in which all operations are limited to a fixed range. In this case, the limit of an operation is the size of the container; an unsigned byte will never go above 255. In the previous example, 128 plus 128 would give something mathematically wrong;

it would attempt to go above 255 and would not go any further. To signal that an overflow has occurred, the Q flag is set in the CPSR.

ARM Saturating instructions work on signed 32-bit boundaries (meaning that the largest number possible is $2^{31} - 1$, and the smallest number possible is -2^{31}), unsigned 32-bit boundaries (ranging from 0 to 2^{32}), and 16-bit signed and unsigned boundaries.

Contrary to the other ARM status flags, the Q bit is a sticky flag. Saturating arithmetic instructions can set the flag, but cannot clear it. In the event of several saturating instructions, if one of the instructions overflows, the Q bit is set. Subsequent instruction will not clear the flag, even if the result does not saturate. In this situation, it is not always possible to know which instruction saturated, but it is possible to know if saturating occurred somewhere during the algorithm.

The following is a discussion of some of the saturating instructions and their uses.

QADD

```
QADD{cond} Rd, Rm, Rn
```

QADD executes a saturating add on two numbers, Rm and Rn, placing the saturated result in Rd. The result will not overflow a signed 32-bit value. It is used in the same way as the ADD instruction, but does not update condition codes.

QSUB

```
QSUB{cond} Rd, Rm, Rn
```

QSUB executes a saturating subtraction, subtracting the value in Rn from the value in Rm. The result is placed in Rd.

QDADD

```
QDADD{cond} Rd, Rm, Rn
```

QDADD (Saturating Double Add) is an instruction that does two things. It calculates the result of a saturating multiply of Rn by two, before performing a saturating addition of the result with Rm. In short, this operation calculates SAT(Rm + SAT(Rn * 2)).

Saturation can occur on the doubling, on the addition, or possibly both. In all cases, the Q flag is set. If saturation occurs on the doubling but not on the addition, the Q flag is set, but the final result is unsaturated.

```
MOV r1, #1 ; r2 contains 1
MOV r2, #0xFF ; r1 contains 255
QDADD r0, r1, r2 ; r0 contains 1 + (255 * 2)
```

In this example, there is no overflow, and no saturation. The Q bit is not set. In the next example, you see what happens during an overflow.

```
MOV r1, #-1 ; r1 contains -1
MVN r2, #0x7f000000 ; r2 contains a very large number
QDADD r0, r1, r2 ; r0 contains 2^31 - 1
```

In this example, the value in r2 was multiplied by 2, but that value was bigger than a signed 32-bit value (0x7F 00 00 00 x 2 = FE 00 00 00, higher than the maximum 7F FF FF FF), so the result was saturated to $2^{31} - 1$. Because the multiplication saturated, the Q bit was set. Now the saturated result is added to the value in r1; in this case, minus one. The end result is $2^{31} - 2$, which is not a saturated number, but because the Q bit was set, you can tell that the multiplication saturated, and the addition did not.

QDSUB

```
QDADD{cond} Rd, Rm, Rn
```

QDSUB (Saturating Double Subtraction) calculates Rm minus two times Rn. In short, it calculates SAT(Rm - SAT(Rn * 2)). Just like QDADD, saturation can occur on the doubling, or the subtraction, or both.

```
MOV r1, #1 ; r2 contains 1
MOV r2, #0xFF ; r1 contains 255
QDSUB r0, r1, r2 ; r0 contains 1 - (255 * 2)
```

DATA TRANSFER

ARM processors use a load-and-store architecture; they cannot do raw calculations directly from system memory. You must first load data from the system memory into one or several registers before performing any calculation.

In architectures before ARMv6, data loaded from or saved to system memory had to be aligned; 32-bit words must be 4-byte aligned, and 16-bit half-words must be 2-byte aligned. Bytes have no restriction. In ARMv6, this restriction was relaxed.

The following is a discussion of some of the data transfer instructions and their uses.

LDR

```
LDR{<cond>}{B|H} Rd, addressing
```

LDR (Load) is an instruction used for moving a single data element from system memory into a register. It supports signed and unsigned words (32 bit), half-words (16 bit), and bytes.

LDRB, short for LDR Byte, is used to load a byte into a register from system memory. LDRH works the same way with a half-word. Signed versions are also available where LDRSB loads a signed byte and LDRSH loads a signed half-word.

To load r0 with the contents of the memory pointed to by the register r1, use the following:

```
LDR r0, [r1]
```

After calculations have been done, the data can be written back out into system memory using STR:

```
STR r0, [r1]
```

Reading in bytes and half-words is just as easy. For example, in the event of a C structure containing bytes and half-words, it is possible to use a pre-index offset to load parts of the structure, using the base address of the structure itself:

```
LDRH r2, [r1, #4]
LDRB r3, [r1, #6]
```

> **NOTE** *Pre-index addressing is explained in Chapter 4, "ARM Assembly Language."*

STR

```
STR{<cond>}{B|H} Rd, addressing
```

STR is the store command. It takes a register and places the 32-bit value into system memory. It supports the same indexing as LDR. Just like LDR, STR also has byte and half-word variants — STRB for bytes, and STRH for half-words.

```
LDR r0, [r1, #20] ; load memory from the address in r1, plus 20 bytes
ADD r0, r0, #1 ; add one to r0
STR r0, [r2, #20] ; save r0 to system memory, in r2 + 20 bytes
```

Example: memcpy

The memcpy routine is one of the most widely studied and optimized routines. The idea is extremely simple; move a portion of memory from one location to another. This happens often in embedded systems, so fine-tuning memcpy is often essential.

You can copy 1 byte at a time, and although the result might not be optimal, it does get the job done. For example, this routine is called wordcopy. The source address goes into r0, and the destination address goes into r1. The amount of words to copy is placed in r2.

```
wordcopy
        LDR     r3, [r0], #4        ; load a word from the source and
        STR     r3, [r1], #4        ; store it to the destination
        SUBS    r2, r2, #1          ; decrement the counter
        BNE     wordcopy            ; ... copy more
```

On the first line, the memory location of the word to read is held in r0. The routine loads the memory location at the location held by r0, and then increments r0 by 4, known as *post-indexing*. The value read is located in r3.

After the value has been read and stored into a register, it is time to write it back out into memory. This is done in the second instruction, STR. Just like the previous line, it writes out the contents of r3 into main memory to the memory address located in r1. When the procedure is complete, SUBS subtracts one from r2 and places the result back into r2, updating the CPSR. Finally, BNE breaks the program and returns to the start only if the Zero flag is set. When r2 reaches zero, the program continues.

An optimized routine would read in several words at a time. You see this later in the "Multiple Register Data Transfer" section.

LOGICAL

Logical operators perform bit-wise operations on two numbers. There are four logical operations: AND, NOT, OR, and EOR. In theory, logical operators can be done on multiple inputs, but with assembly these instructions accept exactly two inputs and produce one output. They can be thought of as:

➤ AND outputs true only if both inputs are true.

➤ OR outputs true if at least one input is true.

➤ EOR outputs true if exactly one input is true.

➤ NOT inverses the input; it will return true if the input is false.

AND is used extensively for "masking"; AND-ing a number with one produces the original output, whereas AND-ing with zero produces zero. Similarly, OR-ing a bit with one produces one as the output, whereas OR-ing a bit with zero produces the original output.

The following is a list of logical instructions used on ARM processors.

AND

AND performs a logical AND between the two operands, placing the result in the destination register.

```
AND r0, r0, #3 ; Keeps bits 0 and 1 of r0, discard the rest
```

EOR

EOR (Exclusive-OR) is a useful instruction when programming bitwise operations. EOR effectively "switches" bits.

```
MOV r0, #0xF ; Put binary 1111 into r0
EOR r0, #2 ; 1111 EOR 0010 = 1101
EOR r0, #2 ; 1101 EOR 0010 = 1111
```

ORR

ORR produces the logical OR between two registers and writes back the result.

```
MOV r1, #42 ; r1 contains b0010 1010
MOV r2, #54 ; r2 contains b0011 0110
ORR r0, r1, r2 ; r0 now contains b0011 1110
```

BIC

BIC is the equivalent of AND NOT; in C, it is equivalent to operand1 & (!operand2).

```
BIC r0, r0, #3 ; clear bits zero and one of r0
```

CLZ

```
CLZ{cond} Rd, Rm
```

CLZ (Count Leading Zeros) is an instruction that takes the register Rm, counts the number of leading zeros, and places the result in Rm. For example, if Rd equals zero, then CLZ returns 32 (because there are 32 zeros). If bit 31 is set, then CLZ returns zero.

COMPARE

Compare instructions are instructions that do not return any results, but set condition codes. They are extremely useful, as they allow the programmer to make comparisons without using a new register, but the CPSR Condition flags are updated. The CPSR is updated automatically; there is no need to specify the S option. There are four instructions, all performing a logical ADD, SUB, OR, and AND.

The following is a list of comparison instructions used on ARM processors.

CMP

The CMP instruction is used to compare two numbers. It does this by subtracting one from the other, and updating the status flags according to the result.

```
MOV r0, #42
MOV r1, #42
CMP r0, r1 ; Compares r0 and r1,
```

CMN

CMN compares two values, updating the CPSR. It is the equivalent to operand1 + operand2.

TST

TST is a test instruction that tests either if one or more bits of a register are clear, or at least one bit is set. There is no output for this instruction; instead, the CPSR condition flags are updated. This is the equivalent of operand1 and operand2.

```
LDR r0, [r1] ; Load the memory pointed by r1 into r0
TEQ r0, 0x80; Is bit 7 of r0 set?
BEQ another_routine ; If so, branch
```

Another way of writing this sequence is:

```
TST r0, #(1<<7) ; is bit 7 set?
BEQ another_routine
```

TEQ

TEQ compares operand1 and operand2 using a bitwise exclusive OR, and tests for equality, updating the CPSR. It is the equivalent to an EORS instruction, except that the result is discarded. This is especially useful when comparing a register and a value, returning zero when the registers are identical, and returning 1 for each bit that is different.

```
LDR r0, [r1] ; Load the memory pointed by r1 into r0
TEQ r0, 0x23 ; Is r0 equal to b0010 0011?
BEQ another_routine ; If so, branch
```

BRANCH

Branch instructions are the core of any microprocessor, providing the possibility to execute portions of code depending on a result. Branch operations are used not only to branch to other routines, but also to do iterations on the current code.

Most assemblers hide the details of a branch instruction by using labels, a convenient way of marking memory locations. Labels are placed at the beginning of a line and are used to mark an address that can be used later by the assembler to calculate the branch offset.

The following is a list of branch instructions used on ARM processors.

B

B (Branch) tells the current program counter that the next instruction will be at the address specified by setting PC to <address>. This is a permanent branch; no return is possible. It is used mainly in loops or to give control to another part of the program.

```
        [ ... ]
        B fwd
        MOV r0, r0 ; This command is never run
    fwd
        [ ... ]
```

In this example, the MOV command is never run because of the unconditional break before it.

Branching is also used to branch backward, creating a simple loop structure, for example:

```
    back
        [ ... ]
        B back
```

Of course, this is especially useful when using condition codes. For example, to loop some instructions waiting for a result to be equal to 42, this code could be used:

```
    back
        [..]
        CMP r0, 42
        BNE back
```

BL

BL (Branch with Link) branches in the same way as the B instruction. The PC will be changed with the address specified, but the address just after BL will be put into r14. This allows the program to return where it was when the subroutine has finished.

```
        [ ... ]
        [ ... ]
        BL calc
        [ ... ] ; next instruction
        [ ... ]
    calc
        ADD r0, r1, r2
        BX lr ;  Return to where we were
```

In this example, during the main application, you branch with link to calc. After the calculation is done, you can return to the main program via a BX instruction.

BX

BX (Branch and Exchange) is an instruction that enables the program to switch between ARM state and Thumb state, for cores supporting both ARM and Thumb states. This enables seamless integration of ARM and Thumb code because the change is done in a single instruction.

The link logic is held in the destination address. Because ARM cores require instructions to be naturally aligned, the lower address bits are not used for instruction fetches. By using this, the BX instruction can know if the destination code is Thumb or ARM. If bit 0 of the destination address is set, then the T flag of the CPSR is set, and the destination code is interpreted as Thumb. If bit 0 of the destination address is clear, then the T flag of the CPSR is cleared, and the destination code is interpreted as ARM.

BLX

BLX (Branch with Link and Exchange) is like the BX instruction. This instruction also changes to and from the Thumb state, but also updates the Link register, allowing to return to the current location.

Example: Counting to Zero

By using the condition Branch if Not Equal, you can create a small loop. In C, this is the equivalent of for (i = 16; i != 0; i--).

```
        MOV r0, #16
countdown:
        SUB r0, r0, #1
        BNE countdown
# Rest of program
```

Example: Thumb Interworking

Switching between Thumb code and ARM code is known as *interworking* and is a critical part of any program that uses both ARM and Thumb. In C, this is perfectly transparent because the compiler and linker automatically handle the state transitions. However, when writing assembly code by hand, or when debugging, you must know how to handle interworking.

Compilers and linkers work together in interlinking, since the compiler does not know if the destination of a branch is in ARM mode or Thumb mode. The compiler will use BX to return, and the linker will look closely at the destination and change the BX instruction to BLX if required, or by inserting veneers.

```
        ; *****
        ; arm.s
        ; *****

        PRESERVE8
        AREA      Arm,CODE,READONLY    ; Name this block of code.
        IMPORT    ThumbProg
        ENTRY                          ; Mark 1st instruction to call.
ARMProg
        MOV   R0,#1                    ; Set R0 to show in ARM code.
        BLX   ThumbProg                ; Call Thumb subroutine.
        MOV   R2,#3                    ; Set R2 to show returned to ARM.
        END

        ; *******
        ; thumb.s
```

```
; *******

        AREA  Thumb,CODE,READONLY      ; Name this block of code.
        THUMB                          ; Subsequent instructions are Thumb.
        EXPORT ThumbProg
ThumbProg
        MOVS  R1, #2                    ; Set R1 to show reached Thumb code.
        BX    lr                       ; Return to the ARM function.
        END                            ; Mark end of this file.
```

What Is MOV pc, lr?

In some legacy code, functions return using MOV pc, lr. This effectively returns the data in the link register to the program counter, which sounds like it would work perfectly, but it doesn't always. ARM deprecated this return method in 1995. The reason is simple: When returning in this fashion, the processor does not change state. If the MOV function was coded for Thumb, and the return code was in ARM, then the processor would not make the switch between the two states, resulting in an exception. While it is possible to return using a MOV pc, lr, it isn't context safe, and it is much safer to always use the BX instruction, even when not changing states.

MULTIPLY

These commands multiply 32-bit numbers into a 32-bit or 64-bit number. ARM cores use a fast hardware multiplier; most multiplication instructions are executed in three cycles or less.

MUL

Multiply two numbers together, where Rd = Rm * Rs.

```
MUL{cond}{S} Rd, Rm, Rs
MOV r1, #42
MOV r2, #4
MUL r0, r1, r2 ; r0 now contains 4 x 42, 168
```

On ARMv5 or earlier architectures, multiplication must never be done using the same register for both values. The results are UNPREDICTABLE, meaning that the result of an instruction cannot be relied upon.

To calculate the square of a number on ARMv5, two registers were necessary:

```
MOV r1, #42
MOV r2, r1
MUL r0, r1, r2
This restriction was relaxed in ARMv6MOV r1, #42
MUL r0, r1, r1
```

MLA

Multiply two numbers together with accumulate. MLA is used to multiply registers to create a 32-bit result, which is then added to another value, producing the final result.

```
MLA{cond}{S} Rd, Rm, Rs, Rn
```

It is the equivalent to `Rd = (Rm * Rs) + Rn`.

```
MOV r1, #4
MOV r2, #10
MOV r3, #2
MLA r0, r1, r2, r3 ; r0 = (r1 x r2) + r3, in this case, 42
```

You cannot use `r15` for any calculations.

UMULL

UMULL (Unsigned Multiply Long) multiplies two unsigned 32-bit numbers to a 64-bit number, stored in two registers, where `RdHi, RdLo = Rm * Rs`.

```
UMULL{cond}{S} RdLo, RdHi, Rm, Rs
```

UMLAL

UMLAL (Unsigned Multiply with Accumulate Long) multiplies two 32-bit numbers to a 64-bit number with accumulation, where `RdHi, RdLo = RdHi, RdLo + ( Rm * Rs )`.

```
UMLAL{cond}{S} RdLo, RdHi, Rm, Rs
```

SMULL

SMULL (Signed Multiply Long) multiplies two signed 32-bit numbers to a 64-bit number, stored in two registers, where `RdHi, RdLo = Rm * Rs`:

```
SMULL{cond}{S} RdLo, RdHi, Rm, Rs
```

SMLAL

SMLAL (Signed Multiply with Accumulate Long) multiplies two signed 32-bit numbers to a 64-bit number with accumulation, where `RdHi, RdLo = RdHi, RdLo + ( Rm * Rs )`.

DIVIDE

In the early days of ARM, some legacy processors did not have hardware division. A design decision traded silicon area against functionality at a time where the speed of division was not critical. It is for this reason that some cores did not have hardware division, and for the same reason, division was done in software. Dividing by powers of two was simple, since it involves shifting, but otherwise, highly optimized software was developed. Today things have changed, and ARM has introduced hardware division on several processors, but not all of them.

In the absence of a hardware divide instruction, division in machine code is exactly the same as division by any other method; it is simply a matter of repeated subtraction. When you divide 42 by 7, what you really want to know is how many times the number 7 fits into the number 42, or in other words, how many times you can subtract the smaller number from the bigger number until the bigger number reaches zero. The answer in this case is, of course, 6. There are several ways to divide, and C libraries contain a lot of information on that subject, but if you need to optimize heavily, you may need to create your own routines in assembly for particular divisions (for example, when a routine will divide a number only by 7, and no other number). For general purpose optimization, standard libraries have gone through years of optimization.

Later cores do support hardware division, namely the Cortex-M3 and Cortex-M4, the Cortex-R4 and the Cortex-R5, and the Cortex-A15 with its sister processor, the Cortex-A7.

You can divide by some numbers using shifts, and the compiler chooses to optimize in this way where it can, but it cannot always simplify. Sometimes you need to be explicit in your code. By using shifts, you can divide by powers of 2.

```
MOV r0, r0, LSR #1 ; Divide r0 by 2
```

SDIV

```
SDIV{cond} {Rd,} Rn, Rm
```

SDIV (Signed Divide) performs a signed integer division of the value in Rn by the value in Rm. If Rd is omitted, the destination register is Rn. Operations on SP and LR are prohibited.

```
SDIV r0, r1, r2 ; r0 = r1/r2
SDIV r3, r4 ; r3 = r3 / r4
```

UDIV

```
UDIV{cond} {Rd,} Rn, Rm
```

UDIV, or Unsigned divide, uses the same syntax as SDIV. UDIV performs integer division on unsigned numbers.

MULTIPLE REGISTER DATA TRANSFER

There are instructions to load and to save a single register to and from memory, but in most applications using several variables, it is often impractical to save a single register each time. Fortunately, ARM has a system to save several registers to memory, and to take into account endianness and memory location.

Before presenting the instructions, you must understand that unlike most instructions, these instructions have a <mode> parameter. These instructions can be programmed to increment or to decrement before or after each transfer. Therefore, when transferring several registers, subsequent registers can either go up in memory space or down. The register used to point to the memory location (the base register) can either be increased or decreased before, or after, each read/write. In short hand, they are written IA, IB, DA, or DB. This is illustrated in the following table. The base register Rn determines the source or destination for the Load/Store Multiple instruction. This register can optionally be updated following the transfer by including an exclamation mark after the register, similar to the single-register load/store command.

ADDRESSING MODE	DESCRIPTION	START ADDRESS	END ADDRESS	RN!
IA	Increment After	Rn	Rn + 4*N -4	Rn + R*N
IB	Increment Before	Rn + 4	Rn + 4*N	Rn + 4*N
DA	Decrement After	Rn – 4*N + 4	Rn	Rn – 4*N
DB	Decrement Before	Rn – 4*N	Rn -4	Rn – 4*?

The easiest way to understand the differences between the modes is by an image. Figure 7-1 shows the result of four store operations, all using a base register of 0x8000.

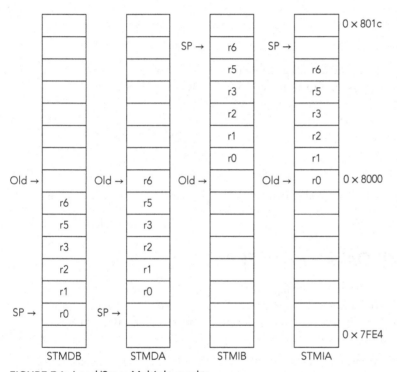

FIGURE 7-1: Load/Store Multiple results

With these options, the program has entire control over the direction of the memory reads/writes and also the resulting stack pointer.

STM

        STM{addr_mode}{cond} Rn{!}, reglist{^}

STM is the "store multiple" instruction. STM takes one or several registers and places them in a block of memory pointed by the base register. The initial registers remain untouched. If the optional "!" is specified, the base register is updated according to the mode.

When encoded into the instruction, the registers are expressed as bits, meaning that any combination (or all the available registers) can be used. The registers are then read in logical order (r0 - r15), not the order expressed on the instruction line.

```
STMFD r9!, {r0-r4, r6, r8} ; Stores the registers in Full Descending mode
```

LDM

LDM is the "load multiple" instruction. Just like STM, LDM takes a list of registers and loads them from memory. The original memory location remains untouched.

```
LDMFD r9!, {r0-r4, r6, r8} ; Loads the registers in Full Descending mode
```

BARREL SHIFTER

The Barrel Shifter is a functional unit that can be used in a number of different circumstances. These commands are not ARM instructions but are added to operand2. They enable complex calculations, still using only one assembly command. They are, however, separate Thumb instructions and cannot be added to the end of an instruction.

Shift operations, basically, move the bits in a register to the left or to the right, filling in vacant bits with 0s or 1s. This is the equivalent to multiplying or dividing by powers of 2. This brings you to the question, "Why aren't shift and rotate operations real instructions, instead of just using the barrel shifter?" Surely this will just complicate things? In reality, it is quite the opposite. A shift or a rotate can be performed at the same time as any ARM-state data processing instruction, increasing speed considerably and providing denser code.

LSL

LSL (Logical Shift Left) is a multiplication by 2^n, equivalent to << in C. It can be used to do simple multiplications but also more complicated calculations. It shifts the value left by the specified amount, padding with zeros. This is illustrated in Figure 7-2, where a binary number is shifted "left" by one.

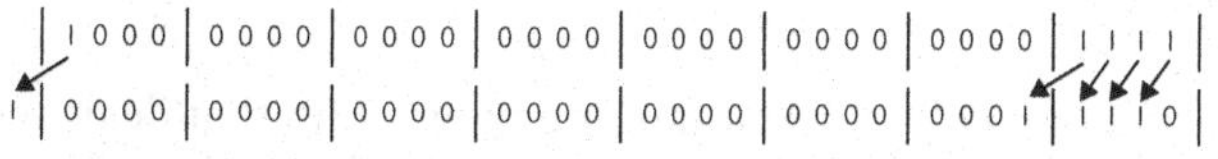

FIGURE 7-2: Binary shift left by one

```
MOV r0, r0, #1 ; Multiply r0 by 2
```

LSL also enables you to do more complicated multiplications, which would take up more time using other instructions:

```
ADD r0, r0, r0, #3 ; Multiply r0 by 9 (r0 = r0 + r0 * 8)
RSB r1, r1, r1, #4 ; Multiply r1 by 15 (r1 = r1 * 16 - r1)
```

Another trick is to use shifts to create a number that cannot be expressed as an immediate number:

```
MOV r0, #0
MOV r1, #0x80000004
MOVS r0, r1, LSL #1
```

This command "moves" the value of r1 into r0, after performing a left shift on the value of r1. The value of r1 is still 0x80000004, but the ARM CPU read in the value of r1 shifted it left one space (the value now being 0x00000008), set the carry bit, and put the result into r0.

LSR

LSR (Logical Shift Right) is just like LSL. LSR is a shift operation and is equivalent to dividing by 2^n. It is the equivalent to >> in C. It shifts the value right by the specified amount, padding with zeros.

```
MOV r0, r0, LSR #2 ; Divide r0 by 4
```

ASR

ASR (Arithmetic Shift Right) is just like LSR: it shifts a number right, the equivalent of dividing by 2^n, but without rounding. The difference with LSR is that ASR keeps the signed bit, the first bit of a 32-bit number, and pads the result. If the number starts with a binary 0, it is padded with 0s. If it starts with a binary 1, the result is padded with 1s.

```
MVN r0, #0 ; r0 = 0xFFFFFFFF
MOV r1, r0, asr #16 ; r1 = 0xFFFFFFFF
MOV r2, r0, lsr #16 ; r2 = 0x0000FFFF
```

ROR

ROR (Rotate Right) rotates a number. Bits moved out of the right end of the register are rotated back into the left end.

```
MOV r0, r0, ROR #16 ; Swap the top and bottom halves of a 32-bit number
```

RRX

RRX (Rotate Right Extended) is just like ROR but with a crucial difference. ROR works with a register but also with the Carry flag. In essence, it performs a shift on a 33-bit number; the C flag is copied into the result before continuing the shift operation.

STACK OPERATIONS

Stack operations are essential for any program that calls subroutines or any program that deals with large amounts of data. Stack operations are like movement instructions but with added functionality that makes them extremely easy to use.

Traditionally, a stack grows down in memory, meaning that the last "pushed" value will be at the lowest address. ARM also supports ascending stacks using LDM and STM, meaning that the stack structure grows up through memory.

PUSH and POP operations are synonyms for STMBD and LDMIA, respectively, with the base register fixed as r13. However, because LDM and STM are not stack-specific, it is necessary to specify the stack pointer.

In ARM state, the core uses LDM and STM for stack operations. See the "Multiple Register Data Transfer" for more information.

PUSH

The PUSH instruction is actually a synonym for STMDB, using SP as the base register. This means that the stack pointer is decreased by 4 and is updated before the push operation occurs.

POP

Just like PUSH, POP is actually a synonym, this time for the LDMIA instruction. The stack pointer is again used automatically and is incremented by 4 after the pop operation.

In Thumb state, PUSH and POP are the only stack operations available.

Example: Returning from a Subroutine

```
subroutine  PUSH    {r5-r7,lr} ; Push work registers and lr
            ; code
            BL      somewhere_else
            ; code
            POP     {r5-r7,pc} ; Pop work registers and pc
```

COPROCESSOR INSTRUCTIONS

The CP15 coprocessor is a powerful tool, one that can help you greatly in your work. The CP15 can be programmed to configure cache, tightly coupled memory, system performance monitoring, and other systems. Architecturally, the CP15, and indeed any and all coprocessors available on the system, are not directly accessible; there are specific instructions to read and to write from coprocessors. If no coprocessors can execute a coprocessor instruction, an undefined instruction abort is generated.

Coprocessor instructions are complicated and require specific documentation from ARM (if using the CP15) or from the manufacturer if using another coprocessor. Do not be worried by their complexity; it is not necessary to know every opcode by heart, but it is important to understand what the instruction intends to do.

Physical coprocessor support was removed from ARM processors n ARMv7. The ARM11 family were the last cores to support external coprocessors. In order to maintain binary compatibility, coprocessor instructions still exist but are mapped directly to system instructions.

The original Thumb instruction set cannot access coprocessors, and therefore, these instructions do not work in Thumb state on processors which do not support Thumb-2. Thumb-2 added coprocessor support.

MRC

MRC (Move to ARM Registers from Coprocessor) has this structure:

```
MRC[condition] coproc, opcode1, dest, cpsource, cpreg[, opcode2]
```

This structure is slightly different from other ARM instructions:

➤ `condition` is one of the 16 condition codes.

➤ `coproc` is the name of the coprocessor (p0 to p15).

➤ `opcode1` is a coprocessor-specific opcode.

➤ `dest` is the destination register.

➤ `cpsource` is the source coprocessor register.

➤ `cpreg` is the additional coprocessor register.

➤ `cpopcode2` is an optional coprocessor cpname operation.

For example:

```
MRC p15, 0, r0, c0, c0, 0
```

In this example, the instruction takes a register from CP15 (p15) and places the result into r0. It requests information from CP15's c0 register, and the opcode2 specifies the subregister. This sounds complicated, and indeed it is complicated to read, but this specific instruction comes straight from ARM's website on CP15. It is the instruction required to read the Main ID Register from CP15.

MCR

MCR (Move to Coprocessor from ARM Registers) has this structure:

```
MRC[condition] coproc, opcode1, dest, cpsource, cpreg[, opcode2]
```

MRC uses the same format at MCR, only the memory transfer direction changes. For example:

```
MCR p15, 0, r0, c13, c0, 3; Write Thread ID Registers
```

This example is, again, cryptic. This particular instruction is copying the value of r0 into the CP15 (p15), into c13. c13 on an ARM11 core is the thread ID register. By issuing this instruction, the ARM core will be given the thread ID for a particular thread, and the opcode2 tells the core that the thread ID number is user readable but needs privileged access to write a new value.

MISCELLANEOUS INSTRUCTIONS

The following are a few instructions that do not belong in any of the previous categories, but are in their own category.

SVC

```
SVC{cond} #immed
```

SVC (Supervisor Call) is an instruction that causes an exception. By issuing this instruction, the processor switches to supervisor mode, the CPSR is saved, and the execution branches to the SVC vector.

SVC can also take an immediate value but is not used by the processor. Instead, an SVC handler can be programmed to recover the value hard-coded into the instruction. In ARM state, this value is a 24-bit immediate value; in Thumb, it is an 8-bit immediate.

SVC used to be called SWI. Some compilers and decompilers still use the SWI name, but newer versions should use SVC.

NOP

```
NOP{cond}
```

NOP is short for No Operation, and put simply, it does nothing. It can be used to make an empty instruction before padding further instructions to a 64-bit boundary, or in some cases used as a handy point to put a breakpoint. In the past, NOP was sometimes used to force the processor to wait for one cycle, but with modern pipelines, this is no longer the case.

MRS

```
MRS{cond} Rd, psr
```

MRS (Move to ARM Register from System coprocessor) moves the content of a PSR to a general purpose register. This instruction is especially useful with saturated arithmetic because it is not possible to get the status of the Q flag directly. By using this instruction, you can get all flags and know if an instruction saturated.

MSR

```
MSR{cond} APSR_flags, Rm
```

MSR (Move to System coprocessor register from ARM Register) loads an immediate value, or the contents of a register, into the specified fields of the Program Status Register (PSR).

SUMMARY

This chapter presented a few of the most common ARM assembly instructions written in UAL, and how they are used. You learned about assembly and understanding instructions when decompiling and debugging. However, this is not a complete list of instructions since every core may have additional instructions added by the manufacturer.

Chapter 5, "First Steps", explains debugging, shows several debugging examples, and discusses just how important it is to read basic assembly.

In the next chapter, you see the NEON processors, which is ARM's advanced single instruction multiple data engine, capable of complex instructions for Digital signal processing and number crunching.

8

NEON

WHAT'S IN THIS CHAPTER?

➤ Presenting NEON

➤ Understanding NEON's registers

➤ Introducing some NEON instructions

➤ Writing a NEON application in assembly

➤ Using NEON intrinsics in C

➤ Writing a NEON application in C

When ARM first released its original SIMD extensions, it was a huge success. Finally, single instructions worked on multiple data values accelerating multimedia applications, and enabling ARM cores access to a whole range of multimedia devices. Single instructions operating on multiple data values packed into registers meant that ARM cores could be used in DSP applications, or simply to obtain better performance. Mobile telephones could decode MP3 music using even less power, meaning longer battery life.

NEON is an extension of the original SIMD instruction set and is often referred to as the Advanced SIMD Extensions. It extends the SIMD concept by adding instructions that work on 64-bit registers (D for double word) and 128-bit registers (Q for quad word).

NEON instructions are executed as part of the ARM instruction stream, simplifying development and debugging.

WHAT ARE THE ADVANTAGES OF NEON?

NEON isn't just about having huge amount of registers. The advantage of SIMD instructions is to execute an operation on several data values packed into a single register in a single instruction, but the data must first be correctly placed into the registers. How exactly is that done?

For example, consider a 24-bit image. There are three channels comprising a total of 24-bits per pixel: 8-bits for red, 8-bits for green, and 8-bits for blue. This is a repetitive structure, one such 24-bit structure per pixel and some digital cameras can make a lot of pixels.

Before doing anything interesting to the image, the data must first be loaded into registers. Without NEON, the operation would possibly have been to load the red component into r5, the blue component into r6, and the green component into r7, after which a filter would be applied, and the three registers would be written back with three reads, at least three operations, and finally three writes, for only one pixel. NEON has a different approach.

NEON registers are 64-bits wide, but you can load several 8-bit values into one register. Presume that the address of the first byte of data is held in r0. Using a NEON instruction, you can load 8 pixels into memory, using one instruction:

```
vld1.8 {d0, d1, d2}, [r0]
```

VLD is the NEON instruction to load data. VLD1.8 means that the processor will be loading 8-bit values, without interleaving. Three registers are also specified, so these three registers will be filled with 8-bit values. Finally, the address of the first byte is taken from a register; in this case, r0. Figure 8-1 shows the result of this operation.

FIGURE 8-1: Loading RGB data with a linear load

In one single instruction, 8 pixels have been loaded into three registers. However, any calculation might be complicated because the different colors have been loaded directly, or linearly. This is where interleaving comes in; the exact order of the data can be specified. By using an interleave of 3, the processor knows that each element is to be loaded, and the first will be placed into the first register, the second into the second, and the third into the third. When reading the fourth element, it will "loop," putting it into the next free space in the first register, and repeating the process.

By rewriting the instruction and specifying an interleave of 3, Figure 8-2 shows the result.

```
vld3.8 {d0, d1, d2}, [r0]
```

The data has now been loaded but this time into a format that is much easier to work with. No more shifting or masking to get the data you want; each color is put directly into one register. Of course, if the data were read in a certain way, the processor can also write data out in the same way.

This brings a question: Because there is now a 64-bit register filled with 8-bit values, how is it possible to do any calculation? The answer is NEON's lanes. A *lane* is a segment of a register, so one instruction can work on multiple values packed into a standard register. In this case, a lane could be 8-bits wide; therefore any calculation

FIGURE 8-2: Loading RGB data with a structured load

wouldn't be done on the entire contents of the register but a series of 8-bit values. Figure 8-3 shows lane calculation on two D registers.

From here, virtually anything is possible. With one single instruction, you can swap two colors. You can do a weighted average of the three colors to create a fourth; effectively grayscaling the image. And when everything is finished, you can also use NEON to accelerate JPEG compression.

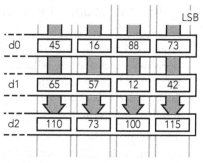

FIGURE 8-3: Lane operation on NEON registers

WHAT DATA TYPES DOES NEON SUPPORT?

NEON instructions support 8-bit, 16-bit, 32-bit, and 64-bit signed and unsigned integers; the same data can be found inside any ARM program. NEON also supports 32-bit single precision floating point numbers, and 8-bit and 16-bit polynomials.

Data types are specified by a letter, and any of the following are supported:

➤ U for unsigned integer

➤ S for signed integer

➤ I for integer of unspecified type

➤ F for single-precision floating-point number

➤ P for polynomial

USING NEON IN ASSEMBLY

Before using NEON in higher level languages like C, you must understand the internals; how NEON reads in data, what sort of data, the instructions that can be used, and how NEON writes the data out to system memory.

Presenting the Registers

NEON has a huge amount of registers: 32 64-bit registers named d0 to d31. They also have another name; they can be seen as 16 128-bit registers named q0 to q15. Actually, they are the same registers; two D (double-word) registers map to one Q (quad-word) register. Figure 8-4 shows the relation between a Q register and two D registers.

The registers are also shared with the VFP if one is present.

q15			q2		q1		q0	
d31	d30			d5	d4	d3	d2	d1	d0

FIGURE 8-4: Q registers and D registers

Why Are the Q and D Registers the Same?

A Q register is effectively two D registers, and filling a Q register overwrites the data in the two D registers. There are several reasons why both names exist, and one of them is that NEON instructions can widen the size of lanes. For example, when multiplying a 16-bit number by another 16-bit number, it is often useful to store the result in a 32-bit number. By using two D-registers to hold 16-bit values, there will be four lanes, or four 16-bit elements. When outputting four 32-bit numbers, the result must be placed into a Q-register, capable of four 32-bit lanes.

The inverse is also true; some NEON instructions can reduce the size of a result, in which case the operands is in a Q register, and the result is placed in a D register.

Loading and Storing Data

Just like the rest of an ARM core, NEON uses a load and store architecture. Data must be loaded into registers before doing any calculation.

There is only one instruction for loading data into NEON registers, and one instruction to save NEON registers back into memory, but the syntax enables a huge amount of customization.

The syntax of the instruction follows:

```
Vopn{cond}. datatype list, [rn]{!}
Vopn{cond}. datatype list, [rn], Rm
```

The structure consists of five parts:

➤ The instruction mnemonic, either VLD for loads or VST for stores

➤ The interleave pattern, the gap between elements

➤ The number of bits of accessed data

➤ A set of NEON registers to load/save data

➤ An ARM register containing the memory location

Understanding the Different Interleaves

The interleave pattern specifies the separation of the data to be either read or written. Interleave 1 (for example, VLD1) is the simplest form. Data is handled sequentially, each element being placed one after another. This is used for loading one-dimensional arrays. Figure 8-5 presents an example of Interleave 1.

With interleave 2, (VLD2), the data is separated into two parts. For example, it can be used on an audio stream, separating data from the left and right channels. Figure 8-6 presents an example of Interleave 2.

Interleave 3 uses three registers and can be used for three-dimensional arrays, for example, loading a graphics image coded in RGB. Figure 8-7 presents an example of Interleave 3.

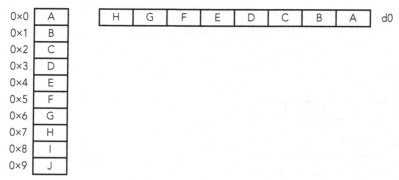

FIGURE 8-5: Interleave 1 example

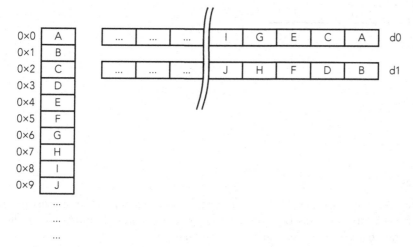

FIGURE 8-6: Interleave 2 example

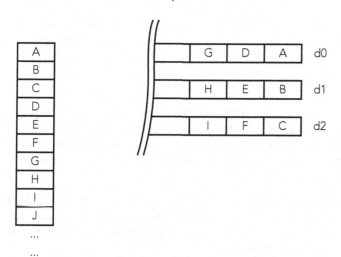

FIGURE 8-7: Interleave 3 example

Interleave 4 uses four registers and can be used for four-dimensional arrays, much like the data found in ARGB images. Figure 8-8 presents an example of Interleave 4.

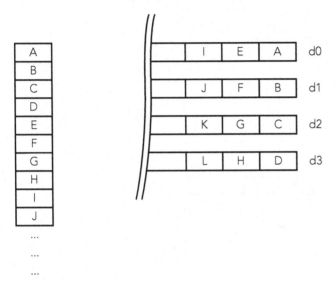

FIGURE 8-8: Interleave 4 example

Selecting the Data Size

You must specify the size of each data element. For a 24-bit graphics file, each pixel color must be coded in 8 bits. By specifying 8 bits in the instruction, the NEON engine knows to interleave on the next occurrence of that data size, effectively separating the pixel data.

Valid data sizes are 8-bits, 16-bits, or 32-bits.

To read 8-bit data with interleave 3, the instruction would be VLD3.8. To save 16-bit data with interleave 4, the instruction would be VST4.16. Lane size can increase or decrease with several operations, and you must take care to specify the correct width.

Defining the NEON Registers

You can define up to four registers depending on the interleave selected. For interleave 4, you must specify four registers because data will be separated into four different registers. For interleave 3, only specify three registers because data will be separated into three groups. For interleave 2, you can specify either two or four registers, depending on the length of the data to be read. For interleave 1, you can specify up to four registers.

Using default values, the ARM core can fill in all the register, using as many elements as possible. It is, however, possible to fill in a single element into one specific lane or to load a single element into all lanes. To do this, the lane must be specified after the register, in brackets. In the previous example, to load a single element into all lanes, use the following:

```
VLD3.8 {d0[2], d1[2], d2[2]}, [r0]
```

By issuing this instruction, the ARM core loads three 8-bit elements into lane 2 of d0, d1, and d2, effectively loading a single pixel into a specific location, as shown in Figure 8-9.

You can also load in a single element into every lane, by leaving out the lane parameter, for example:

```
VLD3.8 {d0[], d1[], d2[]}, [r0]
```

In Figure 8-10, the same 8-bit elements are loaded into all lanes of the registers.

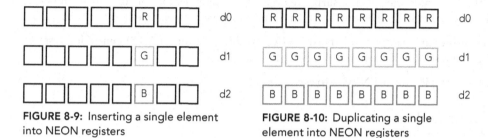

FIGURE 8-9: Inserting a single element into NEON registers

FIGURE 8-10: Duplicating a single element into NEON registers

Vector Sizes

D registers are 64-bits wide, and Q registers are 128-bits wide, but what happens if the data inside the register is too small? In the previous example, eight 8-bit values were loaded into a D register, but what happens if only 6 values are available?

NEON can perform only full register operations, and with the exception of loading a single value into a lane or a register, all instructions execute the same operation on all lanes, including load and save operations. In most cases, this will be transparent; the final two results would give corrupted data because there was no valid input. So long as there is enough system memory free when the write operation occurs, this should not impact your program.

Effective Addressing

You can specify the address for operations in several ways. The simplest form is to specify the address of the memory in an ARM register, without any options. In this case, the data is read in (or written out), and the ARM register is not updated. You can use this on a system where a portion of memory is frequently updated.

Where data is written sequentially over large memory portions, you can use post-increment addressing. Just like on standard ARM instructions, the value of the ARM register can be updated after the memory operation by the amount of memory used, effectively updating the contents of the ARM register to point to the next portion of memory to be read/written. In the example of a graphics image, this would allow the processor to read in all the data sequentially.

```
VLD3.8 {d0-d2}, [r0]! ; update r0 after the data read
```

This doesn't always suffice. The previous example shows how to read in data sequentially, but sometimes more complicated instructions are required. Sometimes, data will not be read in sequentially, but in blocks, for example, a program that will not read in each pixel of a line, but rather the first 8 pixels of each line. In this case, the program would need to read in 8 pixels, and then "jump" to the next line. This is where post-indexing comes in. After memory access, the pointer is incremented by a specific value held in an ARM register.

```
VLD3.8 {d0-d2}, [r0], #40 ; Increase r0 by 40 after the data read
```

Optimized memcpy

Embedded systems often spend a considerable amount of time copying memory from one location to another. With cost constraints, it's not surprising that the system memory on an embedded system is often not the fastest available. Therefore, it is important to develop a fast method for memcpy.

The memcpy routine can change greatly between two systems, but for an ARM embedded system where NEON is present, it is often more effective to use NEON.

Here is a short example of using NEON to replace memcpy:

```
NEONcpy:
VLDM r1!, {d0-d7}
VSTM r0!, {d0-d7}
SUBS r2, r2, #0x40
BGE NEONcpy
```

In this example, r0 holds the source address, r1 holds the destination address, and r2 holds the amount of bytes to copy. Surprisingly, this does not create the speed boost that you would expect. It does, however, have a few advantages. For one, it can be done with minimal instructions and does not overwrite any of the ARM registers; no PUSH and POP required. Secondly, some cores can be configured so that NEON instructions allocate only level-2 cache, therefore not overwriting anything present in level-1 cache. This example is easy to optimize. By adding a simple preload instruction before the reads, the code becomes the following:

```
NEONcpy:
PLD [r1, #0xC0]
VLDM r1!, {d0-d7}
VSTM r0!, {d0-d7}
SUBS r2, r2, #0x40
BGE NEONcpy
```

In this instruction, the preload instruction prompts the processor to attempt to fill in a cache line with the data at the address in r0, but only if the system has the required bandwidth. It does not guarantee that cache lines will be filled, but if they are, subsequent VLDM instructions will result in a cache hit, greatly increasing speed. In tests, this technique showed greatly improved throughput without modifying level one cache lines or ARM registers.

NEON Instructions

NEON instructions can be divided into different categories: arithmetic, logical operations, conversion, shifting, and other advanced features.

Arithmetic

ARM assembly instructions have multiple instructions for arithmetic, for example, adding two numbers, adding with accumulate, and so on. NEON goes a step further, introducing new and advanced instructions. NEON can simply add or subtract, but also add and narrow the high half of an integer, add two numbers dividing the result by two, or execute a pair-wise add, to name but a few.

Multiplication has also been revisited, and new commands exist to automatically double the results of a multiplication or Vector Fused Multiply and Accumulate.

Comparison

NEON benefits from multiple comparison instructions, and the comparison can be a simple bitwise comparison, comparing with another register, extracting maximum/minimum values from a pair of registers, and so on.

General Data Processing

General data processing routines include the possibility to change from one data type to another. For example, it is possible to convert floating-point numbers into integer, and vice versa. NEON also has something called vector extraction (Figure 8-11), extracting 8-bit elements from the bottom end of the second operand vector and the top end of the first, concatenating them, and placing them in the destination vector.

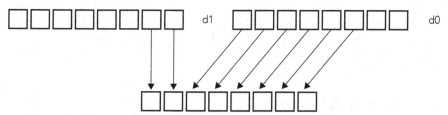

FIGURE 8-11: Vector extract

NEON can also reverse the order of 8, 16, or 32-bit elements within a vector, using the VREV instructions. This can be used to change endianness, or to rearrange components or channels of stream data.

NEON also proposes something that is missing from ARM assembly, the possibility to swap two registers without needing a third register as a temporary store.

> **NOTE** *This is only a small list of NEON data processing instructions. More instructions are listed in Appendix D.*

USING NEON IN C

Just like with ARM Assembly, NEON assembly can make some heavily optimized code at the cost of spending more time writing code. Writing code in C means faster development time and more maintainable code, and compilers normally do a good job of optimizing code. Sometimes, it is necessary to turn to assembly for finely tuned performance, but in most cases, the use of C gives good performance, noticeably better than hand coding using ARM instructions (which are already fast).

A compiler cannot take standard code and use NEON instructions, even if there are many loops, or in cases in which NEON could accelerate code. The compiler has to be specifically told to use the NEON engine. There are several ways to do this as described here.

Presenting Intrinsics

Intrinsic functions and data types, or intrinsics, provide a direct link to assembly, while maintaining higher level functions such as type checking and automatic register allocation. This enables elegant C functions, maintaining the readability and maintainability of C, without the need to write direct assembly instructions. To use NEON intrinsics, include the header file arm_neon.h.

Vector Data Types

C intrinsics enables defining any sort of data type accepted by NEON. NEON data types are names according to this pattern:

```
<type><size>x<number of lanes>_t
```

The type can be an int, uint, float, or poly. The size is the size of each lane, and the number of lanes defines how many lanes will be loaded, and therefore the type of register used (D or Q). To load a series of pixels into a 64-bit D register, each pixel being an 8-bit unsigned value, choose uint8x8_t. The entire list of supported datatypes is presented in Appendix D, "NEON Intrinsics and Instructions."

Loading a Single Vector from Memory

To load data into a NEON register, intrinsics have been made that resemble assembly, but add data types to help compiler checking. They return the data type that the register(s) can hold. To load a single vector, an intrinsic is used that uses the memory address as an argument and returns the data type contained in the register.

```
// VLD1.8 {d0, d1}, [r0]
uint8x16_t  vld1q_u8(__transfersize(16) uint8_t const * ptr);
// VLD1.16 {d0, d1}, [r0]
uint16x8_t  vld1q_u16(__transfersize(8) uint16_t const * ptr);
// VLD1.32 {d0, d1}, [r0]
uint32x4_t  vld1q_u32(__transfersize(4) uint32_t const * ptr);
// VLD1.64 {d0, d1}, [r0]
uint64x2_t  vld1q_u64(__transfersize(2) uint64_t const * ptr);
// VLD1.8 {d0, d1}, [r0]
int8x16_t   vld1q_s8(__transfersize(16) int8_t const * ptr);
// VLD1.16 {d0, d1}, [r0]
int16x8_t   vld1q_s16(__transfersize(8) int16_t const * ptr);
// VLD1.32 {d0, d1}, [r0]
int32x4_t   vld1q_s32(__transfersize(4) int32_t const * ptr);
// VLD1.64 {d0, d1}, [r0]
int64x2_t   vld1q_s64(__transfersize(2) int64_t const * ptr);
// VLD1.16 {d0, d1}, [r0]
float16x8_t vld1q_f16(__transfersize(8) __fp16 const * ptr);
// VLD1.32 {d0, d1}, [r0]
float32x4_t vld1q_f32(__transfersize(4) float32_t const * ptr);
// VLD1.8 {d0, d1}, [r0]
```

```
poly8x16_t  vld1q_p8(__transfersize(16) poly8_t const * ptr);
// VLD1.16 {d0, d1}, [r0]
poly16x8_t  vld1q_p16(__transfersize(8) poly16_t const * ptr);
// VLD1.8 {d0}, [r0]
uint8x8_t   vld1_u8(__transfersize(8) uint8_t const * ptr);
// VLD1.16 {d0}, [r0]
uint16x4_t  vld1_u16(__transfersize(4) uint16_t const * ptr);
// VLD1.32 {d0}, [r0]
uint32x2_t  vld1_u32(__transfersize(2) uint32_t const * ptr);
// VLD1.64 {d0}, [r0]
uint64x1_t  vld1_u64(__transfersize(1) uint64_t const * ptr);
// VLD1.8 {d0}, [r0]
int8x8_t    vld1_s8(__transfersize(8) int8_t const * ptr);
// VLD1.16 {d0}, [r0]
int16x4_t   vld1_s16(__transfersize(4) int16_t const * ptr);
// VLD1.32 {d0}, [r0]
int32x2_t   vld1_s32(__transfersize(2) int32_t const * ptr);
// VLD1.64 {d0}, [r0]
int64x1_t   vld1_s64(__transfersize(1) int64_t const * ptr);
// VLD1.16 {d0}, [r0]
float16x4_t vld1_f16(__transfersize(4) __fp16 const * ptr);
// VLD1.32 {d0}, [r0]
float32x2_t vld1_f32(__transfersize(2) float32_t const * ptr);
// VLD1.8 {d0}, [r0]
poly8x8_t   vld1_p8(__transfersize(8) poly8_t const * ptr);
// VLD1.16 {d0}, [r0]
poly16x4_t  vld1_p16(__transfersize(4) poly16_t const * ptr);
```

Loading Multiple Vectors from Memory

Loading multiple vectors from memory is just like loading a single vector, except that the interleave must be specified. The instructions are almost identical to single instructions; the memory pointer is passed as an argument, and the resulting data type is returned. The interleave is defined in the instruction.

```
uint8x8_t data vld1_u8(src); //Loads one d-word register
uint8x8x2_t data2 vld2_u8(src); //Loads two d-word registers, using interleave 2
uint8x8x3_t data2 vld3_u8(src); //Loads three d-word registers, interleave 3
```

In each case, the instruction resembles the assembly layout.

Using NEON Intrinsics

NEON intrinsics are well designed; they are easily accessible from C without any major change. So long as the logical procedure is respected, read in data using intrinsics, execute NEON instructions, and then write data out, again using intrinsics. Then the routine can benefit from NEON optimization.

It is possible to mix ARM and NEON instructions, but there is sometimes a penalty in doing so; NEON can only use NEON registers, just as ARM can only use ARM instructions. Registers will need to be transferred to and from the NEON engine, costing a slight overhead.

You can also create portions of code that execute only if a NEON engine is present (and defined), by using #ifdef sections.

```
#ifdef __ARM_NEON__
// NEON code
#else
// ARM code
#endif
```

By using this system, you can generate source code that is easily portable from one processor design to another using standard C.

Converting an Image to Grayscale

On almost any modern digital camera, there is an option to convert images to grayscale. This operation is simple; it takes the red, green, and blue components, calculates a weighted average, and then writes the result to a new pixel. This is the sort of repetitive calculation that NEON is well suited for. To do that, following is an example application.

First, a little understanding about the way our eyes see the world. Human eyes are more adapted to seeing green than any other color, so when changing an image to grayscale, simply adding the red, green, and blue component, and then dividing by three is not enough. For clear grayscale images, a certain amount of weight is added to each color. This is known as the luminosity method. It is common to multiply the red channel by 77, the green channel by 151 and the blue channel by 28. The sum of these three numbers is 256, making division simple.

To do that, the program can fill three registers with specific values, the weight ratio. The application must read in a series of pixels, separating the red, green, and blue components into separate registers using interleaving. Next, each color component is multiplied by the weight ratio, and the result is placed into another register. Finally, the new registers are added into a single register, divided, and then written back out into memory. The end result is $((rx) + (gy) + (bz)) / (x + y + z)$.

First, three registers need to be filled with 8-bit values, the ratio values. There are three registers: one for the red components, one for the green, and one for the blue. To take one 8-bit value and to repeat that value over the NEON register, the VDUP instruction is used.

```
uint8x8_t r_ratio = vdup_n_u8(77);
uint8x8_t g_ratio = vdup_n_u8(151);
uint8x8_t b_ratio = vdup_n_u8(28);
```

Note that in C, it is not necessary to specify a register; the compiler can do this automatically and keep track of which variable is held in which register. Now, the data has to be read in, using interleave 3. The variable rgb is defined as a uint8x8x3_t because it uses three registers.

```
uint8x8x3_t rgb  = vld3_u8(src);
```

vld3_u8 does a vector load of unsigned 8-bit values, using interleave 3. Again, you do not need to specify the registers. Now comes the tricky part. Each pixel is 8 bits in size, but you must multiply each one, and add the results of three multiplications together. It isn't possible to do this in an 8-bit lane because there will almost certainly be a data loss. The reason why this example uses only a 64-bit register instead of a 128-bit register is for this reason: The program must widen the lanes from 8-bit to 16-bit and therefore use a larger output register.

Therefore, a temporary register is defined as such:

```
uint16x8_t  temp;
```

This reserves a Q register for a total of 8 16-bit variables. Now, multiply the R component by the ratio, and save it into the temporary register.

```
temp = vmull_u8(rgb.val[0], r_ratio);
```

This instruction is a Vector Multiply, which tells NEON to multiply each lane in rgb.val[0] (the red component of each pixel) by r_ratio (the weight ratio) and to put the results into temp. Because the instruction is VMULL with two L's, it also widens the lane from 8 bits to 16 bits. An example can be seen in Figure 8-12.

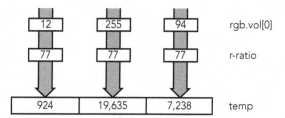

FIGURE 8-12: VMULL multiplying 8-bit values into a 16-bit value

The variable temp now contains each red component of the 8 pixels, multiplied by the red weight. You can do the same thing with the green and blue components: Multiply them into separate registers and then add the results. However, NEON has a more elegant solution: Multiply and Accumulate.

```
temp = vmlal_u8(temp, rgb.val[1], g_ratio);
```

Vector Multiply and Accumulate Long (VMLAL) is the same as Vector Multiply, except it enables adding a value to the result of the multiplication. In this case, VMLAL can multiply the green component of each pixel by the green weight ratio and then add the existing values in temp before writing the data back into temp. Now the variable temp contains the weighted red components plus the weighted green components. All that is left to do is to do the same action with the blue components.

```
temp = vmlal_u8(temp, rgb.val[2], b_ratio);
```

Now temp contains the weighted value of each component of the pixel, multiplied by 256. The value 256 wasn't chosen randomly. The value was chosen because it is a power of 2 and can be shifted to perform a fast division. Also, the largest value possible in an 8-bit value is 256, and the largest possible value of all the weighted values times the pixel components is 65536, the maximum size of a 16-bit value; so there will never be any data loss, even for the highest values possible. Now each weighted pixel must be divided by 256 by shifting and then output the results into 8-bit values. This is a job for VSHRN.

```
result = vshrn_n_u16(temp, 8);
```

Vector Shift Right, Narrow (VSHRN) is an instruction that can take a quad-word register, perform a division by a power of 2, and then output the results into a double-word register, narrowing the lanes. Now you have to write the results back out into memory.

```
vst1_u8(dest, result);
```

And that's it! A simple C function that loops for each 8 pixels of an image and automatically converts RGB pixels into grayscale. The entire C routine looks like this:

```
void neon_grayscale(uint8_t * dest, uint8_t *  src, int num)
{
int i;
uint8x8_t r_ratio = vdup_n_u8(#77);
uint8x8_t g_ratio = vdup_n_u8(#151);
uint8x8_t b_ratio = vdup_n_u8(#28);
```

```
num/=8; //NEON will work on 8 pixels a time

for (i=0; i<n; i++)
{
uint16x8_t temp;
uint8x8x3_t rgb   = vld3_u8(src);
uint8x8_t result;

temp = vmull_u8(rgb.val[0], r_ratio);
temp = vmlal_u8(temp,rgb.val[1], g_ratio);
temp = vmlal_u8(temp,rgb.val[2], b_ratio);
result = vshrn_n_u16(temp, 8);
vst1_u8(dest, result);
src += 8*3; // 3 x 8 pixels in RGB format
dest += 8; // One single 8-bit value per pixel
}
```

SUMMARY

In this chapter, you have seen an overview of the NEON architecture and how it augments ARM's original SIMD instructions. You have seen how to load data into NEON registers, and the different interleave options available. I have shown an example NEON program written directly in C, using NEON intrinsics, and just how easy it is to use the NEON engine from C.

In the next chapter, I will talk about debugging, and software and hardware debuggers, and present some of the techniques available to debug programs and low-level code.

Debugging

WHAT'S IN THIS CHAPTER?

➤ What a debugger can do

➤ The difference between a software debugger and hardware debugger

➤ Debugger terminology

➤ A few software and hardware debuggers

➤ Debugging techniques

➤ When to use a debugger

➤ Effective debugging

A program that works the "first time" is a myth. There will invariably be little problems that need to be fixed: Some of them will be easy; some of them will be hard. Be careful, though; sometimes the easiest problems are the hardest to spot.

There are various techniques for solving problems, but unfortunately, there is no general rule. This is something that is acquired over the years, and it sometimes boils down to instinct.

ARM processors have advanced features that enable developers to easily debug applications or kernels, whatever solution the developer takes.

WHAT IS A DEBUGGER?

For anyone in systems programming, a *debugger* is a software application that can run a program, line by line and show various pieces of data, such as variables and memory contents. You can use debuggers primarily to follow, step by step, the execution of a program and to understand why portions of that program do not function as wanted. Debuggers normally require an operating system to run and to have a method of communication externally: a serial line, Ethernet, monitor, and so on.

For embedded systems, this is often a problem because most do not have outputs, and some do not have an operating system. Even on systems that do have an operating system, sometimes you must look closer at the operating system, something that a normal debugger cannot do. For this, embedded systems use In-Circuit Emulators (ICEs).

ICEs are hardware devices that connect to the embedded system through a special port. ARM processors, and indeed most processors, have a specialized way for debuggers to connect to the heart of the system to enable external devices to take control. Historically, ICEs had their own processor, one that was closer to the debugging computer, which had input and output to the target system. The target CPU was deactivated, and most of the calculation was done on the emulator. Today, this is no longer the case, but these devices tend to keep their historical name of emulators, even if they are debuggers. All calculations are made on the target system, and the ICE communicates only between the processor and the debugging computer.

Some devices are known as In-Circuit Debuggers (ICDs), which is technically a more correct name.

Other ICEs exist, that actually are emulators, but these are designed primarily for the simulation of silicon before making a processor and are out of the scope of this book.

What Can a Debugger Do?

A software debugger, as previously described, can take a binary program and run it exactly as if it were running normally on an operating system. It can pause program executing, perform step-by-step execution and have a look deep into a program.

Hardware debuggers are often a window to embedded systems. Not only can they help debug, but because they have direct access to hardware, they also can upload programs to memory, flash nonvolatile memory, and configure hardware devices.

Hardware debuggers aren't just about debugging software. They can also debug a lot of the hardware, by looking at all the registers on a system, not just the processors. If the serial line isn't giving correct data, checking the serial registers is often a great way of checking without adding any additional code. On some processors, a watchdog is set to automatically reset the processor if the watchdog doesn't hear from the program within a set amount of time. On a Freescale iMX51, it can't be deactivated when activated, except if using a hardware debugger, which is rather useful for long testing sessions.

ARM Debugging Capabilities

ARM processors have excellent debugging capabilities because of integrated hardware. JTAG was originally designed to perform boundary scans to test interconnections on printed circuit boards. Since, JTAG has been used for much more, including debugging. Some classic ARM cores have a hardware macrocell called EmbeddedICE, hardware that can receive debugging instructions, and a small window to the processor and external devices. These devices have hardware support for adding breakpoints and taking control of the processor when a break occurs.

During the development of ARMv6, EmbeddedICE was replaced with CoreSight, an improved debug interface. No longer based on JTAG, this device communicates using Serial Wire Debug (SWD), a low pin count, high-speed alternative to JTAG. Requiring only two pins instead of JTAG's five, this enables debugging for severely pin limited packages, enabling the debugger to take control of even the smallest chips.

CoreSight enables users to have more hardware breakpoints and also enables hardware traces, enabling debuggers to know which routines are used when and for how long. Traces are mainly used for optimization and are explained in the next chapter.

When using debuggers, a lot of technical words might not have any meaning immediately but need to be known to fully use a debugger.

Breakpoint

A *breakpoint* is a location in instruction code in which the processor halts and gives control to the debugger. In software, this halts the program at the specified location, letting the user decide what to do. In hardware, this actually freezes the CPU, so nothing continues in the background.

A breakpoint is triggered when the Program Counter is equal to the address, or when the instruction is about to be executed. ARM cores with on-board debug hardware can have hardware breakpoints, enabling a program to run at full speed before being stopped at a particular memory location. The amount of breakpoints available depends on the core and the architecture; ARM9 cores have two hardware breakpoints, but the Cortex-M0 has four, the Cortex-M3 has eight, and ARMv7A/R cores have six.

Watchpoint

A *watchpoint* is slightly different from a breakpoint, and the two are sometimes confused. Although a breakpoint can halt the processor when a specific instruction is about to be executed, a watchpoint can trigger at a memory location and can be set to trigger on read or write. It is extremely useful to know which part of a program updates a specific portion of memory. What updates that system register? Set a watchpoint on data write, and if the program reads the register, the watchpoint is ignored, but as soon as the program updates the memory, the system halts at the instruction.

Again, ARM cores provide hardware debugging capabilities but usually less than breakpoints. Cortex A/R chips have two watchpoints, the Cortex-M0 also has two, and the Cortex-M3 has four.

Stepping

Stepping is an important feature that enables the debugger to go through code, step by step. When a breakpoint is set, the next instruction becomes visible and waits for the user before continuing. Although you can then have a look at variables before continuing the application, it is sometimes useful to watch the result of each instruction. Stepping does this for you.

Running an application step by step means that each line of code is executed before waiting for user input before performing the next. In a loop, you can watch as each line executes and have variables displayed. Updated variables are often color-coded to show the developer which variables have changed since the last instruction. Most debuggers enable stepping in the native language and in assembly.

Stepping isn't just step by step; the debugger can be ordered to continue execution until it leaves the current routine via a return, to step over a function (after all, you want to debug your own code, not the entire C library) or to specifically step into a function.

Vector Catch

Vector catch is a mechanism used to trap processor exceptions. It is often used early on, before exception handlers are used. Essentially, this technique watches the vector table and interrupts execution when the ARM core enters an exception state.

Stack Frames

Sometimes, the routine that generates the problem won't have a software bug. Routines that normally function perfectly well can have some strange effects if the wrong parameters are sent. This happens often: a division by zero or a string that doesn't contain what was expected. With the stack, you can see the chain of calls; the last function on the list might be creating an exception by printing out the wrong value, but who called this function in the first place? Debuggers can help by printing the entire stack frame.

An example is provided in Figure 9-1. In this example, printf, one of the most used and most reliable routines, generates an exception. It is extremely unlikely that printf itself is the cause, but the problem might be one of the functions calling printf. This example shows the stack frame for this application.

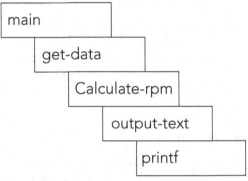

FIGURE 9-1: Example stack frame

TYPES OF DEBUGGING

Debugging is used to correct code. Errors can be of several types; routines can give wrong results or possibly not be called. In embedded systems, there can be more critical errors: An application (or kernel) might be generating exceptions, which need to be debugged and corrected. Exception handlers must sometimes be debugged and can be tricky. Sometimes, a tricky situation requires the use of an external debugger to understand what is happening electronically.

Loops

Loops are the most common elements that go wrong and are also some of the most complicated to read. Nested loops can be tricky, and in some cases, it is almost impossible to write elegant code that is easily readable. When optimized, they can be tricky to read.

Some of the most common mistakes involve variables that are incorrectly initialized, off-by-one errors, and loops that either loop an infinite amount of times or loops that iterate zero number of times.

When debugging loops, it isn't always practical to follow every loop. It is often advisable to debut the first two loops and the last two. Knowing how the loop starts is essential, but often it isn't necessary to see every loop. If the first two start off well, you can begin by presuming that the others will work well. If the first two work, concentrate on the last two to understand how the program exits the loop. Is the loop being terminated too early? Or on the contrary, is the loop being run too many times? By debugging the variables used in the loop, you can often see where errors are coming from.

Be careful checking for equality inside loops. Having a loop depend on an equality to quit is often used, but with floating point numbers especially, a tiny difference can cause the loop to iterate infinitely. Where possible, add a second possibility for leaving a loop. For example, continue until variable *a* is equal, or greater than, variable *b*. A simple equality might have surprising effects if a variable no longer has the value 2, but possibly 2.00001.

Routines

Routines are one of the most common elements to debug, and luckily, one of the easiest. Typically, routines need to be debugged when a return code is erroneous and an inner loop doesn't quite react as it should. This can sometimes be debugged by adding simple serial output text or by using a debugger to follow step by step and analyze variables.

Interrupt Controllers

Interrupt controllers are tricky to debug because they are critical portions of code that need to be executed quickly. There are two ways of debugging them: either by running a simulated environment in which an interrupt can be fed to the controller at will, allowing for step-by-step debugging or in real time. The problem with real time is that it severely limits any interaction; simply printing a line on the console using `printf` can have unexpected results and can change the way the handler works.

Bootloaders

Debugging a bootloader is exceptionally hard with anything else but a hardware debugger. Because this is a portion of code that is at an extremely low level and requires a lot of system calls and/or assembly, it is rarely possible to do this entirely in software except on emulated systems.

DEBUGGERS

Because ARM cores can be used for so many different applications, there are several ways of debugging. Application developers will be at ease on cores running a full operating system because applications such as gdb can be used to debug an application directly on the hardware. On micro-controller applications, external hardware may be required to access the ARM debugging features.

GNU Debugger

The GNU Debugger, or gdb for short, is an excellent piece of software that allows the user to take control of a program; start and stop a program, insert breakpoints, evaluate variables, and a few other important features. It can debug programs written in C, C++ as well as an impressive number of other languages.

There are two ways of running gdb; either running gdb on the target, and configuring gdb to run a target application. The GNU debugger is used regularly to debug PC applications, by running on the same system, but this method is rarely used for embedded systems, simply because running gdb can require too many resources for an embedded system. An example of gdb running an application is illustrated in Figure 9-2. In this instance, gdb is running, and has full control over an application, running on the same system. The application is not separate; it is actually run and controlled by gdb.

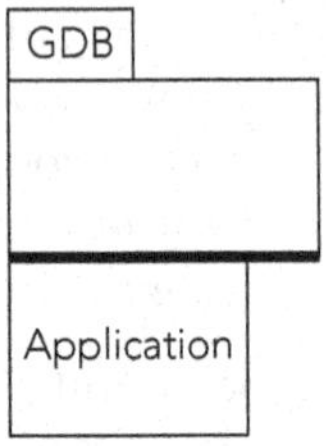

When the previous example is not possible, the GNU Debugger can be used in a master/slave fashion. In this instance, the GNU Debugger works in two stages. First, the gdb server, named gdbserver, must first be compiled for that system, and then be copied onto the target platform. It requires a method of communication to the host compiler computer. This means that the target must have either a working network configuration or a UART connection. Second, on the debugging PC, gdb must be run and then connect to gdbserver. Once again, a specific version of gdb should be used; an ARM version of gdb must be used.

While gdbserver is often software, some hardware implementations exist, and are connected directly to the USB port of the development system. Also, some operating systems allow users to take control via gdb. For example, VxWorks allows users to spawn tasks using gdb, and to take control of tasks spawned from the shell.

Figure 9-3 illustrates an example debugging session on an embedded system, controlled from a development system.

FIGURE 9-2: Running gdb and application on a system

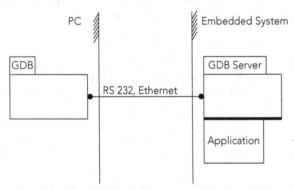

FIGURE 9-3: Running gdb on an embedded system

Running the gdb server is easy; simply define a connection method. For the serial output, you must define the serial port:

```
gdbserver /dev/ttyS0
```

For a networked device, only the port is required:

```
gdbserver :2345
```

The gdb server will start and wait for an incoming connection before continuing.

On the development computer, the GNU Debugger "client," or simply gdb, is required. The GNU Debugger is a command-line program used to communicate with a gdb server. All the calculation will be done by the client, leaving the server to run the program with minimal interference. This has the advantage of having a good debugging capacity on a system with limited RAM or power.

To launch the program using gdb, you must first launch the client and connect to the server.

```
arm-none-eabi-gdb
(gdb) target 192.168.0.2:2345
(gdb) run
```

The GNU Debugger can be configured with multiple parameters; it can be given a program to run or attach to an existing program. By default it quits when the target application exits, but it can be programmed to remain in memory to rerun the binary file.

J-Link GDB Debugger

Using the GNU Debugger often requires an operating system; the network must be active, or the system must report the running processes, and so on. Although in some cases this might be practical, in others, it is impossible. Microcontroller systems, especially, do not have the resources, and in the worst case, the embedded system will not have network capabilities, and might not have a serial line available. In this case, another approach is required.

Silicon Lab's STK3800 evaluation board, first presented in Chapter 5, "First Steps," comes with a J-Link debugger directly on the board. J-Link has a software solution enabling gdb to access a specialized gdbserver, effectively turning the debugging chip into a kernel. This enables the developer to debug a barebones application without the need for any other configuration; there is no need to copy a binary, and there is no need to have an operating system configure a serial port. The J-Link effectively "translates" between the GNU Debugger and the hardware debugger.

EXAMPLE DEBUGGING

The following is a short list of some of the common problems encountered, and some of the ways to detect them and to correct them. They are situations that you may have already faced, either in embedded systems or in systems programming, followed by a brief explanation on how they were solved.

Infinite Loop

An infinite loop is created when a program doesn't run the way it is expected; either because of an unforeseen situation or simply because of a portion of code that wasn't written quite the way it should have been.

This example, contains a portion of code that can run on any machine, not just an embedded ARM system. This code is from the gdb tutorial and explains beautifully how to analyze infinite loops. You can compile this code on an ARM system or on a desktop.

```
#include <stdio.h>
#include <ctype.h>

int main(int argc, char **argv)
{
    char c;

    c = fgetc(stdin);
    while (c != EOF)
    {
        if(isalnum(c))
            printf("%c", c);
        else
            c = fgetc(stdin);
    }
    return 1;
}
```

By looking quickly at the code, it looks obvious that this routine will look at the standard input, and if the char read is alphanumerical, it will be printed to the standard output; otherwise, it waits for another char to restart the loop. However, there is a hidden problem. Running the program gives a hint.

```
> a.out
Hello, world!
HHHHHHHHHHHHHHHHHHHHHHHHHH [...]
```

This is not what was expected. The program continues to print out the first letter, and you have to quit the program. Take a closer look at this program. You can add some printf traces inside the loop, but it is often easier to not modify the program and use a debugger—in this example, the GNU Debugger.

To debug easily, the program must be compiled with the debug flag, -g. By adding this flag, supplemental information is added inside the program, notably the symbol table. It also adds file names and line numbers from where the symbols came from, making it easy to find the exact location of a problem.

```
gcc -g infinite.c
```

Next, this program needs to be run with gdb. Start the program exactly as before; only this time break into it.

```
(gdb) run
Starting program: /local/a.out
Hello
HHHHHHHHHHHHHHHHHH
Program received signal SIGINT, Interrupt.
```

Next, it is time to see where the program is exactly. By issuing the backtrace command, the stack is analyzed.

```
(gdb) backtrace
#0  0x400d8dc4 in write () from /lib/libc.so.6
#1  0x40124bf4 in __check_rhosts_file () from /lib/libc.so.6
#2  0x40086ee8 in _IO_do_write () from /lib/libc.so.6
#3  0x40086e46 in _IO_do_write () from /lib/libc.so.6
```

```
#4  0x40087113 in _IO_file_overflow () from /lib/libc.so.6
#5  0x40087de5 in __overflow () from /lib/libc.so.6
#6  0x40069696 in vfprintf () from /lib/libc.so.6
#7  0x40070d76 in printf () from /lib/libc.so.6
#8  0x80484c2 in main (argc=1, argv=0xbffffaf4) at inf.c:12
#9  0x40037f5c in __libc_start_main () from /lib/libc.so.6
```

The frame that you are interested in is number 8, the "main" routine, your program.

```
(gdb) frame 8
```

Next, you can watch the code, line by line, by using the next command, or "n" for short.

```
(gdb) n
11                  if(isalnum(c))
(gdb)
12                      printf("%c", c);
(gdb)
15          }
(gdb)
11                  if(isalnum(c))
(gdb)
12                      printf("%c", c);
(gdb) n
15          }
(gdb)
11                  if(isalnum(c))
(gdb)
12                      printf("%c", c);
```

There is a pattern here, and one that isn't what was originally intended. If the char c is an alphanumeric, which it is, it is printed out and then repeated forever. The program never gets the next char from the input. By using the debugger for less than a minute, you now know exactly where the problem lies.

```
11:     if(isalnum(c))
12:         printf("%c", c);
13:     else
14:         c = fgetc(stdin);
```

The culprit is line 13; the else statement shouldn't be used. By removing the else statement, the loop works as intended.

The GNU debugger is a powerful tool, even if the learning curve can be a bit steep. Time should be taken to have a closer look and run a few examples. This short example barely scratches the surface of what this powerful debugger can do, but even so, you solved an infinite loop.

Unknown Exception

An exception is one of the more difficult debug situations because there are only a certain number of exceptions available and a lot of situations in which an exception can be made. Using the DS-5 debugger, it can be extremely easy to know exactly what happened.

The DS-5's advanced interface makes debugging easy. On some debuggers, you would place a breakpoint on the vector table, on each element that you are interested in. In the DS-5 interface, this is called *Vector Catch* and can be configured directly to print a message and to pause program execution. For example, imagine that this portion of code gives an error:

```
void bubble(int *p, int N)
{
    int i, j, t;
    for (i = N-1; i >= 0; i--)
    {
        for (j = 1; j <= i; j++)
        {
            if (compare(&p[j-1], &p[j]))
            {
                t = p[j-1];
                p[j-1] = p[j];
                p[j] = t;
            }
        }
    }
}
```

The vector catch informs you that the exception occurs on line 8:

```
if (compare(&p[j-1], &p[j]))
```

So what went wrong? Was it the compare function? The compare function is simple:

```
int compare(int *m, int *n)
{
    return (*m > *n);
}
```

When an exception occurs, the current Program Counter is saved, and DS-5 can trace this. By looking at the process stack, you can see the address that triggers the exception, a Data Access Memory Abort. By clicking this address, the DS-5 environment jumps to the line of code at that address: the compare function. Something went wrong inside this line of code.

In the variables window, you can show the values of each variable in the current section of code, including m and n. In this case, it also shows the memory location. By dragging this variable to the Memory window, you should see what the memory contents at that location are. Except you can't. The memory at that address is defined as invalid; the MMU refuses access, and it looks like your program is attempting to do just that. So it looks like the compare function is the function that is creating the abort, but only because someone is feeding it with wrong information.

Dividing by Zero

Processors are exceptionally well designed for working with integers: real numbers. When working with floating numbers, although still good, they become a little less optimal, and when working with specialized numbers such as imaginary numbers or fractions, operations have to be done in software to emulate these numbers.

Dividing by zero is the software killer; when it crops up, it can crash the sturdiest machines. The mathematics behind this is that dividing a number is equivalent to multiplying by a number's multiplicative inverse; dividing by 2 is the same as multiplying by 1 over 2, or 0.5. The product of a number and its multiplicative inverse is always 1. Two times 1 over 2 is 1. The problem when dividing by zero is that zero doesn't have a multiplicative inverse. The answer is something that therefore cannot be expressed as an integer and something that the processor cannot do. In the face of such an impossibility, it prefers to throw an exception and refuses to continue without a helping hand. Division by zero in a system application is a sure way to crash the entire application, but on an embedded device without an operating system, the results can be disastrous.

The catch in division by zero is that it is not always the instruction that generates the exception that is at fault. It can often occur in a C library, only because the main application passed zero as an argument. Because the C library might not have error checking to see if the user passed zero, as that would cause more cycles to be spent, most libraries rather accept any argument, and specify that zero should never be used. In this case, using a debugger to catch the exception, and then looking at the application stack to see when and how the routine was called, often gives a good indication.

Of course, sometimes the exception is in a line of calculation, and in this case, it is easy to debug. The offending line is the one generating the exception, and after using a debugger to locate the problem, the developer can then correct the offending code.

IN-DEPTH ANALYSIS

Debugging is often considered to be an art, acquired after several in-depth debugging sessions. Many problems can arise during development, and sometimes a bug will be a combination of several problems. So far in this chapter I have listed some of the most common problems. Now I will show a few real-world examples where debugging was required, and where the root cause was not always what it was thought to be.

Data Abort

Situation: A project uses a special R&D-only bootloader to reflash the system in case of corruption. This is a bootloader executed at a privileged level, and all interrupts are disabled. Data is received on a serial line using polling. A watchdog has to be serviced every 60 seconds, or the system reboots. A flash driver has been developed to write the data received; a serial driver has been developed to write standard debug info and to receive a new firmware. Other than that, no systems are needed.

When running the software, the client can connect to the bootloader, send commands, and upload a new flash binary, but the transfer fails and the system freezes. A reconnection isn't possible immediately but is often possible 10 seconds later, so the initial analysis is that it is not a problem with the watchdog. Something is probably wrong with the serial driver.

For this analysis, the development team looked at the C code and initially couldn't find anything wrong. Debug lines were added but to no avail.

On this particular setup, a JTAG debugger was available, and a binary was created and flashed onto the target. Step by step took too long to be of any use, so breakpoints were inserted into the code. Out of habit, a watch was put on the exception vectors, including Data Abort. And indeed, the ARM processor did go into a Data Abort exception.

Data Abort means that the application was trying to read or write an illegal memory location. r14 held the value 0x1FFE7208, and by subtracting 8 from that value (to take into account the instruction queue), the address 0x1FFE7200 resulted. This is the address that caused the data abort. Looking to the C code, it was the macro used to write a specific value into the watchdog register. Nothing looked wrong with the C code, so we went deeper, into the assembly code.

Here is an extract of that code:

```
MOVW r0, #0x8002
MOVT r0, #0x73F9
MOVW r1, 0x5555
STR r1, [r0]
```

Running step by step, we saw that r0 was constructed as 0x73F98002 and r1 contained 0x5555. The processor documentation stated that to clear the watchdog timer, we first had to send 0x5555 and then 0xaaaa to a register, a 16-bit register located at 0x73F98002. The problem with this is that 0x73F98002 is not aligned on a 4-byte boundary. What's more, STR attempted to write a 32-bit number. When this happened, the processor went into a Data Abort exception, and because we didn't handle exceptions, it looped back and forth until the watchdog kicked in.

This was somewhere between a compiler problem and a development problem. The compiler didn't know that we wanted to pass a 16-bit number and so happily tried to write a 32-bit variable into a non-aligned zone. If it had been aligned, the problem would have been different. We would have written a 32-bit variable onto a 16-bit register, plus another register behind it, potentially creating strange side effects. In this case, the short routine was written in assembly to test if the problem had been found, replacing STR with STRH (store half-word), and the program worked perfectly.

Corrupted Serial Line

Situation: A home appliance device using a Cortex-A has a homemade bootloader. This bootloader is designed to enable a user to upload a new flash image in case of flash corruption or in case of a failed firmware upgrade. When testing the firmware upload process, the CPU generates undefined instruction exceptions.

When the firmware is detected as faulty, or when a specific button is pressed to power on, the bootloader waits for data on a UART serial line. When the data has been received, it is flashed into NAND flash, and the system reboots. During tests, we were surprised to see the undefined instruction exception occurring, not every time, but about one in five downloads.

For this problem, we immediately used a hardware debugger. We placed a breakpoint on the Undefined Instruction vector and waited. A few minutes later, we got what we wanted. In RAM, at the exact location, was an instruction that didn't look right.

NAND flash memory is a special soft of memory that requires a bit of software to run. Unlike conventional memory, it cannot be used to run programs directly. NAND memory is fragile and can become worn out over time. To avoid problems, each memory location stores other data, including CRC data. Therefore, software has to be written to extract data from NAND and placed into internal RAM before executing it. Could it be that this routine was somehow wrong?

A hardware debugger gave us access to a lot of information, including the contents of the NAND memory. The hardware debugger "dumped" the contents to a file. Because the contents were copied to memory, at location 0x20000000, we also told the debugger to dump the contents of the RAM. We did a binary compare of the two files, and they were identical up until the last byte of the firmware. Reading from NAND wasn't the problem, so maybe we put bad data into NAND?

The bootloader was designed to receive data from a serial line. It would open a connection and wait for data. When data arrived, it was copied into RAM. An end of file was indicated by two distinct 32-bit values. When the bootloader received those two values, it then copied the firmware stored in RAM into the NAND flash before giving control to the first instruction of the firmware.

The breakpoints were changed, and the system was programmed to break on 0x20000000, the first instruction of the firmware, just after being written to NAND. Again, the contents of RAM and NAND were dumped and compared. And again, they were identical. The NAND routines looked like they were working exactly as intended; so what could be the cause? If the data written to NAND were correct, does that mean that the data received on the serial line was somehow corrupted? We already had the data from RAM, which was supposed to be the exact firmware binary, so we did a comparison. There was indeed a difference; what the processor received was not what we had sent.

The communication method used was RS-232. It needs to be configured with the baud rate, the speed at which data can travel. It is possible to configure the port to detect parity errors, but in standard practice, it isn't used. It was configured for 8N1: 8 bits of data, no parity, and one stop bit. Data was sent as small "packets," resulting in bursts of communication and then a small period of silence. UART devices have small buffers, so we thought that maybe the communications were going too fast and that the buffer filled up, resulting in corrupted data. Again, the debugger helped us to see what was going on. This particular processor had on-board serial ports, and each port had close to a dozen registers to help configure and to read the status. One of the registers contained some valuable information, the amount of buffer overruns, or the amount of times that data was received and the buffer hadn't been emptied. Zero. That wasn't the culprit.

The serial port is used later in the application for debugging output, and we had never seen the slightest problem, so maybe there was a difference in the way it was configured? We noted the contents of all the UART registers and then removed all the breakpoints. We rebooted the system again, reloading a firmware and hoping it wouldn't generate any exceptions. It didn't, and after a few seconds, debugging information was available on the UART port. We then froze the application with the debugger and looked at the contents of the registers. One of them wasn't identical. It was the register that controls speed.

When configuring in software, we normally give the speed directly as bauds, an integer of the amount of bits sent and received in a second. 115200 is a common number. In hardware, however, it is often much more difficult; the baud rate has to be calculated from the system clock and then a calculation, a frequency division. By looking at the values we had in the bootloader, we calculated that we were close to the limits of transmission, and by changing the values slightly, we could no longer upload a binary at all. By changing the values again in the opposite direction, the problem no longer occurred.

The analysis used to find the root of the problem is called why-because analysis and is used frequently in accident analysis. It sometimes applies well to software debugging when the root cause isn't known. It is called why-because because that is exactly the question we ask over and over, why? Why did the exceptions occur? Because the instructions in RAM were corrupted. Why were they corrupted? Because they were incorrectly received. Why were they incorrectly received? Because the serial port configuration wasn't correctly defined, and the speed was unstable, resulting in some packets being transferred incorrectly. There was no security, no checksum, nor even a length verification. When the problem was analyzed, the port speed was set to the one in the main application, and the bootloader was enhanced with some security features.

64-Bit Calculations

Situation: An application was developed that used 64-bit numbers. The 64-bit number was the current time, the number of microseconds since January 1, 1970. This number was derived from two 32-bit registers; one containing the amount of seconds since the January 1, 1970, and the second register the amount of nanoseconds since the last time pulse, sent by some specialized equipment. We were looking for precision time.

It worked perfectly. And one day, it stopped working. Instead of giving us the current time, it gave some strange results; time seemed to slow down. So we were called in to have a look at the code.

```
uint32 secondsU32, usecondsU32
uint64 utctimeU64
[ ... ]
utctimeU64 = (secondsU32 * 1000) + (usecondsU32 / 4);
```

The code is simple enough. UTC Time is the current amount of seconds times 1000, to turn them into milliseconds, and then we add the amount of milliseconds read from another register with a small calculation. Nothing too tricky. So why did it stop working so suddenly? Unit tests were done previous to this, and everything worked fine. We plugged in a debugger to have a closer look. We stepped through the C code, and utctimeU64 did not contain the right value. We stepped through assembly, and we came across this:

```
MOV r3, [r0 + 0x20]
MOV r4, 0x3E8
MUL r4, r4, r3
```

This part caught our attention. The code was easy enough to spot because 0x3E8 in hexadecimal gives 1000 in decimal. What was presumed to be secondsU32 is loaded into r3 and then 1000 into r4. The final calculation, the contents of r3 × r4, is placed into r4. There is one problem with that; when looking at the value of r3, it was clear that any operation on it would immediately overflow the resulting register, and data would be lost. It isn't just a little bit of data that is lost but a full 9 bits of data. What intrigued us was the use of MUL, where UMULL or SMULL would have been appropriate.

The real reason was faulty code. By running step by step in C, the problem wasn't clearly visible. By stepping in assembly, we saw it immediately. The line in C was:

```
utctimeU64 = (secondsU32 * 1000) + (usecondsU32 / 4);
```

That reasoning, although sound, just isn't correctly written. The compiler will take secondsU32, and multiply it by 1000. In other words, it takes the register containing secondsU32 and multiplies that value by 1000, which could possibly result in an overflow, and it did. To correct the code, we copied secondsU32 into a 64-bit value before performing the multiplication, therefore eliminating any possibility of an overflow. The fact that it worked previously was just luck; this was a problem that had been created a few years previously and hadn't an overflow problem until a specific point in time. Unit testing was added to make the test more extreme.

A Timely Response

Situation: An ARM1176 is used in a real-time application in a laser laboratory. Usually used for calculation, the processor use is at approximately 90 percent capacity. Rarely, when a crossbeam is fired, a fast interrupt is issued, and an operation must be executed immediately. The window of operation is only a few nanoseconds wide, but technically, the core should handle it without a problem. However, the core misses the target every time.

When the crossbeam is fired, a drop of fuel is evaporated, and the resonance must be registered. It is not possible to warn the ARM1176 a few nanoseconds before the beam is fired, so it must react immediately.

When this happens, a fast interrupt is issued. The fast interrupt was chosen especially for the speed at which it can be executed and its priority over all other operations. The FIQ code was optimized, helping to shave off a few nanoseconds when starting, but the code was working well; the only problem was the time taken to start the code.

This processor was chosen specifically for the task. The ARM1176 is used in real-time applications, using little energy and clocked at speeds up to 1 GHz. The ARM1176 was chosen over an ARM1156, more suited to real-time applications, because of its computational power and low energy consumption. By using less power than other CPUs, it could be placed next to (or inside) the experiment, and the low heat radiation meant that it could run without interfering. However, it looked like the processor wasn't doing what it was supposed to do, and some staff wanted to return to the ARM1156.

An external team was brought in to see if anything could be done. After some analysis with a debugger, the verdict came back. The vector table and the MMU had not been used correctly.

The MMU did not have a lot of configuration. The memory was mapped according to a layout, but it used only L1 page tables, so only 4096 entries. The SDRAM was mapped to different locations.

When analyzing the vector table, one thing became immediately apparent. The fast interrupt vector was a branch instruction, branching into main memory. The Fast Interrupt vector is placed at the end of the vector table, one of the reasons that code can be placed immediately after the table, saving a branch. Even worse, this branch was sent into SDRAM memory when the ARM1176 has tightly coupled memory.

No code was changed in this project, but the memory layout was slightly changed. The interrupt handler was placed at the end of the vector table and was placed inside tightly coupled memory. This shaved off a few nanoseconds, enough for the interrupt handler to respond as required.

This last example is between two worlds. It required a debugger to look at the system, especially the vectors, but the problem wasn't necessarily the code. The problem came from something known as optimization; the code works, but the code or system needs to be tweaked to obtain satisfactory results. This brings us to the next chapter that discusses optimization.

SUMMARY

This chapter shows different debugger solutions, ranging from software to hardware. Each system has its advantages, and often, a mix of both hardware and software is required. In the next chapter, you see what happens after the debugging phase finishes and another potential use for debuggers: optimization.

10
Writing Optimized C

WHAT'S IN THIS CHAPTER?

➤ Knowing when to optimize

➤ Knowing what to optimize

➤ C optimization techniques

➤ Assembly optimization techniques

➤ Hardware optimization

Optimization is the final part of any project, and it is vitally important to understand. Some developers write optimized code from the start, and on most projects, that is a bad idea. The reason is simple: Optimized code is often difficult to read or to understand, and during the development phase, changes have to be made, often from different people, and in some cases, different departments. It is often best to start with readable, maintainable code before starting the optimization process. In addition, spending an extra two hours on optimizing a section of code might not be worth it; maybe this function will be called only once, or maybe the entire file will be replaced when changes occur in the project.

When the project is finished, when all the functionality has been added and all the bugs have been corrected, now it's time to start optimizing. The problem is, where do you start?

RULES FOR OPTIMIZED CODE

The term *rules* are used, but the truth is there are no set rules. You do not need to follow every rule here, indeed, for some applications; some of these rules might be impractical. You are the only judge as to what should be used and what shouldn't. The previous code used 32-bit integers, but in some cases, you would prefer (or need) to have two 16-bit numbers because space could be critical, and the need for space-saving techniques supersedes the need to optimize for speed.

Don't Start with Optimization

This might sound like a contradiction, but it is also one of the most important unwritten rules. Optimized code of course makes an application or system run faster, but it can make the code less readable. It is also easier to make mistakes in optimized code, simply because the code, being written specifically for a processor, is sometimes written in a less logical manner for humans. Also, is the code that you write going to be used often? It is suggested for most code to write clean code, not necessarily writing heavy optimizations or wasting cycles. The most important part of a project is to get the foundations ready and to get the basic structure. After the project works, then comes the time for optimization.

Like most rules, there are exceptions. One of them concerns interrupt handlers. Interrupts can play a critical role in development and need to be taken care of quickly. On a device that handles multiple interrupts, even during the development phase, handlers need to be at least slightly optimized, and any code that runs in an interrupt context needs to be fast.

Know Your Compiler

The first rule: Know your compiler. A compiler, without any instructions, normally creates a binary that can be used for debugging, but rarely anything optimized. To get the compiler to optimize for speed or size, normally you have to add compiler options. A compiler can be configured to optimize for size, or for speed, or a mixture of both. It can also be configured to not optimize at all, which is useful for debugging.

This is far beyond the scope of this book (and is a subject large enough to merit a book of its own). If your project requires optimized code, you should look closely at ARM's compiler. ARM's compiler contains some of the most advanced optimization routines available, designed by the people who designed the core.

Know Your Code

Again, this sounds like a contradiction. Of course, you know the code; after all, you wrote it, but how many times is your function actually called? How long does this routine take to execute? Knowing the answer to these two questions can also answer another question. What should you optimize? Shaving off 200 milliseconds might be a good optimization, but if that portion of code is run only once, the time spent optimizing might have been wasted. Saving a single millisecond on a routine that is called thousands of times, on the other hand, might have a huge impact.

PROFILING

In software engineering, *profiling* is a form of dynamic program analysis that measures, for example, the amount of memory used or the time a program takes to complete the usage of particular instructions or the frequency and duration of function calls. Using a profiler, you can get a good idea of what your code is doing, which portions of code are called frequently, and most important, the amount of times that certain routines take.

The trouble with embedded systems is that they are so different. What might work well on one embedded system might not work on another. Some systems will have an operating system, others will be bare-metal.

Profiling Inside an Operating System

Profiling on an embedded system with an operating system (especially the Cortex-A line) is relatively easy. For example, on Linux-based systems, GNU's gprof is an excellent tool to use, but using such a tool requires several things to be present (disk space, for one).

To prepare a program to be profiled via gprof, it must be compiled with a special option, telling the compiler to add little bits of code to your own. To compile for profiling, simply add the -pg option:

```
arm-none-linux-gcc -o myprog myprog.c utils.c -g -pg
```

By adding this option, calls are added to monitor functions before each function call. This is used for creating statistical data about which function was run, how many times, and the amount of time spent.

After the program is compiled for profiling, it must be run to generate the information that gprof needs. Simply run the program as you would normally, using the same command-line options, and the program will run and create the necessary data files. The program will run slightly slower because debug routines have been added, but it shouldn't be noticeable.

When the program has completed, it's time to use gprof, which requires two files: the output file that was created, and the executable file itself. If you omit the executable filename, the file a.out is used. If you give no profile data filename, the file gmon.out is used. If any file is not in the proper format, or if the profile data file does not appear to belong to the executable file, an error message prints.

Gprof can output statistical data to an output file for analysis.

```
Flat profile:

Each sample counts as 0.001 seconds.
  %   cumulative   self              self     total
 time   seconds   seconds    calls  ms/call  ms/call  name
80.24     5.84     5.120     4000     1.28     1.28   calcfreq
20.26     1.45     1.280     4000     0.32     0.32   getio
00.00     0.01     0.009        1     8.96     8.96   precalc
```

This example printout shows a program that was run with the GNU profiler. This program is designed to get data from a GPIO and then calculate the frequency of the input signal. There are three functions: calcfreq, getio, and precalc. calcfreq takes (on average) 1.28 ms to execute and getio only 0.32, but precalc takes a whopping 8.96 ms. At first, it is tempting to optimize the function that takes the most time, but have a closer look. precalc is called only once, but calcfreq, which takes only one-eighth of the time to run, is called 4,000 times. If optimization is required, this is the function to optimize because saving even one-tenth of a millisecond in this function results in a savings of more than the precalc function itself.

Profilers like this work by analyzing the program's program counter at regular intervals. It requires operating system interrupts, and as such, cannot be used on barebones systems. It also gets its data by statistical approximation, so the results are not accurate, but they are precise enough to give you a general idea.

For Linux systems, oprofile is an excellent tool. This tool, released under the GNU GPL, leverages the hardware performance counters of the CPU to enable profiling for a wide variety of statistics.

No special recompilations are required, and even debug symbols are not always necessary. It can be used to profile a single application, or it can be used to profile the entire system.

Profiling on a Bare Metal System

Profiling on a bare metal system is slightly more complicated because often there isn't an operating system running that enables OS interrupts. There are, however, other options.

Hardware Profiler

As shown in the previous chapter, you can connect hardware devices to development boards for debugging. Some of these devices use the same interface for more advanced functions, including profiling.

Hardware profilers are more accurate than software profilers and have the advantage of not modifying code. The company Segger (http://www.segger.com) develops JTAG emulators for ARM systems, called the J-Link, which can be used to profile applications. Lauterbach Trace32 systems also have advanced profiling solutions. The DS-5 debugger from ARM is also a professional solution, offering advanced features.

Some manufacturers provide debugging interfaces directly onto evaluation boards, something that is important for the first steps of development.

For example, Silicon Labs provides evaluation boards equipped with J-Link technology. These boards not only give information about the routines being run, but they also correlate the amount of energy that each routine uses. Because Silicon Labs EFM32 series are heavily focused on energy efficiency, its tools also show some advanced statistics on energy usage. For example, when profiling an application, you can tell not only how often a particular routine is called, but also the amount of energy that it uses. This greatly helps specific profiling; optimization will not only be for the amount of time a routine takes, but also the amount of energy, which is an embedded engineer's biggest dilemma. This solution provides the tools required to fully understand what portions of code require optimization, and what type.

Silicon Labs energyAware Profiler shows a real-time graph of power consumption, and with all the points of interest. It is possible to see that IRQ awoke the microcontroller, the event that returned it to sleep mode, the functions run, and the amount of CPU time for each routine. Of course, there is also an external debug port if you want to use your own tools.

GPIO Output

Another technique that you can use to profile specific functions is an available GPIO line. With the help of an oscilloscope, it is easy to see exactly how much time a routine takes.

For example, imagine an interrupt function on a Cortex-M microcontroller. Some Cortex-M devices have fast I/O capable of switching in two cycles or less. This is perfect for such a routine. At the beginning of the interrupt, set the I/O to a logical 1. At the end of the routine, switch the I/O back to a logical 0. On the oscilloscope, set a trigger on the output, and you can see exactly how long each routine or each specific event takes. You aren't tied to an entire routine, but just about any section of code.

Cycle Counter

Some ARM cores have a Performance Monitor Unit, a small unit that can be programmed to gather statistics on the operation of the processor and memory system. In this case, you can use it to calculate the number of cycles a portion of code takes.

You can access the Performance Monitor Unit through the CP15 coprocessor, which is available on select cores. Because you access it through CP15, it requires system privileges, and thus can be programmed only by the kernel or through privileged code. By default, the counters are disabled. First, user-mode access to the performance counter must be enabled.

```
/* enable user-mode access to the performance counter*/
asm ("MCR p15, 0, %0, C9, C14, 0\n\t" :: "r"(1));
```

When this command is issued, the cycle counter starts incrementing. The cycle counter can then be read in user space, with a simple command:

```
static inline unsigned int get_cyclecount (void)
{
  unsigned int cycles;
  // Read CCNT Register
  asm volatile ("MRC p15, 0, %0, c9, c13, 0\t\n": "=r"(cycles));
  return cycles;
}
```

You can use this counter by comparing the number of cycles before and after the code section, or reset it as required. Also, for long routines, it has a divider, which can increment once every 64 cycles.

```
static inline void init_perfcounters (int32_t do_reset, int32_t enable_divider)
{
  // in general enable all counters (including cycle counter)
  int32_t value = 1;

  // peform reset:
  if (do_reset)
  {
    value |= 2;     // reset all counters to zero.
    value |= 4;     // reset cycle counter to zero.
  }

  if (enable_divider)
    value |= 8;     // enable "by 64" divider for CCNT.

  value |= 16;

  // program the performance-counter control-register:
  asm volatile ("MCR p15, 0, %0, c9, c12, 0\t\n" :: "r"(value));

  // enable all counters:
  asm volatile ("MCR p15, 0, %0, c9, c12, 1\t\n" :: "r"(0x8000000f));

  // clear overflows:
  asm volatile ("MCR p15, 0, %0, c9, c12, 3\t\n" :: "r"(0x8000000f));
}
```

C OPTIMIZATIONS

Although assembly language gives you full control over the processor, it isn't practical to write large portions of software in assembly. For embedded projects, most engineers prefer C. C is portable, is much easier to write and maintain than assembly, and yet can still make highly optimized code. However, again, there is a difference between application development and embedded development. There are a few rules to follow, and to fully understand what is going on, you need to know about what the compiler is doing and the assembly it generates.

Basic Example

Start with a simple program.

```
void loopit(void)
{
    u16 i; //Internal variable
iGlobal = 0; //Global variable

//16 bit index incrementation
for (i = 0; i < 16: i++)
{
iGlobal++;
}
}
```

This is an extremely simple program; it creates a loop that runs 16 times, each time incrementing a global variable. The code was compiled, transferred, and then run with a debugger capable of advanced performance monitoring. The application code comes in at 24 bytes, and on an ARM926EJ-S evaluation board, it runs in 138 µs. Most people would think that is great, but embedded engineers go pale with this. There is nothing strictly wrong with the code; it is perfectly good C code, highly maintainable, but there are things that can be done to make it run faster. ARM systems, and indeed a lot of systems, actually do better when they count down to zero. The reason is simple; every time the processor makes a calculation, the processor automatically compares it to zero and sets a processor flag. On this platform, the bit in question is Z in the CPSR register. At the end of each loop, i is compared to an integer. If you decreased to zero, you could add a jump condition if z is true, saving cycles. So, make a quick change, and count down to zero:

```
void loopit(void)
{
u16 i; //Internal variable

//16 bit index decrementation

for (i = 16; i != 0: i--)
{
iGlobal++;
}
}
```

The size of the code remains unchanged; you are still at 24 bytes, but the execution time is faster, 124 µs. That is a bit of a speed gain, but there is still a lot you can do. The code uses a variable that is 16 bits long, presumably to save space. The loop can loop only 16 times, so why bother having a 32-bit variable? 16 should do. Actually, it does, but it isn't always a good idea. This particular ARM core is 32-bit native, and using 16-bit values takes up valuable processor power because the processor has to convert a 16-bit variable to 32 bits, work with it, and then retransform it to 16 bits. Working with the native size can help. So turn that into a 32-bit variable:

```
void loopit(void)
{
    u32 i; //Internal variable
    iGlobal = 0; //Global variable

    //32 bit index decrementation
    for (i = 16; i != 0: i--)
    {
        iGlobal++;
    }
}
```

Now, when debugging, you notice something. The size has gone down to 20 bytes because there are fewer instructions needed. Execution time has also gone down to 115 µs, again, because there are fewer instructions to execute. The joys of optimizing! But you aren't done yet. That global variable is a nightmare; every time you loop, the processor needs to access the RAM to change a variable, and that uses up valuable time. So, now define a variable, keep it local, and at the end of the loop, copy it back to the global variable:

```
void loopit(void)
{
    u32 i; //Internal variable
    u32 j;
    iGlobal = 0; //Global variable

    //32 bit index decrementation
    for (i = 16; i != 0: i--)
    {
        j++;
    }
    iGlobal = j; //Copy the local variable's value to the global variable
}
```

You haven't done a lot here; all you have done is to declare a new variable and use that for the loop instead. Again, there is no size change; there are new codes for accessing a register, but you don't have the codes to access RAM. Because the variable is now in a register, it is a considerable speed boost; the execution time is now down to 52 µs. But you can still do better. The loop creates a lot of overhead, and where possible, unrolling a loop can help:

```
void loopit(void)
{
    u32 i; //Internal variable
    u32 j;
    iGlobal = 0; //Global variable

    //32 bit index decrementation
    for (i = 4; i != 0: i--)
```

```
    {
        j++; j++; j++; j++;
    }
    iGlobal = j; //Copy the local variable's value to the global variable
}
```

This time, you loop only 4 times, instead of 12, and doing 4 times the work inside the loop. This might sound strange, but this saves considerable overhead time; looping and forking take up valuable cycles. With this new routine, the size has gone up slightly to 22 bytes, but the execution time is down to 26 μs. There wasn't anything wrong with the code, but there are always ways to optimize, and time should be taken for code optimization, especially on embedded systems. That isn't an excuse for not being careful on powerful platforms; just because processors go faster and faster, it isn't a reason to use up valuable cycles.

In total, optimization saved 112μs, a reduction of 81 percent. However, to achieve this result, several optimization cycles were performed. The code was profiled, then optimized, and then tested, repeating the cycle. Optimization can be a long procedure, testing multiple theories, possibly keeping the results, or reverting to the previous configuration. The cycle is illustrated in Figure 10-1.

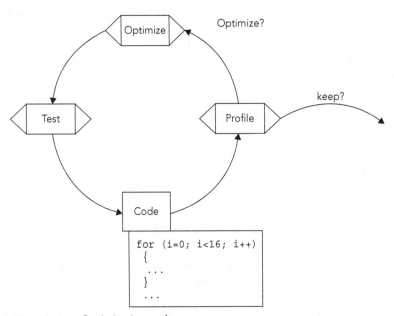

FIGURE 10-1: Optimization cycle

Count Down, Not Up

It's common to see code counting up, but as far as the processor is concerned, it is faster to count down to zero. To fully understand why, you need to look at the assembly code.

When you start the for loop, you initialize one of the registers to zero. Then you do the calculation, or break to another portion of code. At this point, increment the register. Compare the register to another number, and this takes up one cycle. If the result is lower, return to the beginning of the loop.

```
      MOV r0, 0 @The amount of loops we have done
loop:

   [ ... ]

      ADD r0, r0, #1 @ Add one
      CMP r0, #15
      BLE loop
```

If you start at a certain number and count down to zero, things are slightly different. Initialize one of the registers to the number you want. Then, again, do the calculation or break to another portion of code. Here, you can decrement the register and force a status update. In the previous code, you would have compared the register to another number, but you don't need to here. The CPSR would have been updated, so instead of comparing, you can simply Branch if Not Equal.

```
      MOV r0, 16 @The amount of loops left to do
loop:

   [ ... ]

      SUBS r0, r0, #1 @ Subtract one
      BNE loop
```

As you can see, you no longer have the CMP instruction. You have just saved a cycle per iteration. Not the most drastic speed-up possible, but if a routine has to loop thousands of times, it starts to build up.

Integers

Integers are a vital part of any development. Processors were designed to handle integers, not floating point or any other type of numeral. Ever since their introduction, special instructions or coprocessors for handling floating point numbers have been added on select cores, but despite optimization and engineering, they take longer to execute than integer arithmetic. You invariably use integers for standard calculation.

Most integer operations can be done in just a few cycles, with one notable exception, division, discussed in the next section. Generally, always use integers that are the same width as the system bus to avoid unwanted calculations later. Although a u16 might be all you need to hold in the data, if the variable is heavily used on a 32-bit system, making it a u32 can speed things up. When reading in a u16, the processor invariably reads in a u32 and then does some operations to transform it into a u16, which costs cycles.

Also, if you know that your variable can handle only positive numbers, make it unsigned. Most processors can handle unsigned integer arithmetic considerably faster than signed. (This is also good practice and helps make for self-documenting code.) Always try to make your code use integers. If you need two decimal places, multiply your figures by 100 instead of using a floating point.

Division

In the early days of ARM processors, ARM studied the needs for their processor carefully, and made a choice to not integrate a hardware division unit. This made the processor simpler, cheaper, and faster. Divisions were not all too common, and the divisions that were required could still be performed in software using highly optimized routines.

Division is complicated and requires a substantial number of transistors to be performed quickly. Some ARM processors have hardware division integrated, but some do not. Hardware division (present on Cortex-M3, Cortex-M4, and Cortex-A15/Cortex-A7 cores to name but a few) takes between 2 and 12 cycles.

General rule: If you can avoid dividing, avoid it. A 32-bit division in software can take up to (and in some cases more than) 120 cycles.

Sometimes you can get away with multiplying instead of dividing, especially when comparing. (a / b) > c can sometimes be rewritten as a > (c * b).

You can use shifting, although not technically dividing, as division. Where possible, the compiler attempts to shift rather than divide, but that works only for few cases. If the compiler cannot shift, it falls back to software routines for division.

Knowing what is required is essential to optimization. For example, if a program often divides by 10, you can write a small function that multiplies a number by 3277 and then divides the result by 32768.

```
add r1, r0, r0, lsl #1
add r0, r0, r1, lsl #2
add r0, r0, r1, lsl #6
add r0, r0, r1, lsl #10
mov r0, r0, lsr #15
```

This function does have a limited range, and care must be taken to ensure that the multiplication does not overflow. In some cases this can also be an approximation, not an exact result, but it is an example of what you can do by carefully rethinking routines to change them into shifts. In certain circumstances, when the maximum value of a variable is known, dividing in this fashion can save cycles.

Don't Use Too Many Parameters

When writing C code, some developers are tempted to use large functions with multiple parameters. Some coding conventions call for small routines to be used, no longer than a printed page in length, but go into little detail about the parameters.

When you call a function in C, generally this is translated as a branch in assembly. The standard ARM calling convention dictates that parameters are passed by placing the parameter values into registers r0 through r3 before calling the subroutine. This means that a C routine typically uses up to four 32-bit integers as parameters, and any other parameters will be put onto the stack. You could just use higher registers, putting parameters into r4, r5, and so on, but at some point, something must be decided, and ARM chose this to be its calling convention. If you design a small assembly program, you can do anything you want, but a compiler sticks to the rules to simplify things.

Compilers can be configured to use a certain number of registers before pushing further variables onto the stack.

The ARM calling convention states that r0 to r3 are used as parameters for functions (r0 is also used as a return variable), and r4 to r12 are caller-save, meaning that a subroutine must not modify the value on return. A subroutine may of course modify any registers, but on return, the contents must have been restored. To do this, the subroutines must push the registers it needs to the stack and then pop them on return.

Pointers, Not Objects

When a subroutine is called, the first four parameters are passed as registers; all the others are pushed onto the stack. If a parameter is too big, it is also pushed onto the stack. Calling a subroutine by giving it a table of 64 integers can create considerably more overhead than giving it one parameter, the address of the table. By giving our subroutine the address of the object, you no longer need to push anything onto the stack, saving time and memory. The routine can then fetch the data with the memory address, and it is quite possible that only a few elements are required, not the entire table.

Don't Frequently Update System Memory

In the previous example, you updated a global variable. When updating a global variable, or any variable that is not enclosed in your subroutine, the processor must write that variable out to system memory, waiting for the pipeline. In the best case, you get a cache hit, and the information will be written fairly quickly, but some zones are non-cacheable, so the information needs to be written out to system memory. Keeping a local variable in your subroutine means that in the best case, you update a register, keeping things extremely fast. After your routine finishes, you can write that value back out to system memory, incurring a pipeline delay only once.

Be careful when doing this, however, to make sure that you can keep a local copy in register memory. Remember that an interrupt breaks the current process, and your interrupt might need the real value. Also, in threaded applications, another thread may need the variable, in which case the data needs to be protected before writing (and frequently before reading, too).

This is one of the optimizations that can drastically improve performance, but great care must be taken.

Alignment

Alignment is vitally important in ARM-based systems. All ARM instructions must be aligned on a 32-bit boundary. NEON instructions are also 32-bits long, and must be aligned similarly. Thumb instructions are different and can be aligned on a 16-bit boundary. If instructions are to be injected from an external source (data cartridge, memory card, and so on), great care must be taken to put the data in the right location, since misaligned instructions will be interpreted as an undefined instruction.

Data alignment is a little different. Although it is advisable to use data that has the same width as the system bus, sometimes this isn't possible. Sometimes, data needs to be packed, such as hardware addresses, network packets, and so on. ARM cores are good at fetching 32-bit values, but in a packet structure, an integer could be on a boundary between two double words. In the best case, this requires multiple instructions to fetch the memory and by using shifts, get the final result. In the worst case, it can result in an alignment trap, when the CPU tries to perform a memory access on an unaligned address.

ASSEMBLY OPTIMIZATIONS

When C optimizations are not enough, sometimes it is necessary to go a step further and look at assembly. Normally the compiler will do an excellent job in translating C to assembly, but it cannot know exactly what you want to do, and the scope of the action requested. Sometimes the compiler needs a hand, and sometimes you have to write short routines.

Specialized Routines

C compilers have to take your functions and translate them into assembly, without knowing all the possible use cases. For example, a multiplication routine might have to automatically take any number (16-bit, 32-bit, or maybe even 64-bit) and multiply that with any other combination. The list is endless. In most cases, there will be only a few use cases. For example, in an accounting program, maybe the only division possible will be dividing by 100, converting a number in cents to a number in dollars.

In embedded systems, it is often useful to create highly optimized routines for specific functions, mainly mathematical operations. For example, a quick routine for multiplying a number by 10 could be written as follows, taking only two cycles to complete.

```
MOV r1, r0, asl #3 ; Multiply r0 by 8
ADD r0, r1, r0, asl #1 ; Add r0 times 2 to the result
```

Don't hesitate to create several routines like this in a helper file. In some cases, optimized libraries are available for use.

Handling Interrupts

Interrupts are events that force the processor to stop its normal operation and respond to another event. *Interrupt handlers* should be designed to be as fast as possible, signaling the interrupt to the main program through a flag or system variable before returning to the main application. The kernel (if available) can reschedule the applications to take into account an interrupt; if an interrupt handler is given the task of calculation, or any other routine that takes a long time, other interrupts might have to wait for the first interrupt to finish, resulting in surprising results.

For critical interrupts, FIQ is available. FIQ has a higher priority than IRQ, and on ARMv7A/R cores, the FIQ vector is at the end of the vector table, meaning that it is not necessary to jump to another portion of memory. The advantage is that this saves a branch instruction and also saves a potential memory reread. On most systems, the memory located at 0x00000000 is internal memory and doesn't suffer from the same latency as external memory.

Interrupt Handling Schemes

There are several ways to handle interrupt, all depending on the project. Each has its own advantage and disadvantage, and choosing the right scheme is important for any project.

➤ A non-nested interrupt handler handles interrupts sequentially.

➤ A nested interrupt handler handles multiple interrupts, last in first out.

➤ A re-entrant interrupt handler handles multiple interrupts and prioritizes them.

On a system with few interrupts, a non-nested handler is often enough and can be easily made to be extremely fast. Other projects handling lots of interrupts may need a nested handler, and projects with interrupts coming from multiple sources might require a re-entrant interrupt handler.

Non-Nested Interrupt Handler

The simplest interrupt handler is the non-nested interrupt handler. When entering this handler, all interrupts are disabled, and then the interrupt handler handles the incoming request. When the interrupt handler has completed its task, interrupts are re-enabled, and control is returned to the main application.

Nested Interrupt Handler

The nested interrupt handler is an improvement over the non-nested handler; it re-enables interrupts before the handler has fully serviced the current interrupt. Mainly used on real-time systems, this handler adds complexity to a project but also increases performance. The downside is that the complexity of this handler can introduce timing problems that can be difficult to trace, but with careful planning and by protection context restoration, this handler can handle a large amount of interrupts.

Re-Entrant Interrupt Handler

The main difference between a re-entrant interrupt handler and a nested interrupt handler is that interrupts are re-enabled early on, reducing interrupt latency. This type of handler requires extra care because all the code will be executed in a specific mode (usually SVC). The advantage of using a different mode is that the interrupt stack is not used and, therefore, will not overflow.

A re-entrant interrupt handler must save the IRQ state, switch processor modes, and save the state for the new processor mode before branching.

HARDWARE CONFIGURATION OPTIMIZATIONS

Far from the software side of a project, it is often important to configure the processor at the lowest level. These optimizations do not make the most out of coding rules or clever software techniques, but rather configure the processor to make the most out of the hardware.

Frequency Scaling

In situations in which intensive calculation is required from time to time, frequency scaling routines can be added to the software. When the processor needs to run at full speed, a system call can be made to let the processor run at maximum speed, therefore accelerating executes speed at the expense of consuming more energy. When the calculation finishes, it can be put back to a slower speed, saving energy while waiting for the next calculation.

Configuring Cache

Cache can be one of the biggest boosts available on any processor. Before the invention of cache memory, computer systems were simple. The processor asked for data in system memory and wrote data to the system memory. When processors became faster and faster, more and more cycles were wasted, waiting for system memory to respond to be able to continue, so a buffer was created between the processor and the system memory. Embedded systems especially, with price constraints, can often have slow system memory.

Cache, put simply, is a buffer between the processor and the external memory. Memory fetches can take a long time, so processors can take advantage of cache to read in sections of system memory into cache, where data access is quicker.

Cache isn't simply about buffering memory between the system memory and the processor; it is sometimes the other way around, buffering between the processor and the system memory. This is where things become complicated. Sooner or later, that data must be written back to system memory, but when? There are two write policies: write-though and write-back. In a *write-through cache*, every write to the cache results in a write to main memory. In *write-back*, the cache is kept but marked as "dirty"; it will be written out to system memory when the processor is available, when the cache is evicted, or when the data memory is again read. For this reason, write-back can result in two system memory accesses: one to write the data to system memory and another one to reread the system memory.

Cache is separated into *cache lines*, blocks of data. Each block of data has a fixed size, and each cache has a certain amount of cache lines available. The time taken to fetch one cache line from memory (read latency) matters because the CPU will run out of things to do while waiting for the cache line. When a CPU reaches this state, it is called a *stall*. The proportion of accesses that result in a cache hit is known as the *hit rate* and can be a measure of the effectiveness of the cache for a given program or algorithm. Read misses delay execution because they require data to be transferred from memory much more slowly than the cache itself. Write misses may occur without such penalty because the processor can continue execution while data is copied to the main memory in the background.

Instruction Cache

On modern ARM-cores with cache, instructions and memory are separated into two channels. Because data memory might be changed frequently, and instruction memory should never be changed, it simplifies things if the two are separated. By activating instruction cache, the next time the core fetches an instruction, the cache interface can fetch several instructions and make them available in cache memory.

Setting the I-Cache is done via the CP15 system coprocessor and should be active for most projects.

```
mrc p15, 0, r0, c1, c0, 0
orr r0, r0, #0x00001000 @ set bit 12 (I) I-cache
mcr p15, 0, r0, c1, c0, 0
```

Data Cache

Data cache is slightly more complicated. Data access may be accesses to read-sensitive or write-sensitive peripherals, or to system components that change the system in some way. It isn't safe to enable global data cache because caching some of these devices could result in disastrous side effects.

When the MMU is configured, it can be programmed to allow or deny access to specific regions of memory; for example, it might be programmed to deny read accesses to a section of memory just after a stack, resulting in an exception if there is a stack overflow.

For the D-Cache to be active, a table must be written to system memory, known as the translation table. This table "describes" sections of memory and can tell the MMU which regions of memory are to be accessible—and if they are accessible, what cache strategy should be put in place.

The ARM MMU supports entries in the translation tables, which can represent either an entire 1 MB (section), 64 KB (large page), 4 KB (small page), or 1 KB (tiny page) of virtual memory. To provide flexibility the translation tables are multilevel; there is a single top-level table that divides the address space into 1 MB sections, and each entry in that table can either describe a corresponding area of physical memory or provide a pointer to a second level table.

The ARM MMU design is well designed because it enables mixing of page sizes. It isn't necessary to divide the system memory into 1-KB blocks; otherwise, the table would be massive. Instead, it is possible to divide memory only when required, and it is indeed possible to use only sections if required.

The translation table enables some system optimization, but care must be taken with the translation table. When the hardware performs a translation table walk, it has to access physical memory, which can be slow. Fortunately, the MMU has its own dedicated cache, known as the translation lookaside buffer (TLB). However, this cache can contain only a certain amount of lines before having to reread system memory. If the translation table is complicated, it is sometimes worth putting this table into internal memory (if space is available).

Locking Cache Lines

You can make a few tweaks to cache configurations to optimize system performance.

Consider an application where IRQ latency is critical. When an IRQ arrives, it must be dealt with as soon as possible. If the IRQ handler is no longer present in cache memory, it is necessary to reread a cache line containing the IRQ handler before executing, something that can take a certain amount of cycles to complete. It is possible to "lock" a cache line, to tell the hardware to never replace that cache line, and to always keep it ready if needed. For an IRQ handler, this might be an option if no faster system memory is available, but it comes at a price; by doing so, there is less cache available for the rest of the application.

Use Thumb

As seen in Chapter 6, Thumb instructions are 16-bits long. Thumb-2 adds some 32-bit instructions, but even with those instructions Thumb instruction density is higher than with ARM instructions.

For this reason, if a portion of code needs to remain in cache, it is sometimes worth coding in Thumb. Because Thumb code is denser, more instructions can be placed in the same cache size, which makes Thumb code often more cache efficient.

SUMMARY

In this chapter, you realized the importance of profiling your code to see which portions of code require optimization, and some of the different techniques used. You also saw some of the possibilities for optimizing code, both in C and in assembly, and just a few techniques to boost the processing capacities with software and hardware techniques.

PART II
Reference

➤ **APPENDIX A:** Terminology

➤ **APPENDIX B:** ARM Architecture Versions

➤ **APPENDIX C:** ARM Core Versions

➤ **APPENDIX D:** NEON Intrinsics and Instructions

➤ **APPENDIX E:** Assembly Instructions

Terminology

When studying embedded systems, and reading through technical documentation, there are a lot of terms that, at first, make no sense. A processor might be capable of obtaining a certain amount of MIPS, or maybe it supports JTAG debugging, or even support SIMD, but what exactly does that mean? In this appendix, you will see some of the most common terms and an explanation of each.

BRANCH PREDICTION

During a branch operation, when branching to a new portion of code, there can be a performance hit while the processor gets new instructions from another portion of memory. To reduce this performance hit, branch prediction hardware is included in some ARM implementations, fetching instructions from memory according to what the branch predictor thinks will be the result. Newer branch prediction hardware can obtain 95 percent accuracy, greatly increasing branch performance. Some branch prediction hardware can obtain a 100 percent accuracy by speculatively executing both branch results, and discarding one of the two when the result is known.

CACHE

When memory became cheaper and systems started using more of it, it became clear that too much time was spent fetching data from the memory or putting data back into the memory. Analysis showed that most of the time the system would read in data from the spatial locality; in essence, if an access is made to a particular location in memory, there is a high probability that other accesses will be made to either that or neighboring locations within the lifetime of a program. To speed up the process, a cache was put in place.

A CPU cache is a faster form of memory used to reduce the average time to access memory. The cache is much smaller, but much faster than the system memory, and can store copies of the system memory. When the CPU requests data, if it is present in the cache, the CPU fetches it directly from cache, resulting in much faster access times. Modified cache, known as *Dirty Data*, is written back to memory when the cache space is required for new data, or during explicit maintenance operations.

All application-class ARM processors since ARM9 have had a Harvard cache architecture, where instruction cache and data cache are separated. Most Cortex-A processors support a two-level cache architecture in which the most common configuration is a pair of separate L1 caches, backed by a unified L2 cache.

Cache Hit

Memory was requested from the processor and found in cache. This is known as a cache hit, and access to system memory is not required.

Cache Line

Instead of reading single words from memory, data is transferred between memory and cache in blocks of fixed sizes, called cache lines. The requested memory is written or read, including some memory located surrounding the requested memory block, because it is highly likely that data located near this location will be used in the near future.

Cache Miss

Memory was requested from the processor and was not found in cache. This is known as a cache miss — the processor must now access system memory before the operation can be completed.

COPROCESSORS

In the early days of ARM, cores supported a coprocessor architecture. Although ARM processors do not have any instructions similar to Intel's x86 CPUID commands, ARM chips enable up to 16 coprocessors to be connected to a core. The ARM architecture provided an elegant way to extend the instruction set using "coprocessors" — a command that is not recognized by the ARM core is sent to each coprocessor until one of them accepts the instruction. Coprocessors are a way for designers to add extended functionality without the need to heavily modify an ARM core. By keeping the power and the simplicity of an ARM core, a designer can add a coprocessor to handle things that the ARM core was not designed to do. For example, Xscale processors have a DSP coprocessor and advanced interrupt handling functions directly on a coprocessor, and virtually any integrator could integrate an HD video decoder.

The last ARM core to support the coprocessor architecture was the ARM1176. Today, the ARM architecture still defines the coprocessor instruction set, and uses "coprocessor instructions," but the coprocessor architecture no longer exists. Configuration, debug, trace, VFP, and NEON instructions still exist, but they do not have any external hardware associated with what they do — all the functions are now internal.

CP10

CP10 defines coprocessor instructions for Vector Floating Point (VFP).

CP11

CP11 defines coprocessor instructions for NEON. NEON is an extension of the original SIMD instruction set, and is often referred to as the Advanced SIMD Extensions.

CP14

CP14 defines coprocessor instructions for the debug unit. These features assist the development of application software, operating systems, systems, and hardware. It enables stopping program execution, examining and altering processor and coprocessor states, altering memory and peripheral state, and restarting the processor core.

CP15

CP15 is a special coprocessor, designed for memory and cache management, designated as the system control coprocessor. CP15 is used to configure the MMU, TCM, cache, cache debug access, and system performance data. Each ARM processor can have up to 16 coprocessors, named CP0 to CP15, and CP15 is reserved by ARM.

CYCLE

Each CPU has a frequency, in Hertz. The Hertz is a unit of frequency, defined as the number of cycles per second of a periodic phenomenon. A processor's clock is, basically, a repeating signal from a logical 0 to a logical 1, and then back again to a logical 0, millions of times a second. A "cycle" is activated every time the signal goes from a logical 0 to a logical 1. In an 800 MHz processor, or a processor running at 800,000,000 Hz, there are 800 million cycles a second. Different operations require a different number of cycles to complete. Although some instructions may take only one cycle to complete, access to memory subsystems can sometimes take thousands — if not tens of thousands — of cycles. Also, some processors can do several things in one cycle; although one part of the CPU is busy executing an instruction, another is already busy fetching the next instruction.

EXCEPTION

An exception is a condition that is triggered when normal program flow is interrupted, either by an internal or external event. It can be caused by attempting to read protected memory (or a memory section that does not exist) or when dividing by zero. When an exception occurs, normal execution is halted, and the Program Counter is placed onto the relevant exception handler for execution.

INTERRUPT

An interrupt is an internal or external signal to the application, informing the processor that something requires its attention. There are several types of interrupts: normal interrupts, fast interrupts, and software interrupts. They are called interrupts because of their impact on the processor, which has to "interrupt" its execution sequence to service the interrupt. This is done by an interrupt handler.

JAZELLE

Jazelle was originally designed to enable Java bytecode execution directly by the processor, implemented as a third execution state alongside ARM and Thumb-mode. Support for Jazelle is indicated by the letter J in the processor name (for example, the ARM926EJ-S), and is a requirement for ARMv6; however, newer devices include only a trivial implementation. With the advances in processor speeds and performance, Jazelle has been deprecated and should not be used for new applications.

JTAG

Short for Joint Test Action Group, it is the common name for the IEEE 1149.1 test access port and boundary scan architecture. Although originally devised by electronic engineers as a way of testing printed circuit boards using boundary scans, today it is used to debug embedded systems. Several JTAG probes exist, enabling programmers to take control of processors and to help debugging and performance checking.

MIPS

Short for Million Instructions per Second, MIPS was an early attempt at benchmarking. A one Megahertz processor, executing one instruction per clock, is a 1 MIPS processor. However, not every instruction is executed in a single clock, far from it. The Intel 4004, the first single-chip CPU, was benchmarked at 0.07 MIPS.

MIPS was a popular benchmarking method until processors arrived at a speed of more than 1 GHz, where MIPS no longer had any real meaning. Because single instructions carry out varying amounts of work, the idea of comparing computers by numbers of instructions became obsolete. Today, the Dhrystone benchmark, while dated, is often quoted in benchmark results. To accurately estimate a processor's speed, a variety of benchmarks are used.

NEON

NEON is an extension of the original SIMD instruction set, and is often referred to as the Advanced SIMD Extensions. It extends the SIMD concept by adding instructions that work on 64-bit registers (D for double word) and 128-bit registers (Q for quad word).

OUT-OF-ORDER EXECUTION

Processors with out-of-order Execution can reorganize the order of instructions inside the pipeline to optimize efficiency, avoiding pipeline stalls. When an instruction creates a stall situation, the pipeline may attempt to execute another instruction that does not depend on an imminent result, even if it is later on in the pipeline.

PIPELINE

To accelerate instruction throughput, pipelines were introduced. Instead of the processor working on a single instruction, fetching, and writing data as required, these steps are part of a pipeline. A pipeline is composed of several stages, and each stage is responsible for one specific action: fetch, decode, execute, data write, and so on. An instruction makes its way through the pipeline, passing through each stage. On each clock cycle, each stage is run; while one instruction is being decoded, another is being executed, and so on.

REGISTER

A register is a small amount of storage available directly inside the CPU. When doing calculations, operations are done directly into registers only; an ARM CPU will not write results directly into system memory. To complete an operation, memory must be read into a register. Then after the calculation is completed, the register will be written back to system memory.

Registers are the fastest of all memories, capable of being read and written in a processor single cycle.

SIMD

Short for Single Instruction Multiple Data, these instructions can operate on several items packed into registers, which is useful for multimedia applications where the same mathematical operations must be performed on large data segments. This has since been augmented by NEON.

SOC

System on a Chip designates a computer chip containing a processor core and all the required external devices embedded directly onto the same microchip. They tend to have built-in memory, input and output peripherals, and sometimes graphics engines, but often require external devices to be effective (especially flash and memory).

SYNTHESIZABLE

ARM cores are available in two formats: hard die, where the physical layout of the ARM core is defined, and peripherals are added to the existing form, or as synthesizable, where the ARM core is delivered as a Verilog program. In this form, device manufacturers can perform custom modifications, tweaking the design to obtain higher clock speeds, optimizations for size, or low power consumption.

TRUSTZONE

TrustZone is a security extension for select ARM processors, providing two virtual processors backed by hardware-based access control. The application core can switch between the two states (referred to as worlds), to prevent data being leaked from one world to another. TrustZone is typically used to run a rich operating system in a less trusted world, and more specialized security code (for example, DRM management) in the more trusted world.

VECTOR TABLES

A vector table is a place in memory containing responses to exceptions. On ARMv7-AR, it is eight words long, containing simple jump instructions. On ARMv7-M, it is much larger and doesn't contain instructions, only memory locations. Put simply, it contains pointers to where the real code lies. For example, when an ARMv7-AR CPU receives an interrupt, an exception is made, setting the PC to a specific location, somewhere in the vector table. This instruction makes the processor jump to the area of code that is responsible for handling that particular exception. It is your job to correctly populate the vector table and to make sure that the vectors are correct.

B

ARM Architecture Versions

ARM architecture versions are often a source of confusion. ARM architecture versions (designs) are written as ARMv, whereas ARM cores (the CPU) are written as ARM. Also, ARM cores do not always have the same first number as their architecture. The ARM940T is based on the ARMv4 architecture, whereas the ARM926EJ-S is based on the ARMv5 architecture. The following table lists the different ARM Architectures and their associated families.

ARCHITECTURE	FAMILY
ARMv1	ARM1
ARMv2	ARM2, ARM3
ARMv3	ARM6, ARM7
ARMv4	StrongARM, ARM7TDMI, ARM8, ARM9TDMI
ARMv5	ARM7EJ, ARM9E, ARM10E, XScale
ARMv6	ARM11
ARMv6-M	Cortex-M0, Cortex-M0+, Cortex-M1
ARMv7-A	Cortex-A5, Cortex-A7, Cortex-A8, Cortex-A9, Cortex-A12, Cortex-A15
ARMv7-R	Cortex-R4, Cortex-R5, Cortex-R7
ARMv7-M	Cortex-M3
ARMv7E-M	Cortex-M4
ARMv8-A	Cortex-A53, Cortex-A57

ARMV1

The first ARM processor was created April 26, 1985. It was targeted as a coprocessor for the BBC Micro, one of Acorn's best-selling computers. Only a few hundred were ever made. It was originally designed to help Acorn work on the ARM2 processor but was sold to third-party developers to accustom them to the new architecture. You can imagine the thrill of using an 8-bit CPU running with a 32-bit coprocessor.

The ARM1 was a revolution for its time; it was a fully functional 32-bit processor with 26-bit addressing. It had 16 general-purpose 32-bit registers, all instructions were 32-bit, and the instruction set was orthogonal, meaning that the instructions were not tied to any particular register. This was contrary to the 6502, which had LDA and LDX instructions and loaded only one particular register. Acorn's philosophy, from the start, was simplicity.

ARMV2

Following on the success of the ARM1, Acorn started work on the ARM2. Less than a year after the release of ARM1, ARM2 became the first commercially available RISC processor. The ARM2 was also based on the second version of the ARM architecture, called ARMv2.

The major weak point for ARM1 was the lack of hardware multiplication support. Multiplication was done in software using shifts and additions, but the general effect was considered to be "horribly slow." ARMv2 fixed this, adding two instructions: MUL and MLA.

Another weakness of the ARMv1 structure was the lack of floating-point hardware. Acorn decided to address this problem by adding hardware support for coprocessors and intended to develop and deliver a floating-point coprocessor at a later date.

Another change was in the Fast Interrupt controller. Two new registers were added. Instead of banking registers R10 to R15, R8 and R9 were added to the list, increasing performance by reducing memory access to the stack.

ARM3, still based on the ARMv2 architecture, was released in 1989. The clock speed was increased to 25MHz, giving a performance of approximately 13 MIPS (compared to the 4 MIPS of ARM2). It contained approximately 300,000 transistors.

The ARM3 was the first ARM processor to use cache. ARM elected to use a fairly simple caching model: a 64-way set-associative cache with random write through a replacement method and 128-bit cache lines. Alterations were made to the coprocessor interface to support this, and the cache system was designated coprocessor zero.

ARMV3

This was the period where ARM spun itself away from Acorn. Thus, for some reason, there was no ARM4 or ARM5.

ARM6 introduced 32-bit addressing support, while still retaining compatibility to the previous 26-bit mode. Two new processor modes were added for handling memory fetch errors and undefined instructions, and two new registers were added: the Current Processor State Register (CPSR) and the Stored Processor State Register (SPSR). This now enabled ARM cores to use virtual memory without the need for previous, tedious tasks.

ARM6 was clocked at 20, 30, and 33 MHz and produced approximately 17, 26, and 28 MIPS average, respectively. It was also power-efficient, enabling a low (for the time) 3.3 v core voltage. This was the beginning for mobile embedded systems because the first product to use an ARM6 was the Apple Newton MessagePad.

ARM7 continued on the success of ARM6. The company, ARM Limited, was a huge success and added more features as the wider market requested them.

ARM7 doubled the size of the cache to 8 k and also doubled the size of the translation look-aside buffer. These changes increased performance over ARM6 by 40 percent.

ARM7 also introduced an extended instruction set which, quite logically for an ARM extension, has been named Thumb. Thumb is a second 16-bit instruction set, allowing (theoretically) programs to be one-half of their memory size. However, by using only eight registers, and a lack of conditional execution support, it ran slower but was a response to other embedded 8-bit and 16-bit processors.

ARM7 also introduced hardware debugging. Previously, engineers had to rely on the software ARMulator for debugging, but with the ARM7, on-chip debugging was possible. The target system can be run as normal, but with external hardware and software, the developer can set breakpoints, step through code, and examine registers and memory.

ARM7 also included advanced multiplication; it included both 32-bit and 64-bit multiplication and multiplication/accumulation, enabling ARM processors to be used in applications where DSPs were more traditionally used. The advanced multiplication core was so successful that it was used in ARM8, ARM9, and StrongARM processor cores.

ARMV4

ARM7-TDMI (Thumb + Debug + Multiplier + ICE) is an improvement of the original ARM7 core, based on the ARMv4T architecture. It is capable of 130 MIPS and was one of the most widely used cores for embedded systems. They were used on Apple iPods, Nintendo's Game Boy Advance, and most of the major mobile telephones.

ARM9-TDMI is a successor to the popular ARM7-TDMI, still using the ARMv4T architecture. They have reduced heat production and clock frequency improvements, both at the cost of adding more transistors. A lot of work was done on the ARM9, the pipeline was greatly improved, and most instructions were executed in only one clock cycle.

ARMV5

The ARMv5 architecture, used in ARM9 and ARM10, introduced Jazelle DBX, or Direct Bytecode Execution, enabling execution of Java bytecode in hardware. Aimed mainly at the mobile phone market, Jazelle enabled Java ME applications and games to run faster by converting recognized bytecodes into native ARM instructions. ARM claims that approximately 95 percent of bytecode in typical programs ends up being directly processed in hardware.

The ARMv5 introduced saturating arithmetic instructions, enabling more intense calculations without the risk of overflow. With four dedicated instructions, calculations can be made that, when exceeding the maximum size of a 32-bit integer, set the overflow bit but return the maximum allowed value (−231 or 231 −1).

The ARM926EJ-S, one of the most popular ARM cores, is based on the ARMv5 architecture.

ARMV6

In 2002, ARM started licensing the ARMv6 core, namely, the ARM11 family. The ARMv6 architecture implemented Single Instruction, Multiple Data instructions (SIMD), heavily used in the mobile telephone market for MPEG-4. The addition of SIMD instructions effectively doubled MPEG-4 processing speed.

ARMv6 also solved some of the problems faced with data alignment; from then on, unaligned data access and mixed-endian data access was supported.

The core pipeline was increased from a five-stage pipeline to an eight-stage pipeline, increasing clock speeds with expected speeds at 1 GHz.

ARMV6-M

The ARMv6 architecture addressed the most demanding applications, but ARM was faced with a problem. With more and more clients requiring higher clock speeds and more data crunching power, it was clear that ARM was giving its customers everything they needed. However, some clients were no longer interested in such a complex architecture and were looking for something more light-weight, while still retaining all the advantages of ARM's technological research. The ARMv6-M architecture was created.

The ARMv6-M architecture introduced the Cortex-M core, designed for Microcontroller applications, and uses the Thumb subset. This microcontroller was much smaller than previous processors, and addressed clients that needed ultralow-powered devices with a small footprint. NXP's UM10415, based on the Cortex M0, ran at 48 MHz and had 32 Kb of flash memory and 8 Kb of RAM. With 25 GPIO lines, a UART port, SPI and I2C controllers, it was designed for ultramobility. Its footprint was 7 mm by 7 mm.

The ARMv6-M architecture was designed for simplicity. Simplicity for the developer, who could develop an entire embedded system from C without even touching assembly, but also simplicity from an electronics point of view, vastly reducing power and heat. It no longer included the ARM instruction set; it relied solely on Thumb-1 and Thumb-2 instructions. The pipeline was reduced to a two-stage pipeline, slightly decreasing performance, but vastly decreasing power usage. Although performance is lower on an ARMv6-M compared to an ARMv5, target devices did not need the processing power delivered by ARM11 processors. Cortex M processors are designed for microcontroller applications, with advanced I/O capability, but reduced processing power.

ARMV7-A/R

With the success of the ARMv6, and with the introduction of the new Cortex line, ARM introduced the ARMv7. This subset of the architecture is used for Cortex-A and Cortex-R processors. Cortex-M uses its own architecture subset.

ARMv7 includes optional virtualization technology, and for the processors that include this (Cortex-A7 and Cortex-A15), hardware division is also supported.

ARMV7-M

The ARMv7-M architecture is derived from the ARMv7-AR but excludes all the functions that the Cortex-M cannot use; it does not contain the ARM assembly language, but only Thumb and Thumb-2. The ARMv6-M architecture was a huge success, and the v7-M architecture extended the architecture to enable the full subset of Thumb and Thumb-2 to be used. It also added something that was missing: divide instructions. Processors based on the ARMv7-M architecture (the Cortex-M3 and Cortex-M4) support hardware division, saturated math, and an accelerated hardware multiplier.

ARMV8

The ARMv8 architecture is a switch to 64-bit computing. Featuring the new A64 instruction set, these 64-bit processors remain binary-compatible with 32-bit versions and can run 32-bit applications inside a 64-bit operating system. They also retain full compatibility with Thumb and Thumb-2, easing new development.

Capable of addressing 64-bits of memory, they also have advanced features for cache management and SIMD instructions, making them the ideal processors for demanding mobile applications, like video editing and extreme multimedia. ARMv8 is also an excellent processor for server applications, and numerous manufacturers are looking closely at this design to solve some of the age old problems of server farms—heat, power consumption, and space requirements.

Today, there are two processor designs in ARMv8; the Cortex-A53 and the Cortex-A57. Both of these designs can be used together using ARM's big.LITTLE technology, and support up to 16 cores.

C

ARM Core Versions

Everything started with the ARM1, and ARM2 quickly fixed or improved any weak points of the ARM1. ARM3 was once again an internal chip, and no major projects used these chips. ARM's commercial success started with the ARM6 chip.

ARM6

ARM6 was based on the ARMv3 architecture and was the first core to have full 32-bit memory address space (previous cores were 26-bit). It ran at 5V and had 33,500 transistors. The ARM60 was capable of 10 MIPS running at 12 MHz, but the later ARM600 was capable of 28 MIPS running at 33 MHz. The ARM600 also included 4 KB of unified cache, something that was previously developed for the ARM3. A cheaper version was soon delivered: the ARM610. Like its predecessor, it had 4 KB of cache but had no coprocessor bus and was slightly less powerful (17 MIPS at 20 MHz).

Panasonic introduced the 3DO Interactive Multiplayer, a games console based on the ARM60 in 1993. The Apple Newton 100 series were powered with an ARM610 core, one of the first mobile devices using ARM cores.

ARM7

In 1993, ARM introduced the ARM700 processor, using the ARMv3 core. It doubled the ARM6's cache, to a full 8 KB of unified cache. It was also the first processor that could be powered by a 3.3V supply. Its performance improvement was between 50 and 100 percent, and the 3.3V version also used one-half the power of a 5V ARM6. ARM worked hard on the power consumption of the ARM7, using 0.8µm CMOS technology instead of 1µm CMOS technology. ARM7 was ARM's push into the mobile sector and was extremely well received.

ARM7TDMI

The ARM7TDMI was the first ARM core to use the new ARMv4T architecture and introduced the Thumb extension. It ran at a clock speed of 70 MHz but did not include any cache. ARM710T and ARM720T versions included cache and MMUs but ran at lower clock speeds. The ARM740T included a cache and an MPU.

ARM7TDMI is one of ARM's great success stories, being used in hundreds of devices where low power and good performance need to go hand in hand. It was used in the Apple iPod, the Lego Mindstorms NXT, the Game Boy Advance, and a huge range of mobile phones from Nokia. Samsung also used them directly inside its line of microSD cards.

ARM8

The ARM810 core used the previous ARMv4 architecture but included branch prediction and double-bandwidth memory, vastly improving performance. For most applications, ARM8 doubled performance compared to an ARM710 processor. It introduced a five-stage pipeline, whereas ARM7 had only three. At the cost of a little silicon, processor speeds could be roughly doubled by still using the same silicon fabrication process.

A few companies licensed the ARM8 core, but the arrival of StrongARM changed everything, being theoretically more than four times as powerful.

STRONGARM

The StrongARM project was a collaborative project between ARM and Digital Equipment Corporation to create a faster ARM core. The StrongARM was designed to address the needs of the high-end, low-power embedded market, where users needed more performance than ARM processors could deliver. Target devices were PDAs and set-top boxes.

To develop StrongARM, DEC became ARM's first architecture licensee. This entitled it to design an ARM-compatible processor without using one of ARM's own implementations as a starting point. DEC used its own in-house tools and processes to develop an efficient implementation.

In early 1996, the SA-110 was born. The first versions operated at 100, 160, and 200 MHz, with faster 166 and 233 MHz versions appearing at the end of 1996. The SA-110 was designed to be used with slow memory, and therefore it featured separate instruction cache and data cache, and each had a generous capacity of 16 Kb. It powered the Apple MessagePad 2000, contributing to its success.

In 1997, DEC announced the SA-1100. The SA-1100 was more specialized for mobile applications and added an integrated memory controller, a PCMCIA controller, and an LCD controller. These controllers came at a price; the data cache was reduced from 16 Kb to 8 Kb. The SA-1100 powered the Psion Series 7 subnotebook family.

In 1997, DEC agreed to sell its StrongARM group to Intel, as a lawsuit settlement. Intel took over the StrongARM project, using it to replace its line of RISC processors — the i860 and i960.

The SA-1110 was Intel's derivative of the SA-110 targeted at the mobile sector. It added support for 66 MHz and 103 MHz SDRAM modules. A companion chip was available, the SA-1111, providing additional support for peripherals. It was used in part of the Compaq iPaq series, a hugely successful PocketPC range.

The SA-1500 was a derivative of the SA-110 project, created by DEC, but was never put into production by Intel. Intel replaced the StrongARM series by another family, the XScale.

ARM9TDMI

Even before the StrongARM was released, ARM was already busy developing the ARM9T.

With the ARM9, ARM moved from the classic von Neumann architecture to a modified Harvard architecture, separating instruction and data cache. At the cost of added silicon, this modification alone greatly improved speed. By separating instructions from data, instruction fetches and data accesses could occur simultaneously. ARM9 also used the five5-stage pipeline introduced by the ARM8 core version.

ARM9TDMI was a replacement for the hugely popular ARM7TDMI. Applications designed for ARM7TDMI were roughly 30 percent faster on an ARM9TDMI.

ARM9E

ARM9E implemented the ARM9TDMI pipeline but added support for the ARMv5TE architecture, adding some DSP instructions. The multiplier unit width was also doubled, halving the time required for most multiplication operations.

ARM10

The ARM10 was a highly anticipated successor to the ARM9 family and was announced in October 1998. ARM10's aim was to double ARM9's performance by using optimization and advanced fabrication. To increase performance, ARM worked on two main aspects of the processor: pipeline optimization and instruction execution speed.

The pipeline in ARM9 processors was already advanced, but a pipeline is only as fast as its slowest element. Several optimizations were proposed, but most were rejected because they added too much complexity to the pipeline, which increased power consumption or overall price. A weak point was identified in the Decode stage. To increase pipeline speed, the original Decode section was split into two parts, Issue and Decode, where Issue partially decodes the instruction, and Decode reads registers with the rest of the decode sequence.

Further optimizations came from instruction optimization. The ARM10 came with a new multiplication core, a fast 16×32 hardware multiplier. This enabled the ARM10 processor to perform one 32-bit multiply and accumulate operation every clock cycle, a vast improvement from the previous 3–5 cycles on ARM9.

The ARM10 also supported Hit-Under-Miss in the data cache and included a static branch prediction scheme to offset the effect of a longer pipeline.

XSCALE

The XScale processor from Intel was the continuation of the StrongARM series. Following Intel's acquisition of the StrongARM, XScale replaced Intel's RISC systems and also powered an entire generation of hand-held devices.

In the mid-1990s, the PC sector was going mobile. Hewlett-Packard's HP200LX computer was a palm top, a complete system held in a hand, and although far less powerful than a portable computer, it could be put into a pocket. Users could finally keep their agenda, notes, and contacts in a small-factor computer, available at any time. The HP200LX was based on an Intel CISC-compatible 80186 and contained an entire version of Windows. Boot-up times were relatively fast, but although the general idea was there, the technology wasn't quite available. In 1996, Microsoft created Windows CE 1.0, which was the start of the Pocket PC era. It was a change of technology; it was no longer based on x86 processors that were fast but power hungry. The logical choice was to look at RISC processors, and the name Pocket PC was a marketing choice by Microsoft. Pocket PC referred to a specific set of hardware based on an ARMv4T-compatible CPU.

ARM11

ARM1136 introduced the ARMv6 architecture, adding SIMD instructions, multiprocessor support, TrustZone, and Thumb-2. It had a significantly improved pipeline, now comprised of 8 stages (though the ARM1156 pipeline architecture was slightly different, having limited dual-issue capability). It included dynamic branch prediction, reducing the risk of stalling the pipeline.

ARM11 also supported limited out-of-order completion, allowing the pipeline to continue execution if the result of a previous instruction is not needed by the following instructions. By giving the pipeline some time for memory reads and writes, it is possible to increase performance by avoiding pipeline stalls.

With the advanced pipeline, the ARM11 ran at speeds up to 1 GHz.

The ARM11 also had SIMD instructions, meaning single-instruction-multiple-data. Much like Intel's MMX instruction set, these instructions are designed to perform repetitive instructions on multiple data sets, heavily used in audio and video codecs.

CORTEX

ARM11 was a huge success, and ARM processors were becoming more and more powerful, but also larger, and more expensive. Companies who had specific projects were having a hard time choosing which processor to use; either a powerful, latest generation ARM, or for smaller devices, an older ARM, without the recent advantages. ARM processors were being used for more and more devices, and not all of them required a fast CPU; some systems required slower processors, or even very small factor systems. Some ARM systems are so small that they are located inside an SD card, or even directly inside a cable. ARM rearranged their line of processors to target specific fields, and in 2004, the Cortex family was announced, beginning with the Cortex-M3.

The Cortex family has 3 classes of processors; the Cortex-A, the Cortex-R and the Cortex-M. ARM's mastery of those three letters became almost obsessional. Cortex-A processors were designed for Application designs, where an entire multitasking operating system would be run. Cortex-R was designed for real-time applications, where very fast reaction times were required. Cortex-M was designed for ultra-low power microprocessor applications.

The very first Cortex processor was announced in 2004, with the Cortex-M3. The next year, the first Cortex-A design was announced, the Cortex-A8. The Cortex-R family was announced in 2011. Figure C-1 shows a timeline of the Cortex family, as well as some milestones from ARM.

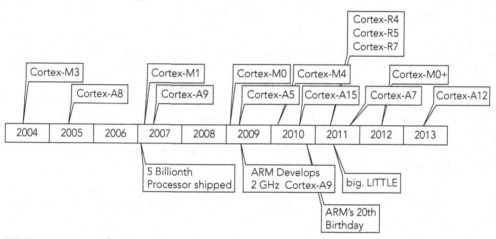

FIGURE C-1: Cortex family timeline

Cortex-A

The Cortex-A processor is designed for Application systems. Application processors are the powerhouse chips, running complete operating systems, high-performance multimedia codecs, and demanding applications.

The Cortex-A series includes everything needed for devices hosting a rich operating system. They are sufficiently powerful and come with an MMU. By adding a few external components, it is possible to create advanced platforms. They are targeted at mobile devices that require advanced calculations or graphics. Smartphones, tablets, digital TVs, and infotainment systems are powered by a Cortex-A, and even laptops have been developed running on multi-core Cortex-A cores.

The first Cortex-A core was announced in 2005, and development has continued since. Cortex-A processors can include an optional NEON engine and FPU logic.

Cortex-A5

The Cortex-A5 was announced in 2007. It is designed to be used on entry-level smartphones, some feature phones, and digital multimedia devices. The Cortex-A5 was proposed as a replacement for 2 hugely popular CPUs; the ARM-926EJ-S and the ARM1176JZ-S. The Cortex-A5 is more powerful than an ARM1176JZ-S, while using about as much power as the ARM926EJ-S.

The Cortex-A5 is an in-order processor, meaning it has a simplified instruction prefetcher and decoder, meaning more power efficient, but more prone to processor stalls, and therefore not as advanced or as fast as other designs. The Cortex-A5 remains a budget processor.

Cortex-A7

The Cortex-A7 was announced a year after the Cortex-A15. It is architecturally identical to the Cortex-A15, as it contains the same technologies. Binary applications that run on a Cortex-A15 will run on the Cortex-A7. Heralded at the time as ARM's most power-efficient application processor, it provided 50 percent greater performance than the Cortex-A8.

While the performance of the Cortex-A7 is overshadowed by the more powerful Cortex-A15, ARM also announced their big.LITTLE technology, linking both processors together. The Cortex-A15 is available as stand-alone, as is the Cortex-A7, but the Cortex-A7 can become a companion CPU to the Cortex-A15. Inside an operating system, the kernel can decide which processor to run an application on. Low-powered applications (like background applications, alarm clocks, and e-mail reading) can run on the energy efficient Cortex-A7, and demanding applications can run on the more powerful Cortex-15. By migrating applications from one processor to another, the kernel can also turn off one processor or the other when no processes are assigned to it, further reducing energy consumption.

The A7 itself is an in-order processor, with an 8-stage pipeline. To be binary compatible with the A15, it also supports LPAE, allowing it to address one terabyte of address space. It also includes Virtualization extensions.

Cortex-A8

The Cortex-A8 was the first Cortex-A processor. Using a superscalar design, it achieves roughly twice as many instructions executed per clock cycle as previous designs, and is binary compatible to the ARM926, ARM1136 and ARM1176 processors. It also integrates advanced branch prediction, with ARM claiming up to 95 percent accuracy. The Cortex A8 is designed to be run up to frequencies of 1 GHz.

Cortex-A9

The Cortex-A9 is a more advanced version of the Cortex-A8, capable of higher clock speeds (up to 2 GHz), and with a multi-core architecture, allowing up to four processors in a single coherent cluster.

The Cortex-A9 is a speculative issue superscalar processor. By using advanced techniques, the processor executes code that might not actually be needed. For example, in branch code, both results might be calculated. If it turns out that some work was not needed, the results are discarded. The philosophy is to do work before knowing if it is needed, then discarding where appropriate, rather than creating a stall when new work is requested. If the execution was not required, then the changes are reverted. If the execution is required, then the changes are "committed," effectively eliminating any processor stalls due to branch prediction, memory prefeteches or pipeline execution. This technology is especially useful in processors that handle databases, where lots of speculative execution is required.

Cortex-A12

The Cortex-A12 is a newcomer in the Cortex-A family. Released in 2013, it is designed as the successor to the Cortex-A9. It is an out-of-order speculative issue superscalar processor, providing more performance per watt than the Cortex-A9. Like the Cortex-A9, it can be configured with up to 4 cores. It has the NEON SIMD instruction set extension, includes TrustZone security extensions, and 40-bit Large Physical Address extensions, allowing the Cortex-A12 to address up to one terabyte of memory space.

This core targets mid-range devices, offering advanced functionality while retaining backwards compatibility with Cortex-A15, Cortex-A7, and Cortex-A9 processors, but offers 40 percent more performance than the Cortex-A9.

Cortex-A15

The Cortex-A15 processor is the most advanced processor of the 32-bit Cortex-A series. ARM has confirmed that the Cortex-A15 is 40 percent faster than the Cortex-A9, at an equivalent number of cores and clock speed. The Cortex-A15 is an out-of-order superscalar multi-core design, running at up to 2.5 GHz.

The Cortex-A15 can have four cores per coherent cluster, and can use the Cortex-A7 processor as a companion CPU, using ARM's big.LITTLE technology.

With ultra-high powered applications in mind, it became clear that the 4 gigabyte memory limit imposed by the 32-bit design, a limit that seemed unobtainable a few years ago, was about to be broken, and would be a limitation. To counter this, the Cortex-A15 has 40-bit Large Physical Address Extensions (LPAE), allowing for a total addressable space of one terabyte.

The Cortex-A15 itself is an out-of-order speculative issue superscalar processor, using some of ARM's most advanced technology to make this ARM's fastest 32-bit processor.

Cortex-A50 Series

The Cortex-A50 series is the latest range of processors based on the 64-bit ARMv8 architecture. It supports the new AArch64, an execution state that runs alongside an enhanced version of ARM's existing 32-bit instruction set. The Cortex-A53 and Cortex-A57 are only the beginning of the 64-bit revolution; more processors will follow soon.

Cortex-R

The Cortex-R profile is for real-time applications — for critical systems where reliability is crucial and speed is decisive. Real-time systems are designed to handle fast-changing data, and to be sufficiently responsive to handle the data throughput without slowing down. For this reason, Cortex-R processors are found in hard drives, network equipment, and embedded into critical systems, such as car brake assistance.

In the multi-core design, up to 4 cores can be used on the same chip, and a single-core version is also available.

In order to maximize reactivity, Cortex-R chips can contain tightly-coupled memory, but do not have a full MMU, instead they rely on memory protection units.

Cortex-R4

The first in the Cortex-R line, the Cortex-R4 is based on the ARMv7-R architecture, and was launched in May 2006. It is available in a synthesizable form. It slightly outperforms an ARM1156 at the same clock speed, and with a 40nm production, can obtain clock frequencies of almost 1 GHz. It includes branch prediction and instruction pre-fetch, allowing for fast reaction times.

For safety-critical applications, the Cortex-R4 has optional parity and ECC checks on all RAM interfaces, and the optional TCM can be completely configured as a separate instruction/data, or unified memory. It is equipped with a Memory Protection Unit, capable of handling 12 regions. Cortex-R4 supports dual-core lockstep configuration for safety-critical applications.

Cortex-R5

The Cortex-R5 was released in 2010, 4 years after the Cortex-R4, and complements the Cortex-R4 with an enriched feature set. It remains binary compatible with the Cortex-R4. Cortex-R5 provides improved support for multi-processing in a dual-core configuration.

Cortex-R7

The Cortex-R7 increased the pipeline length from 8 to 11, and allows for out-of-order execution. The Memory Protection Unit was also changed from previous models, now allowing for up to 16 regions. Cortex-R7 provides full support for SMP/AMP multi-processing in a fully-coherent dual-core configuration.

Cortex-M

The Cortex-M processor is designed for microcontroller applications. These applications typically require little processing power, but need lots of input and output lines, very small form factor, deterministic interrupt response and exceptionally low power consumption. Cortex-M chips are used heavily in Bluetooth devices, touchscreen controllers, remote control devices and even embedded directly into some cables. Some devices using Cortex-M boast a battery life of years, not just hours.

The Cortex-M package footprint is often extremely small, in some cases, just a few millimeters squared (NXP's LPC1102 chips are 2.17 × 2.32mm, containing 32 kbytes of flash and 8 kbytes or RAM).

Cortex-M chips are designed for rapid development, since the entire application, including the vector tables, can be written in C.

Cortex-M0

The Cortex-M0 design uses the ARMv6-M architecture. It uses only Thumb instructions with the Thumb-2 technology, allowing both 16-bit and 32-bit instructions. However, not all instructions are available. The entire 16-bit Thumb subset can be used, with the exception of CBZ, CBNZ, and IT. Of the 32-bit instructions, only BL, DMB, DSB, ISB, MRS and MSR can be used.

The Cortex-M0 has a 3-stage pipeline without branch prediction. It handles one non-maskable interrupt and up to 32 physical interrupts, with an interrupt latency of 16 cycles. It also implements some advanced sleep functions, including deep sleep.

Cortex-M0+

The Cortex-M0+ design is an augmented version of the Cortex-M0. It is more power efficient, and uses the same instruction set as the M0. It has some features from the Cortex-M3 and Cortex-M4, such as the Memory Protection Unit and the relocatable vector table, but also adds its own features, such as the Micro Trace Buffer and single-cycle I/O interface. The pipeline was decreased from 3 to 2, improving power usage.

Cortex-M1

The Cortex-M1 design is an optimized core that was created specifically to be loaded into FPGA chips. It supports all the instructions supported by the Cortex-M0, and the only difference is a very slightly degraded 32-bit hardware multiply unit. Where the Cortex-M0 could do multiplications in either 1 or 32 cycles, the Cortex-M1 executes the same instruction in either 3 or 33 cycles.

Cortex-M3

The Cortex-M3 is the first Cortex to use the new ARMv7-M architecture. It uses a 3-stage pipeline, and also includes branch speculation, attempting to increase speed by guessing the output of a branch, and pre-loading instructions into the pipeline.

The Cortex-M3 has 240 prioritizable interrupts, and non-maskable interrupt. Interrupt latency was reduced to 12 cycles.

Compared to the Cortex-M0, the Cortex-M3 uses slightly more power, but has a huge advantage; it uses the entire Thumb instruction set. While the Cortex-M0, Cortex-M0+, and Cortex-M1 could only use very few 32-bit instructions, a much larger set of 32-bit instructions can be used, including division instructions. Finally, an ARM processor was able to use hardware division.

The Cortex-M3 also has a memory protection unit, allowing read-write access or prevention for up to 8 memory regions.

Cortex-M4

The Cortex-M4 is almost identical to a Cortex-M3, but with the addition of DSP instructions for more mathematical intense applications in binary data. It is also slightly faster than the Cortex-M3, since its pipeline includes advanced branch speculation. The Cortex-M4 supports an optional Floating Point Unit.

NEON Intrinsics and Instructions

This appendix contains information on, and a list of instructions used with, the NEON engine. Data types, lane types, and intrinsics are listed.

DATA TYPES

Table D-1 lists the different data types supported on the NEON engine, and the corresponding C data types.

TABLE D-1: NEON Data Types

DATA TYPE	D-REGISTER (64 BITS)	Q-REGISTER (128 BITS)
Signed integers	int8x8_t	int8x16_t
	int16x4_t	int16x8_t
	int32x2_t	int32x4_t
	int64x1_t	int64x2_t
Unsigned integers	uint8x8_t	uint8x16_t
	uint16x4_t	uint16x8_t
	uint32x2_t	uint32x4_t
	uint64x1_t	uint64x2_t
Floating-point	float16x4_t	float16x8_t
	float32x2_t	float32x4_t
Polynomial	poly8x8_t	poly8x16_t
	poly16x4_t	poly16x8_t

LANE TYPES

Table D-2 lists the different lane types per class, and the amount of possible types for each class.

TABLE D-2: Data Lane Types

CLASS	COUNT	TYPES
int	6	int8, int16, int32, uint8, uint16, uint32
int/64	8	int8, int16, int32, int64, uint8, uint16, uint32, uint64
sint	3	int8, int16, int32
sint16/32	2	int16, int32
int32	2	int32, uint32
8-bit	3	int8, uint8, poly8
int/poly8	7	int8, int16, int32, uint8, uint16, uint32, poly8
int/64/poly	10	int8, int16, int32, int64, uint8, uint16, uint32, uint64, poly8, poly16
arith	7	int8, int16, int32, uint8, uint16, uint32, float32
arith/64	9	int8, int16, int32, int64, uint8, uint16, uint32, uint64, float32
arith/poly8	8	int8, int16, int32, uint8, uint16, uint32, poly8, float32
floating	1	float32
any	11	int8, int16, int32, int64, uint8, uint16, uint32, uint64, poly8, poly16, float32

ASSEMBLY INSTRUCTIONS

Table D-3 contains a list of NEON instructions, as well as a brief description of each instruction.

TABLE D-3: NEON Instructions

INSTRUCTION	DESCRIPTION
VABA	Absolute difference and Accumulate
VABD	Absolute difference
VABS	Absolute Value
VACGE	Absolute Compare Greater Than or Equal
VACGT	Absolute Compare Greater Than
VACLE	Absolute Compare Less Than or Equal

INSTRUCTION	DESCRIPTION
VACLT	Absolute Compare Less Than
VADD	Add
VADDHN	Add, Select High Half
VAND	Logical AND
VBIC	Bitwise Bit Clear
VBIF	Bitwise Insert if False
VBIT	Bitwise Insert if True
VBSL	Bitwise Select
VCEQ	Compare Equal
VCGE	Compare Greater Than or Equal
VCGT	Compare Greater Than
VCLE	Compare Less Than or Equal
VCLS	Count Leading Sign bits
VCLT	Compare Less Than
VCLZ	Count Leading Zeroes
VCNT	Count set bits
VCVT	Convert between different number formats
VDUP	Duplicate scalar to all lanes of vector
VEOR	Bitwise Exclusive OR
VEXT	Extract
VFMA	Fused Multiply and Accumulate
VFMS	Fused Multiply and Subtract
VHADD	Halving Add
VHSUB	Halving Subtract
VLD	Vector Load
VMAX	Maximum
VMIN	Minimum
VMLA	Multiply and Accumulate
VMLS	Multiply and Subtract

continues

TABLE D-3 *(continued)*

INSTRUCTION	DESCRIPTION
VMOV	Move
VMOVL	Move Long
VMOVN	Move Narrow
VMUL	Multiply
VMVN	Move Negative
VNEG	Negate
VORN	Bitwise OR NOT
VORR	Bitwise OR
VPADAL	Pairwise Add and Accumulate
VPADD	Pairwise Add
VPMAX	Pairwise Maximum
VPMIN	Pairwise Minimum
VQABS	Absolute Value, Saturate
VQADD	Add, Saturate
VQDMLAL	Saturating Double Multiply Accumulate
VQDMLSL	Saturating Double Multiply and Subtract
VQDMUL	Saturating Double Multiply
VQDMULH	Saturating Double Multiply returning High half
VQMOVN	Saturating Move
VQNEG	Negate, Saturate
VQRDMULH	Saturating Double Multiply returning High half
VQRSHL	Shift left, Round, Saturate
VQRSHR	Shift Right, Round, Saturate
VQSHL	Shift Left, Saturate
VQSHR	Shift Right, Saturate
VQSUB	Subtract, Saturate

INSTRUCTION	DESCRIPTION
VRADDH	Add, Select High Half, Round
VRECPE	Reciprocal Estimate
VRECPS	Reciprocal Step
VREV	Reverse Elements
VRHADD	Halving Add, Round
VRSHR	Shift Right and Round
VRSQRTE	Reciprocal Square Root Estimate
VRSQRTS	Reciprocal Square Root Step
VRSRA	Shift Right, Round and Accumulate
VRSUBH	Subtract, select High half, Round
VSHL	Shift Left
VSHR	Shift Right
VSLI	Shift Left and Insert
VSRA	Shift Right, Accumulate
VSRI	Shift Right and Insert
VST	Vector Store
VSUB	Subtract
VSUBH	Subtract, Select High half
VSWP	Swap Vectors
VTBL	Vector Table Lookup
VTBX	Vector Table Extension
VTRN	Vector Transpose
VTST	Test Bits
VUZP	Vector Unzip
VZIP	Vector Zip

INTRINSIC NAMING CONVENTIONS

Intrinsics provide an elegant way to write NEON instructions using C. NEON intrinsics are created using the following structure:

v[q][r]name[u][n][q][_lane][_n][_result]_type

where:

➤ q indicates a saturating operation.

➤ r indicates a rounding operation.

➤ name is the descriptive name of the operation.

➤ u indicates signed-to-unsigned saturation.

➤ n indicates a narrowing operation.

➤ q indicates an operation on 128-bit vectors.

➤ _n indicates a scalar operand supplied as an argument.

➤ _lane indicates a scalar operand taken from the lane of a vector.

➤ result is the result type in short form.

For example, vmul_s16 multiplies two vectors of signed 16-bit values and is equivalent to VMUL. I16. Some examples in C include:

```
uint32x4_t vec128 = vld1q_u32(i); // Load 4 32-bit values
uint8x8_t vadd_u8 (uint8x8_t,
    uint8x8_t); //Add two lanes
int8x16_t vaddq_s8 (int8x16_t, int8x16_t); //Saturating add two lanes
```

Assembly Instructions

This appendix lists the different assembly instructions used on ARM cores, and what architecture each instruction introduced.

ARM INSTRUCTIONS

The following is a list of ARM-state instructions, separated into various categories.

Arithmetic Instructions

Arithmetic instructions do basic mathematical calculations: addition, subtraction, multiplication, and division. These instructions are listed in Table E-1, as well as the architecture in which they were introduced.

TABLE E-1: List of Arithmetic Instructions

MNEMONIC	FUNCTION	ARCHITECTURE	ASSEMBLER	ACTION
ADD	Add	4	ADD{S}{cond} {S}{cond} Rd, Rn, <Operand2>	Rd := Rn + Operand2
ADC	Add with Carry	4	ADC{S}{cond} Rd, Rn, <Operand2>	Rd := Rn + Operand2 + Carry
QADD	Add Saturating	5TE	QADD{cond} Rd, Rm, Rn	Rd := SAT(Rm + Rn)
QDADD	Add Double Saturating	5TE	QDADD{cond} Rd, Rm, Rn	Rd := SAT(Rm + SAT(Rn * 2))
SUB	Subtract	4	SUB{S}{cond} Rd, Rn, <Operand2>	Rd := Rn - Operand2
SBC	Subtract with Carry	4	SBC{S}{cond} Rd, Rn, <Operand2>	Rd := Rn – Operand2 - NOT(Carry)
RSB	Reverse Subtract	4	RSB{S}{cond} Rd, Rn, <Operand2>	Rd := Operand2 - Rn
RSC	Reverse Subtract with Carry	4	RSC{S}{cond} Rd, Rn, <Operand2>	Rd := Operand2 – Rn - NOT(Carry)
QSUB	Saturating Subtract	5TE	QSUB{cond} Rd, Rm, Rn	Rd := SAT(Rm - Rn)
QDSUB	Saturating Double Subtract	5TE	QDSUB{cond} Rd, Rm, Rn	Rd := SAT(Rm – SAT(Rn * 2))
MUL	Multiply	4	MUL{S}{cond} Rd, Rm, Rs	Rd := (Rm * Rs)[31:0]
MLA	Multiply and Accumulate	4	MLA{S}{cond} Rd, Rm, Rs, Rn	Rd := ((Rm * Rs) + Rn) [31:0]
UMULL	Unsigned Multiply Long	4	UMULL{S}{cond} RdLo, RdHi, Rm, Rs	RdHi,RdLo := unsigned(Rm * Rs)
UMLAL	Unsigned Multiply and Accumulate Long	4	UMLAL{S}{cond} RdLo, RdHi, Rm, Rs	RdHi,RdLo := unsigned(RdHi,RdLo + Rm * Rs)
UMAAL	Unsigned Multiply Double Accumulate Long	6	UMAAL{cond} RdLo, RdHi, Rm, Rs	RdHi,RdLo := unsigned(RdHi + RdLo + Rm * Rs)

SMULL	Signed Multiply Long	4	SMULL{S}{cond} RdLo, RdHi, Rm, Rs	RdHi,RdLo := signed(Rm * Rs)
SMLAL	Signed Multiply Long and Accumulate	4	SMLAL{S}{cond} RdLo, RdHi, Rm, Rs	RdHi,RdLo := signed(RdHi,RdLo + Rm * Rs)
SMUL	Signed Multiply 16 x 16 Bits	5TE	SMULxy{cond} Rd, Rm, Rs	Rd := Rm[x] * Rs[y]
SMULW	Signed Multiply 32 x 16 Bits	5TE	SMULWy{cond} Rd, Rm, Rs	Rd := (Rm * Rs[y])[47:16]
SMLA	Signed Multiply 16 x 16 Bits and Accumulate	5TE	SMLAxy{cond} Rd, Rm, Rs, Rn	Rd := Rn + Rm[x] * Rs[y]
SMLAW	Signed Multiply 32 x 16 Bits and Accumulate	5TE	SMLAWy{cond} Rd, Rm, Rs, Rn	Rd := Rn + (Rm * Rs[y]) [47:16]
SMLAL	Signed Multiply 16 x 16 Bits and Accumulate Long	5TE	SMLALxy{cond} RdLo, RdHi, Rm, Rs	RdHi,RdLo := RdHi,RdLo + Rm[x] * Rs[y]
SMUAD	Dual Signed Multiply, Add	6	SMUAD{X}{cond} Rd, Rm, Rs	Rd := Rm[15:0] * RsX[15:0] + Rm[31:16] * RsX[31:16]
SMLAD	Dual Signed Multiply, Add and Accumulate	6	SMLAD{X}{cond} Rd, Rm, Rs, Rn	Rd := Rn + Rm[15:0] * RsX[15:0] + Rm[31:16] * RsX[31:16]
SMLALD	Dual Signed Multiply, Add and Accumulate Long	6	SMLALD{X}{cond} RdHi, RdLo, Rm, Rs	RdHi,RdLo := RdHi,RdLo + Rm[15:0] * RsX[15:0] + Rm[31:16] * RsX[31:16]
SMUSD	Dual Signed Multiply, Subtract	6	SMUSD{X}{cond} Rd, Rm, Rs	Rd := Rm[15:0] * RsX[15:0] – Rm[31:16] * RsX[31:16]
SMLSD	Dual Signed Multiply, Subtract and Accumulate	6	SMLSD{X}{cond} Rd, Rm, Rs, Rn	Rd := Rn + Rm[15:0] * RsX[15:0] – Rm[31:16] * RsX[31:16]
SMLSLD	Dual Signed Multiply, Subtract and Accumulate Long	6	SMLSLD{X}{cond} RdHi, RdLo, Rm, Rs	RdHi,RdLo := RdHi,RdLo + Rm[15:0] * RsX[15:0] – Rm[31:16] * RsX[31:16]

continues

TABLE E-1 *(continued)*

MNEMONIC	FUNCTION	ARCHITECTURE	ASSEMBLER	ACTION
SMMUL	Signed Most Significant Word Multiply	6	SMMUL{R}{cond} Rd, Rm, Rs	Rd := (Rm * Rs)[63:32]
SMMLA	Signed Most Significant Word Multiply and Accumulate	6	SMMLA{R}{cond} Rd, Rm, Rs, Rn	Rd := Rn + (Rm * Rs) [63:32]
SMMLS	Signed Most Significant Word Multiply and Subtract	6	SMMLS{R}{cond} Rd, Rm, Rs, Rn	Rd := Rn − (Rm * Rs) [63:32]
CLZ	Count Leading Zeroes	5	CLZ{cond} Rd, Rm	Rd := number of leading zeroes in Rm

Parallel Arithmetic

Parallel arithmetic instructions are instructions that work on two or more values packed into 32-bit data. Parallel arithmetic instructions use prefixes, listed in Table E-2.

TABLE E-2: Parallel Arithmetic Prefixes

PREFIX	FUNCTION
S	Signed arithmetic modulo 2^8 or 2^{16}. Sets APSR GE flags
Q	Signed saturating arithmetic
SH	Signed arithmetic, halving the results
U	Unsigned arithmetic modulo 2^8 or 2^{16}. Sets APSR GE flags
UQ	Unsigned saturating arithmetic
UH	Unsigned arithmetic, halving the results

Table E-3 lists parallel arithmetic instructions, their usage, and their effect.

TABLE E-3: Parallel Arithmetic Instructions

MNEMONIC	FUNCTION	ARCHITECTURE	ASSEMBLER	ACTION
ADD16	Halfword-Wise Addition	6	<prefix>ADD16{cond} Rd, Rn, Rm	Rd[31:16] := Rn[31:16] + Rm[31:16], Rd[15:0] := Rn[15:0] + Rm[15:0]
SUB16	Halfword-Wise Subtraction	6	<prefix>SUB16{cond} Rd, Rn, Rm	Rd[31:16] := Rn[31:16] − Rm[31:16], Rd[15:0] := Rn[15:0] − Rm[15:0]
ADD8	Byte-Wise Addition	6	<prefix>ADD8{cond} Rd, Rn, Rm	Rd[31:24] := Rn[31:24] + Rm[31:24], Rd[23:16] := Rn[23:16] + Rm[23:16], Rd[15:8] := Rn[15:8] + Rm[15:8], Rd[7:0] := Rn[7:0] + Rm[7:0]
SUB8	Byte-Wise Subtraction	6	<prefix>SUB8{cond} Rd, Rn, Rm	Rd[31:24] := Rn[31:24] − Rm[31:24], Rd[23:16] := Rn[23:16] − Rm[23:16], Rd[15:8] := Rn[15:8] − Rm[15:8], Rd[7:0] := Rn[7:0] − Rm[7:0]
ASX	Halfword-Wise Exchange, Add, Subtract	6	<prefix>ADDSUBX {cond} Rd, Rn, Rm	Rd[31:16] := Rn[31:16] + Rm[15:0], Rd[15:0] := Rn[15:0] − Rm[31:16]
SAX	Halfword-Wise Exchange, Subtract, Add	6	<prefix>SUBADDX {cond} Rd, Rn, Rm	Rd[31:16] := Rn[31:16] − Rm[15:0], Rd[15:0] := Rn[15:0] + Rm[31:16]
USAD8	Unsigned Sum of Absolute Differences	6	USAD8{cond} Rd, Rm, Rs	Rd := Abs(Rm[31:24] − Rs[31:24]) + Abs(Rm[23:16] − Rs[23:16]) + Abs(Rm[15:8] − Rs[15:8]) + Abs(Rm[7:0] − Rs[7:0])
USADA8	Unsigned Sum of Absolute Differences and Accumulate	6	USADA8{cond} Rd, Rm, Rs, Rn	Rd := Rn + Abs(Rm[31:24] − Rs[31:24]) + Abs(Rm[23:16] − Rs[23:16]) + Abs(Rm[15:8] − Rs[15:8]) + Abs(Rm[7:0] − Rs[7:0])

Movement

Movement instructions take data from one register before moving it to a second register, optionally negating the data first. Movement instructions can also place data into registers from operands. These instructions are listed in Table E-4.

TABLE E-4: Movement Instructions

MNEMONIC	FUNCTION	ARCHITECTURE	ASSEMBLER	ACTION
MOV	Move	4	MOV{S}{cond} Rd, <Operand2>	Rd := Operand2
MVN	Move Negated	4	MVN{S}{cond} Rd, <Operand2>	Rd := 0xFFFFFFFF EOR Operand2
MRS	Move PSR to Register	4	MRS{cond} Rd, <PSR>	Rd := PSR
MSR	Move Register to PSR	4	MSR{cond} <PSR>_<fields>, Rm	PSR := Rm (selected bytes only)
MSR	Move Immediate to PSR	4	MSR{cond} <PSR>_<fields>, #<immed_8r>	PSR := immed_8r (selected bytes only)
CPY	Copy	6	CPY{cond} Rd, <Operand2>	Rd := Operand2, does not update flags

The MSR instruction uses a field parameter that specifies the SPSR or CPSR fields to be moved. They are listed in Table E-5.

TABLE E-5: MSR Fields Parameters

FIELD	DESCRIPTION
C	Control field mask byte, PSR[7:0]
X	Extension field mask byte, PSR[15:8]
S	Status field mask byte, PSR[23:16]
F	Flags field mask byte, PSR[31:24]

Load

Load instructions take memory addresses and put the contents of those locations into registers. They are listed in Table E-6.

TABLE E-6: Load Instructions.

MNEMONIC	FUNCTION	ARCHITECTURE	ASSEMBLER	ACTION
LDR	Load Word	All	LDR{cond} Rd, <a_mode2>	Rd := [address]
LDRT	Load Word, User Mode Privilege	All	LDR T {cond} Rd, <a_mode2P>	Rd := [address]
LDRB	Load Byte	All	LDR B {cond} Rd, <a_mode2>	Rd := ZeroExtend[byte from address]
LDRBT	Load Byte, User Mode Privilege	All	LDR BT {cond} Rd, <a_mode2P>	Rd := ZeroExtend[byte from address]
LDRSB	Load Signed Byte	4	LDR SB {cond} Rd, <a_mode3>	Rd := SignExtend[byte from address]
LDRH	Load Halfword	4	LDR H {cond} Rd, <a_mode3>	Rd := ZeroExtend[halfword from address]
LDRSH	Load Signed Halfword	4	LDR SH {cond} Rd, <a_mode3>	d := SignExtend[halfword from address]
LDRD	Load Doubleword	5TE	LDR D {cond} Rd, <a_mode3>	Rd := [address], R(d+1) := [address + 4]
LDM	Load Multiple	All	LDM{cond}<a_mode4L> Rn{!}, <reglist-PC>	Load list of registers from [Rn]
LDM	Load Multiple, Return and Exchange	All	LDM{cond}<a_mode4L> Rn{!}, <reglist+PC>	Load registers, R15 := [address][31:1] (5T: Change to Thumb if [address][0] is 1)
LDM	Load Multiple, Return and Exchange, Restore CPSR	All	LDM{cond}<a_mode4L> Rn{!}, <reglist+PC>^	Load registers, branch (5T: and exchange), CPSR := SPSR

continues

TABLE E-6 *(continued)*

MNEMONIC	FUNCTION	ARCHITECTURE	ASSEMBLER	ACTION
PLD	Preload Data (Memory System Hint)	5TE	PLD <a_mode2>	Memory may prepare to load from address
PLDW	Preload Data with Intention to Write (Memory System Hint)	7	PLDW<a_mode2>	Memory may prepare to load from address
LDREX	Load Exclusive	6	LDREX{cond} Rd, [Rn]	Rd := [Rn], tag address as exclusive access Outstanding tag set if not shared address

Store

Store instructions place memory from registers into system memory. The data size can vary, and multiple registers can be stored to memory in a single instruction. Store instructions are listed in Table E-7.

TABLE E-7: Store Instructions

MNEMONIC	FUNCTION	ARCHITECTURE	ASSEMBLER	ACTION
STR	Store Word	All	STR{cond} Rd, <a_mode2>	[address] := Rd
STRT	Store Word, User Mode Privilege	All	STR T {cond} Rd, <a_mode2P>	[address] := Rd
STRB	Store Byte	All	STR B {cond} Rd, <a_mode2>	[address][7:0] := Rd[7:0]
STRBT	Store Byte, User Mode Privilege	All	STR BT {cond} Rd, <a_mode2P>	[address][7:0] := Rd[7:0]
STRH	Store Halfword	4	STR H {cond} Rd, <a_mode3>	[address][15:0] := Rd[15:0]
STRD	Store Doubleword	5TE	STR D {cond} Rd, <a_mode3>	[address] := Rd, [address + 4] := R(d+1)
STM	Store Multiple	All	STM{cond}<a_mode4S> Rn{!}, <reglist>	Store list of registers to [Rn]

| STM | Store Multiple, User Mode Registers | All | STM{cond}<a_mode4S> Rn{!}, <reglist>^ | Store list of User mode registers to [Rn] |
| STREX | Store Exclusive | 6 | STREX{cond} Rd, Rm, [Rn] | [Rn] := Rm if allowed, Rd := 0 if successful, else 1 |

Logical

Logical instructions perform logical bit-wise operations on registers. They are listed in Table E-8.

TABLE E-8: Logical Instructions

MNEMONIC	FUNCTION	ARCHITECTURE	ASSEMBLER	ACTION
AND	AND	All	AND{S}{cond} Rd, Rn, <Operand2>	Rd := Rn AND Operand2
EOR	EOR	All	EOR{S}{cond} Rd, Rn, <Operand2>	Rd := Rn EOR Operand2
ORR	ORR	All	ORR{S}{cond} Rd, Rn, <Operand2>	Rd := Rn OR Operand2
BIC	Bit Clear	All	BIC{S}{cond} Rd, Rn, <Operand2>	Rd := Rn AND NOT Operand2

Comparison

Comparison instructions compare a register to another register, or to static data, and test bitwise data. The instructions are listed in Table E-9.

TABLE E-9: Comparison Instructions

MNEMONIC	FUNCTION	ARCHITECTURE	ASSEMBLER	ACTION
TST	Test	All	TST{cond} Rn, <Operand2>	Update CPSR flags on Rn AND Operand2
TEQ	Test Equivalence	All	TEQ{cond} Rn, <Operand2>	Update CPSR flags on Rn EOR Operand2
CMP	Compare	All	CMP{cond} Rn, <Operand2>	Update CPSR flags on Rn – Operand2
CMN	Compare Negative	All	CMN{cond} Rn, <Operand2>	Update CPSR flags on Rn + Operand2

Saturate

Saturating instructions are arithmetic instructions that saturate; they will not overflow their containers, and will return the maximum or minimum value possible when an overflow would occur. They are listed in Table E-10.

TABLE E-10: Saturating Arithmetic Instructions

MNEMONIC	FUNCTION	ARCHITECTURE	ASSEMBLER	ACTION
SSAT	Signed Saturate Word	6	SSAT{cond} Rd, #<sat>, Rm{, ASR <sh>}	Rd := SignedSat((Rm ASR sh), sat). <sat> range 0-31, <sh> range 1-32.
			SSAT{cond} Rd, #<sat>, Rm{, LSL <sh>}	Rd := SignedSat((Rm LSL sh), sat). <sat> range 0-31, <sh> range 0-31.
SSAT16	Signed Saturate Two Halfwords	6	SSAT16{cond} Rd, #<sat>, Rm	Rd[31:16] := SignedSat(Rm[31:16], sat), Rd[15:0] := SignedSat(Rm[15:0], sat). <sat> range 0-15.
USAT	Unsigned Saturate Word	6	USAT{cond} Rd, #<sat>, Rm{, ASR <sh>}	Rd := UnsignedSat((Rm ASR sh), sat). <sat> range 0-31, <sh> range 1-32.
			USAT{cond} Rd, #<sat>, Rm{, LSL <sh>}	Rd := UnsignedSat((Rm LSL sh), sat). <sat> range 0-31, <sh> range 0-31.
USAT16	Unsigned Saturate Two Halfwords	6	USAT16{cond} Rd, #<sat>, Rm	Rd[31:16] := UnsignedSat(Rm[31:16], sat), Rd[15:0] := UnsignedSat(Rm[15:0], sat). <sat> range 0-15.

Branch

Branch instructions order the processor or microcontroller to execute code elsewhere, conditionally or unconditionally. Branching instructions can link, and can change processor modes if required. They are listed in Table E-11.

TABLE E-11: Branch Instructions

MNEMONIC	FUNCTION	ARCHITECTURE	ASSEMBLER	ACTION
B	Branch	All	B{cond} label	R15 := label (+/-32M)
BL	Branch with Link	All	BL{cond} label	R14 := address of next instruction, R15 := label (+/-32M)
BX	Branch and Exchange	4T, 5T	BX{cond} Rm	R15 := Rm, Change to Thumb if Rm[0] is 1
BLX	Branch with Link and Exchange	5T	BLX label	R14 := address of next instruction, R15 := label, Change to Thumb
		5T	BLX{cond} Rm	R14 := address of next instruction, R15 := Rm[31:1] Change to Thumb if Rm[0] is 1
BXJ	Branch and Change to Java State	5TEJ, 6	BXJ{cond} Rm	Change to Java state
TBB	Table Branch Byte	6	TBB Rn, Rm	PC-relative forward branch of base Rn, index Rm
TBH	Table Branch Halfword	6	TBH Rn, Rm, LSL #1	PC-relative forward branch of base Rn, index Rm
CBZ	Compare and Branch on Zero	6	CBZ Rn, Label	Branch to Label if Rn = 0, no status flag update
CBNZ	Compare and Branch on Non-Zero	6	CBNZ Rn, Label	Branch to Label if Rn != 0, no status flag update

Extend

Extend instructions change a value's size, for example, extending a 16-bit signed or unsigned value to 32-bits. They are listed in Table E-12.

TABLE E-12: Extend Instructions

MNEMONIC	FUNCTION	ARCHITECTURE	ASSEMBLER	ACTION
SXTH	Signed Extend Halfword to Word	6	SXTH{cond} Rd, Rm{, ROR #<sh>}	Rd[31:0] := SignExtend((Rm ROR (8 * sh))[15:0]). sh 0-3.
SXTB16	Signed Extend 2 Bytes to Halfword	6	SXTB16{cond} Rd, Rm{, ROR #<sh>}	Rd[31:16] := SignExtend((Rm ROR (8 * sh))[23:16]), Rd[15:0] := SignExtend((Rm ROR (8 * sh))[7:0]). sh 0-3.
SXTB	Signed Extend Byte to Word	6	SXTB{cond} Rd, Rm{, ROR #<sh>}	Rd[31:0] := SignExtend((Rm ROR (8 * sh))[7:0]). sh 0-3.
UXTH	Unsigned Extend Halfword to Word	6	UXTH{cond} Rd, Rm{, ROR #<sh>}	Rd[31:0] := ZeroExtend((Rm ROR (8 * sh))[15:0]). sh 0-3.
UXTB16	Unsigned Extend 2 Bytes to Halfwords	6	UXTB16{cond} Rd, Rm{, ROR #<sh>}	Rd[31:16] := ZeroExtend((Rm ROR (8 * sh))[23:16]), Rd[15:0] := ZeroExtend((Rm ROR (8 * sh))[7:0]). sh 0-3
UXTB	Unsigned Extend Byte to Word	6	UXTB{cond} Rd, Rm{, ROR #<sh>}	Rd[31:0] := ZeroExtend((Rm ROR (8 * sh))[7:0]). sh 0-3
SXTAH	Signed Extend Halfword to Word, Add	6	SXTAH{cond} Rd, Rn, Rm{, ROR #<sh>}	Rd[31:0] := Rn[31:0] + SignExtend((Rm ROR (8 * sh))[15:0]). sh 0-3
SXTAB16	Signed Extend 2 Bytes to Halfword, Add	6	SXTAB16{cond} Rd, Rn, Rm{, ROR #<sh>}	Rd[31:16] := Rn[31:16] + SignExtend((Rm ROR (8 * sh))[23:16]), Rd[15:0] := Rn[15:0] + SignExtend((Rm ROR (8 * sh))[7:0]). sh 0-3
SXTAB	Signed Extend Byte to Word, Add	6	SXTAB{cond} Rd, Rn, Rm{, ROR #<sh>}	Rd[31:0] := Rn[31:0] + SignExtend((Rm ROR (8 * sh))[7:0]). sh 0-3.

UXTAH	Unsigned Extend Halfword to Word, Add	6	UXTAH{cond} Rd, Rn, Rm{, ROR #<sh>}	Rd[31:0] := Rn[31:0] + ZeroExtend((Rm ROR (8 * sh))[15:0]). sh 0-3.
UXTAB16	Unsigned Extend 2 Bytes to Halfword, Add	6	UXTAB16{cond} Rd, Rn, Rm{, ROR #<sh>}	Rd[31:16] := Rn[31:16] + ZeroExtend((Rm ROR (8 * sh))[23:16]), Rd[15:0] := Rn[15:0] + ZeroExtend((Rm ROR (8 * sh))[7:0]). sh 0-3
UXTAB	Unsigned Extend Byte to Word, Add	6	UXTAB{cond} Rd, Rn, Rm{, ROR #<sh>}	Rd[31:0] := Rn[31:0] + ZeroExtend((Rm ROR (8 * sh))[7:0]). sh 0-3

Miscellaneous

These are instructions that do not belong to any previous category. They are listed in Table E-13.

TABLE E-13: Miscellaneous Instructions

MNEMONIC	FUNCTION	ARCHITECTURE	ASSEMBLER	ACTION
PKHBT	Pack Halfword Bottom + Top	6	PKHBT{cond} Rd, Rn, Rm{, LSL #<sh>}	R15 := label (+/-32M) Rd[15:0] := Rn[15:0], Rd[31:16] := (Rm LSL sh)[31:16]. sh 0-31
PKHTB	Pack Halfword Top + Bottom	6	PKHTB{cond} Rd, Rn, Rm{, ASR #<sh>}	Rd[31:16] := Rn[31:16], Rd[15:0] := (Rm ASR sh)[15:0]. sh 1-32.
REV	Reverse Bytes in Word	6	REV{cond} Rd, Rm	Rd[31:24] := Rm[7:0], Rd[23:16] := Rm[15:8], Rd[15:8] := Rm[23:16], Rd[7:0] := Rm[31:24]
REV16	Reverse Bytes in Both Halfwords	6	REV16{cond} Rd, Rm	Rd[15:8] := Rm[7:0], Rd[7:0] := Rm[15:8], Rd[31:24] := Rm[23:16], Rd[23:16] := Rm[31:24]
REVSH	Reverse Bytes in Low Halfword, Sign Extend	6	REVSH{cond} Rd, Rm	Rd[15:8] := Rm[7:0], Rd[7:0] := Rm[15:8], Rd[31:16] := Rm[7] * &FFFF

continues

TABLE E-13 *(continued)*

MNEMONIC	FUNCTION	ARCHITECTURE	ASSEMBLER	ACTION
SEL	Select Bytes	6	SEL{cond} Rd, Rn, Rm	Rd[7:0] := Rn[7:0] if GE[0] = 1, else Rd[7:0] := Rm[7:0] Bits[15:8], [23:16], [31:24] selected similarly by GE[1], GE[2], GE[3]
CPSID	Change Processor State, Disable Interrupts	6	CPSID \<iflags\> {, #\<p_mode\>}	Disable specified interrups, optional change mode
CPSIE	Change Processor State, Enable Interrupts	6	CPSIE \<iflags\> {, #\<p_mode\>}	Enable specified interrups, optional change mode
CPS	Change Processor Mode	6	CPS #\<p_mode\>	Set processor mode to p_mode
SETEND	Set Endianness	6	SETEND \<endianness\>	Sets endianness for loads and saves. \<endianness\> can be BE (Big Endian) or LE (Little Endian).
SRS	Store Return State	6	SRS\<a_mode4S\> #\<p_mode\>{!}	[R13m] := R14, [R13m + 4] := CPSR
RFE	Return from Exception	6	RFE\<a_mode4L\> Rn{!}	PC := [Rn], CPSR := [Rn + 4]
BKPT	Breakpoint	5T	BKPT \<immed_16\>	Prefetch abort or enter debug state
SVC	Supervisor Call (Previously SWI)	All	SVC{cond} \<immed_24\>	Supervisor Call (SVC) exception
NOP	No Operation	6	NOP	Does nothing. Timing not guaranteed.

THUMB INSTRUCTIONS ON CORTEX-M CORES

Cortex-M cores support only a subset of Thumb instructions, or the entire Thumb instruction set, depending on the core. Table E-14 lists the different Cortex-M cores, and the supported instructions.

TABLE E-14: Thumb Instructions on Cortex-M Cores

MNEMONIC	FUNCTION	SIZE	M0/M0+/M1	M3	M4	M4F
ADC	Add with Carry	16	Yes	Yes	Yes	Yes
ADC	Add with Carry	32	No	Yes	Yes	Yes
ADD	Add	16	Yes	Yes	Yes	Yes
ADD	Add	32	No	Yes	Yes	Yes
ADR	Load Address to Register	16	Yes	Yes	Yes	Yes
ADR	Load Address to Register	32	No	Yes	Yes	Yes
AND	Logical AND	16	Yes	Yes	Yes	Yes
AND	Logical AND	32	No	Yes	Yes	Yes
ASR	Arithmetic Shift Right	16	Yes	Yes	Yes	Yes
ASR	Arithmetic Shift Right	32	No	Yes	Yes	Yes
B	Branch	16	Yes	Yes	Yes	Yes
B	Branch	32	No	Yes	Yes	Yes
BFC	Bit Field Clear	32	No	Yes	Yes	Yes
BFI	Bit Field Insert	32	No	Yes	Yes	Yes
BIC	Logical AND NOT	16	Yes	Yes	Yes	Yes
BIC	Logical AND NOT	32	No	Yes	Yes	Yes
BKPT	Breakpoint	16	Yes	Yes	Yes	Yes
BL	Branch and Link	32	Yes	Yes	Yes	Yes
BLX	Branch with Link and Exchange	16	Yes	Yes	Yes	Yes
BX	Branch and Exchange	16	Yes	Yes	Yes	Yes
CBNZ	Compare and Branch on Not Zero	16	No	Yes	Yes	Yes
CBZ	Compare and Branch on Zero	16	No	Yes	Yes	Yes
CDP	Coprocessor Data Operation	32	No	Yes	Yes	Yes
CLREX	Clear Exclusive	32	No	Yes	Yes	Yes
CLZ	Count Leading Zeroes	32	No	Yes	Yes	Yes
CMN	Compare Negative	16	Yes	Yes	Yes	Yes
CMN	Compare Negative	32	No	Yes	Yes	Yes

continues

TABLE E-14 *(continued)*

MNEMONIC	FUNCTION	SIZE	M0/M0+/M1	M3	M4	M4F
CMP	Compare	16	Yes	Yes	Yes	Yes
CMP	Compare	32	No	Yes	Yes	Yes
CPS	Change Processor State	16	Yes	Yes	Yes	Yes
DBG	Debug Hint	32	No	Yes	Yes	Yes
DMB	Data Memory Barrier	32	Yes	Yes	Yes	Yes
DSB	Data Synchronization Barrier	32	Yes	Yes	Yes	Yes
EOR	Logical Exclusive OR	16	Yes	Yes	Yes	Yes
EOR	Logical Exclusive OR	32	No	Yes	Yes	Yes
ISB	Instruction Synchronization Barrier	32	Yes	Yes	Yes	Yes
IT	If Then	16	No	Yes	Yes	Yes
LDC	Load Coprocessor	32	No	Yes	Yes	Yes
LDM	Load Multiple Registers	16	Yes	Yes	Yes	Yes
LDMIA	Load Multiple Registers, Increment After	32	No	Yes	Yes	Yes
LDMDB	Load Multiple Registers, Decrement Before	32	No	Yes	Yes	Yes
LDR	Load Register	16	Yes	Yes	Yes	Yes
LDR	Load Register	32	No	Yes	Yes	Yes
LDRB	Load Register from Byte	16	Yes	Yes	Yes	Yes
LDRB	Load Register from Byte	32	No	Yes	Yes	Yes
LDRBT	Load Register from Byte Unprivileged	32	No	Yes	Yes	Yes
LDRD	Load Register Dual	32	No	Yes	Yes	Yes
LDREX	Load Register Exclusive	32	No	Yes	Yes	Yes
LDREXB	Load Register Exclusive from Byte	32	No	Yes	Yes	Yes
LDREXH	Load Register Exclusive from Halfword	32	No	Yes	Yes	Yes
LDRH	Load Register from Halfword	16	Yes	Yes	Yes	Yes
LDRH	Load Register from Halfword	32	No	Yes	Yes	Yes
LDRHT	Load Register from Halfword Unprivileged	32	No	Yes	Yes	Yes

LDRSB	Load Register from Signed Byte	16	Yes	Yes	Yes	Yes
LDRSB	Load Register from Signed Byte	32	No	Yes	Yes	Yes
LDRSBT	Load Register from Signed Byte Unprivileged	32	No	Yes	Yes	Yes
LDRSH	Load Register from Signed Halfword	16	Yes	Yes	Yes	Yes
LDRSH	Load Register from Signed Halfword	32	No	Yes	Yes	Yes
LDRSHT	Load Register from Signed Halfword Unprivileged	32	No	Yes	Yes	Yes
LDRT	Load Register Unprivileged	32	No	Yes	Yes	Yes
LSL	Logical Shift Left	16	Yes	Yes	Yes	Yes
LSL	Logical Shift Left	32	No	Yes	Yes	Yes
LSR	Logical Shift Right	16	Yes	Yes	Yes	Yes
LSR	Logical Shift Right	32	No	Yes	Yes	Yes
MCR	Move to Coprocessor from ARM Register	32	No	Yes	Yes	Yes
MCRR	Move to Coprocessor from ARM Register	32	No	Yes	Yes	Yes
MLA	Multiply and Accumulate	32	No	Yes	Yes	Yes
MLS	Multiply-Subtract	32	No	Yes	Yes	Yes
MOV	Move	16	Yes	Yes	Yes	Yes
MOV	Move	32	No	Yes	Yes	Yes
MOVT	Move to Top	32	No	Yes	Yes	Yes
MRC	Move to ARM Register from Coprocessor	32	No	Yes	Yes	Yes
MRRC	Move to ARM Register from Coprocessor	32	No	Yes	Yes	Yes
MRS	Move from ARM Register to Status Register	32	Yes	Yes	Yes	Yes
MSR	Move from Status Register to ARM Register	32	Yes	Yes	Yes	Yes
MUL	Multiply	16	Yes	Yes	Yes	Yes

continues

TABLE E-14 *(continued)*

MNEMONIC	FUNCTION	SIZE	M0/M0+/M1	M3	M4	M4F
MUL	Multiply	32	No	Yes	Yes	Yes
MVN	Move Negated	16	Yes	Yes	Yes	Yes
MVN	Move Negated	32	No	Yes	Yes	Yes
NOP	No Operation	16	Yes	Yes	Yes	Yes
NOP	No Operation	32	No	Yes	Yes	Yes
ORN	Logical OR NOT	32	No	Yes	Yes	Yes
ORR	Logical OR	16	Yes	Yes	Yes	Yes
ORR	Logical OR	32	No	Yes	Yes	Yes
PKH	Pack Halfword	32	No	No	Yes	Yes
PLD	Preload Data	32	No	Yes	Yes	Yes
PLDW	Preload Data	32	No	Yes	Yes	Yes
PLI	Preload Instruction	32	No	Yes	Yes	Yes
POP	Pop Register(s)	16	Yes	Yes	Yes	Yes
POP	Pop Register(s)	32	No	Yes	Yes	Yes
PUSH	Push Register(s)	16	Yes	Yes	Yes	Yes
PUSH	Push Register(s)	32	No	Yes	Yes	Yes
QADD	Saturating Add	32	No	No	Yes	Yes
QADD16	Saturating Two 16-Bit Integer Addition	32	No	No	Yes	Yes
QADD8	Saturating Four 8-Bit Integer Addition	32	No	No	Yes	Yes
QASX	Saturating Add and Subtract with Exchange	32	No	No	Yes	Yes
QDADD	Saturating Double and Add	32	No	No	Yes	Yes
QDSUB	Saturating Double and Subtract	32	No	No	Yes	Yes
QSAX	Saturating Subtract and Add with Exchange	32	No	No	Yes	Yes
QSUB	Saturating Subtract	32	No	No	Yes	Yes
QSUB16	Saturating Two 16-Bit Integer Subtraction	32	No	No	Yes	Yes

QSUB8	Saturating Four 8-Bit Integer Subtraction	32	No	No	Yes	Yes
RBIT	Reverse Bit Order	32	No	Yes	Yes	Yes
REV	Reverse Byte Order	16	Yes	Yes	Yes	Yes
REV	Reverse Byte Order	32	No	Yes	Yes	Yes
REV16	Reverse Byte Order in Halfword	16	Yes	Yes	Yes	Yes
REV16	Reverse Byte Order in Halfword	32	No	Yes	Yes	Yes
REVSH	Reverse Byte Order in Bottom Halfword	16	Yes	Yes	Yes	Yes
REVSH	Reverse byte Order in Bottom Halfword	32	No	Yes	Yes	Yes
ROR	Rotate Right	16	Yes	Yes	Yes	Yes
ROR	Rotate Right	32	No	Yes	Yes	Yes
RRX	Rotate Right with Extend	32	No	Yes	Yes	Yes
RSB	Reverse Subtract	16	Yes	Yes	Yes	Yes
RSB	Reverse Subtract	32	No	Yes	Yes	Yes
SADD16	Signed Add 16 Bits	32	No	No	Yes	Yes
SADD8	Signed Add 8 Bits	32	No	No	Yes	Yes
SASX	Signed Add and Subtract with Exchange	32	No	No	Yes	Yes
SBC	Subtract with Carry	16	Yes	Yes	Yes	Yes
SBC	Subtract with Carry	32	No	Yes	Yes	Yes
SBFX	Signed Bit-Field Exchange	32	No	Yes	Yes	Yes
SDIV	Signed Division	32	No	Yes	Yes	Yes
SEL	Select Bytes	32	No	No	Yes	Yes
SEV	Send Event	16	Yes	Yes	Yes	Yes
SEV	Send Event	32	No	Yes	Yes	Yes
SHADD16	Signed Halving Add 16	32	No	No	Yes	Yes
SHADD8	Signed Halving Add 8	32	No	No	Yes	Yes
SHASX	Signed Halving Add and Subtract with Exchange	32	No	No	Yes	Yes

continues

TABLE E-14 *(continued)*

MNEMONIC	FUNCTION	SIZE	M0/M0+/M1	M3	M4	M4F
SHSAX	Signed Halving Subtract and Add with Exchange	32	No	No	Yes	Yes
SHSUB16	Signed Halving Subtract 16	32	No	No	Yes	Yes
SHSUB8	Signed Halving Subtract 8	32	No	No	Yes	Yes
SMLABB	Signed Multiply Accumulate – Bottom Bottom	32	No	No	Yes	Yes
SMLABT	Signed Multiply Accumulate – Bottom Top	32	No	No	Yes	Yes
SMLAD	Signed Multiply Accumulate Dual	32	No	No	Yes	Yes
SMLAL	Signed Multiply Accumulate Long	32	No	Yes	Yes	Yes
SMLALBB	Signed Multiply Accumulate Long – Bottom Bottom	32	No	No	Yes	Yes
SMLALBT	Signed Multiply Accumulate Long – Bottom Top	32	No	No	Yes	Yes
SMLALD	Signed Multiply Accumulate Long Dual	32	No	No	Yes	Yes
SMLALTB	Signed Multiply Accumulate Long – Top Bottom	32	No	No	Yes	Yes
SMLALTT	Signed Multiply Accumulate Long – Top Top	32	No	No	Yes	Yes
SMLATB	Signed Multiply Accumulate – Top Bottom	32	No	No	Yes	Yes
SMLATT	Signed Multiply Accumulate – Top Top	32	No	No	Yes	Yes
SMLAWB	Signed Multiply Accumulate Word, Bottom	32	No	No	Yes	Yes
SMLAWT	Signed Multiply Accumulate Word, Top	32	No	No	Yes	Yes
SMLSD	Signed Multiply with Subtraction Dual	32	No	No	Yes	Yes
SMLSLD	Signed Multiply with Subtraction Acculumation Dual	32	No	No	Yes	Yes
SMMLA	Signed Most Significant Word Multiply Accumulate	32	No	No	Yes	Yes
SMMLS	Signed Most Significant Word Subtract Accumulate	32	No	No	Yes	Yes

SMMUL	Signed Most Significant Word Multiply	32	No	No	Yes	Yes
SMUAD	Signed Dual Multiply Add	32	No	No	Yes	Yes
SMULBB	Signed Multiply – Bottom Bottom	32	No	No	Yes	Yes
SMULBT	Signed Multiply – Bottom Top	32	No	No	Yes	Yes
SMULL	Signed Long Multiply	32	No	Yes	Yes	Yes
SMULTB	Signed Long Multiply – Top Bottom	32	No	No	Yes	Yes
SMULTT	Signed Long Multiply – Top Top	32	No	No	Yes	Yes
SMULWB	Signed Multiply by Word – Bottom	32	No	No	Yes	Yes
SMULWT	Signed Multiply by Word – Top	32	No	No	Yes	Yes
SMUSD	Signed Dual Multiply Subtract	32	No	No	Yes	Yes
SSAT	Signed Saturate	32	No	Yes	Yes	Yes
SSAT16	Signed Saturate 16 Bits	32	No	No	Yes	Yes
SSAX	Signed Subtract and Add with Exchange	32	No	No	Yes	Yes
SSUB16	Signed Subtract 16 Bits	32	No	No	Yes	Yes
SSUB8	Signed Subtract 8 Bits	32	No	No	Yes	Yes
STC	Store Coprocessor	32	No	Yes	Yes	Yes
STM	Store Multiple Registers	16	Yes	Yes	Yes	Yes
STMDB	Store Multiple Registers, Decrement Before	32	No	Yes	Yes	Yes
STMIA	Store Multiple Registers, Increment After	32	No	Yes	Yes	Yes
STR	Store	16	Yes	Yes	Yes	Yes
STR	Store	32	No	Yes	Yes	Yes
STRB	Store Byte	16	Yes	Yes	Yes	Yes
STRB	Store Byte	32	No	Yes	Yes	Yes
STRBT	Store Byte Unprivileged	32	No	Yes	Yes	Yes
STRD	Store Register Dual	32	No	Yes	Yes	Yes
STREX	Store Register Exclusive	32	No	Yes	Yes	Yes
STREXB	Store Register Exclusive Byte	32	No	Yes	Yes	Yes

continues

TABLE E-14 *(continued)*

MNEMONIC	FUNCTION	SIZE	M0/M0+/M1	M3	M4	M4F
STREXH	Store Register Exclusive Halfword	32	No	Yes	Yes	Yes
STRH	Store Halfword	16	Yes	Yes	Yes	Yes
STRH	Store Halfword	32	No	Yes	Yes	Yes
STRHT	Store Halfword Unprivileged	32	No	Yes	Yes	Yes
STRT	Store Register Unprivileged	32	No	Yes	Yes	Yes
SUB	Subtract	16	Yes	Yes	Yes	Yes
SUB	Subtract	32	No	Yes	Yes	Yes
SVC	Supervisor Call	16	Yes	Yes	Yes	Yes
SXTAB	Sign and Extend Byte	32	No	No	Yes	Yes
SXTAB16	Sign and Extend to Bytes	32	No	No	Yes	Yes
SXTAH	Sign and Extend Halfword	32	No	No	Yes	Yes
SXTB	Sign Extend Byte	16	Yes	Yes	Yes	Yes
SXTB	Sign Extend Byte	32	No	Yes	Yes	Yes
SXTB16	Sign Extend Two Bytes	32	No	No	Yes	Yes
SXTH	Sign Extend Halfword	16	Yes	Yes	Yes	Yes
SXTH	Sign Extend Halfword	32	No	Yes	Yes	Yes
TBB	Table Branch Byte	32	No	Yes	Yes	Yes
TBH	Table Branch Halfword	32	No	Yes	Yes	Yes
TEQ	Test Equivalence	32	No	Yes	Yes	Yes
TST	Test	16	Yes	Yes	Yes	Yes
TST	Test	32	No	Yes	Yes	Yes
UADD16	Unsigned Add 16	32	No	No	Yes	Yes
UADD8	Unsigned Add 8	32	No	No	Yes	Yes
UASX	Add and Subtract with Exchange	32	No	No	Yes	Yes
UBFX	Unsigned Bit-Field Extract	32	No	Yes	Yes	Yes
UDIV	Unsigned Division	32	No	Yes	Yes	Yes
UHADD16	Unsigned Halving Add 16	32	No	No	Yes	Yes

UHADD8	Unsigned Halving Add 8	32	No	No	Yes	Yes
UHASX	Unsigned Halving Add and Subtract with Exchange	32	No	No	Yes	Yes
UHSAX	Unsigned Halving Subtract and Add with Exchange	32	No	No	Yes	Yes
UHSUB16	Unsigned Halving Subtract 16	32	No	No	Yes	Yes
UHSUB8	Unsigned Halving Subtract 8	32	No	No	Yes	Yes
UMAAL	Unsigned Multiply Accumulate Accumulate Long	32	No	No	Yes	Yes
UMLAL	Unsigned Long Multiply and Accumulate	32	No	Yes	Yes	Yes
UMULL	Unsigned Long Multiply	32	No	Yes	Yes	Yes
UQADD16	Unsigned Saturating Add 16	32	No	No	Yes	Yes
UQADD8	Unsigned Saturating Add 8	32	No	No	Yes	Yes
UQASX	Unsigned Saturating Add and Subtract with Exchange	32	No	No	Yes	Yes
UQSAX	Unsigned Saturating Subtract and Add with Exchange	32	No	No	Yes	Yes
UQSUB16	Unsigned Saturating Subtract 16	32	No	No	Yes	Yes
UQSUB8	Unsigned Saturating Subtract 8	32	No	No	Yes	Yes
USAD8	Unsigned Sum of Absolute Differences 8	32	No	No	Yes	Yes
USADA8	Unsigned Sum of Absolute Differences 8 and Accumulate	32	No	No	Yes	Yes
USAT	Unsigned Saturate	32	No	Yes	Yes	Yes
USAT16	Unsigned Saturate 16	32	No	No	Yes	Yes
USAX	Subtract and Add with Exchange	32	No	No	Yes	Yes
USUB16	Unsigned Subtract 16	32	No	No	Yes	Yes
USUB8	Unsigned Subtract 8	32	No	No	Yes	Yes
UXTAB	Zero Extend and Add Byte	32	No	No	Yes	Yes
UXTAB16	Zero Extend and Add 2 Bytes	32	No	No	Yes	Yes

continues

TABLE E-14 *(continued)*

MNEMONIC	FUNCTION	SIZE	M0/M0+/M1	M3	M4	M4F
UXTAH	Zero Extend and Add Halfword	32	No	No	Yes	Yes
UXTB	Zero Extend Byte	16	Yes	Yes	Yes	Yes
UXTB	Zero Extend Byte	32	No	Yes	Yes	Yes
UXTB16	Zero Extend 2 Bytes	32	No	No	Yes	Yes
UXTH	Zero Extend Halfword	16	Yes	Yes	Yes	Yes
UXTH	Zero Extend Halfword	32	No	Yes	Yes	Yes
VABS	Floating-Point Absolute Value	32	No	No	No	Yes
VADD	Floating-Point Add	32	No	No	No	Yes
VCMP	Floating-Point Compare	32	No	No	No	Yes
VCMPE	Floating-Point Compare with Invalid Operation Check	32	No	No	No	Yes
VCVT	Vector Convert	32	No	No	No	Yes
VCVTR	Vector Convert with Rounding	32	No	No	No	Yes
VDIV	Floating-Point Divide	32	No	No	No	Yes
VLDM	Extension Register Load Multiple	32	No	No	No	Yes
VLDR	Extension Register Load Register	32	No	No	No	Yes
VMLA	Floating-Point Multiply and Accumulate	32	No	No	No	Yes
VMLS	Floating-Point Multiply and Subtract	32	No	No	No	Yes
VMOV	Extension Register Move	32	No	No	No	Yes
VMRS	Move to ARM Core Register from Floating-Point System Register	32	No	No	No	Yes
VMSR	Move to Floating-Point System Register from ARM Core Register	32	No	No	No	Yes
VMUL	Floating-Point Multiply	32	No	No	No	Yes
VNEG	Floating-Point Negate	32	No	No	No	Yes
VNMLA	Floating-Point Negated Multiply and Accumulate	32	No	No	No	Yes
VNMLS	Floating-Point Negated Multiply and Subtract	32	No	No	No	Yes

VNMUL	Floating-Point Negated Multiply	32	No	No	No	Yes
VPOP	Extension Register Pop	32	No	No	No	Yes
VPUSH	Extension Register Push	32	No	No	No	Yes
VSQRT	Floating-Point Square Root	32	No	No	No	Yes
VSTM	Extension Register Store Multiple	32	No	No	No	Yes
VSTR	Extension Register Store Register	32	No	No	No	Yes
VSUB	Floating-Point Subtract	32	No	No	No	Yes
WFE	Wait For Event	16	Yes	Yes	Yes	Yes
WFE	Wait For Event	32	No	Yes	Yes	Yes
WFI	Wait For Interrupt	16	Yes	Yes	Yes	Yes
WFI	Wait For Interrupt	32	No	Yes	Yes	Yes
YIELD	Yield	16	Yes	Yes	Yes	Yes
YIELD	Yield	32	No	Yes	Yes	Yes

INDEX

Symbols

@ (at sign), comments, 61
! (exclamation mark), pre-index addressing, 68
[] (square brackets), compiler, 68

A

Abort mode, 43
absolute branches, 69
Acorn, 3–6, 5, 23, 103, 200
Active Book, 5
ADC, 126, 222
ADD, 61, 66, 114–115, 125, 222
ADD8, 225
ADD16, 225
addressing
    assembly language, 66–69
    NEON, 151–152
    physical address, 45
    post-index, 68, 130
    pre-index, 68, 129
    virtual address, 45
Advanced Technology Group (ATG), 5–6
aeabi_idiv, 82
AL, 62
alignment, C optimization, 185–186
ALU. See Arithmetic Logic Unit
AMD, 20
AND, 131, 229
Android, 25
Apple Computer, 5–6, 20, 25
architecture, 7, 29–51
    cache, 31–33
    calculation unit, 37

coprocessor, 39–40
CPU
    pipeline, 37–39
    register, 30
exceptions, 40–43
GCC, 25
internal RAM, 31
load and store, 30, 148
MMU, 32, 45–47
multiplication, 48–49
processor register, 33–35
stack, 31
subsystems, 33–40
TCM, 39
technologies, 47–50
Thumb, 49
TrustZone, 49–50
Vector Floating Point, 48
vector tables, 44–45
versions, 199–203
Architecture Reference Manual, 11
Arduino Due, 23
arithmetic instructions, 125–127, 152–153, 202, 221–224
    parallel, 224–225
    saturating, 127–129, 230
Arithmetic Logic Unit (ALU), 18, 36, 37
ARM6, 22, 200–201, 205
ARM7, 10, 47, 205
ARM7EJ-S, 47
ARM7TDMI, 22, 201, 206
    ARM926EJ-S, 9–10
    16-bit, 108
    Thumb, 49
        instructions, 107, 108

ARM8, 201, 206
ARM9, 7, 49, 111, 194, 201
ARM9E, 48, 207
ARM9TDMI, 207
ARM10, 49, 207–208
ARM11, 30, 49, 208
ARM250, 16
ARM926EJ-S, 9–10, 79, 202
ARM1156T2-S, 49, 111
ARM1176, 22, 173
ARM1176JZF-S, 24, 102
arm-non-eabi-objdump, 77
ARMv1, 200
ARMv2, 200
ARMv2a, 16
ARMv3, 200–201
ARMv4, 49, 201
ARMv5, 10, 135, 201–202
ARMv5T, 47
ARMv5TEJ, 48
ARMv6, 36, 111, 196, 202, 208
ARMv6-M, 113, 203, 212
ARMv7, 10, 124
ARMv7-A/R, 198, 203
ARMv7-M, 113, 203
ARMv8, 12, 203
ASF. *See* Atmel Software Framework
ASIC, 49
ASR, 140, 235
assembly instructions, 121–143, 221–245
    barrel shifter, 139–140
    branch instructions, 132–135
    compare instructions, 131–132
    coprocessor, 141–142
    data transfer, 129–130
    division, 136–137
    logical operators, 130–131
    mathematics, 125–127
    multiple register data transfer, 137–139
    multiplication, 135–136
    NEON, 152–153, 216–219
    RISC, 121
    saturating arithmetic, 127–129
    stack, 140–141
    32-bit, 123–125

assembly language, 53–71
    addressing modes, 66–69
    bootloader, 59
    branching, 69–70
    comments, 61
    compiler, 57–58
    condition codes, 62–66
    GCC, 80
    instructions, 61
    label, 61
    loading and storing, 69
    mathematics, 70
    optimization, 60
    reverse engineering, 59–60
    setting values, 69
    size, 56–57
    speed, 55–56
ASX, 225
ATG. *See* Advanced Technology Group
Atmel, D20 Xplained Pro, 95–101
Atmel Software Framework (ASF), 96
Atom N550, 21
AVR, 95

B

B, 133, 231
BACKGROUND_HEIGHT, 92
BACKGROUND_WIDTH, 92
backtrace, 166–167
banked register, 33, 44
bare metal system, 178–179
barrel shifter, 67, 115, 139–140
BBC. *See* British Broadcasting Corporation
BBC Micro, 5, 23, 103, 200
Beagleboard, 24
Beaglebone, 24
Bemer, Bob, 19
BIC, 131, 229
big.LITTLE, 50–51, 203
BIOS, 79
bitfield instructions, 117
BKPT, 234
BL, 110, 133, 231
BLX, 134, 231

`bootcode.bin`, 104
Booth's Algorithm, 48
bootloader, 56–57, 170, 171. *See also* U-Boot
    assembly language, 59
    debugging, 163
    recovery, 78–79
branch instructions, 132–135, 231
branch prediction, 39, 193
branching, 114
    assembly language, 69–70
    Thumb-2, 117
breakout boards, 24
breakpoints, 161, 170, 171
British Broadcasting Corporation (BBC), 4–5
`BUTTON_0`, 97
`BX`, 133–134, 231
`BXJ`, 231

C

    Data Abort, 170
    NEON, 153–158, 220
C optimization, 175–190
    alignment, 185–186
    cache, 188–190
    compiler, 176, 186
    D-cache, 189
    division, 183–184
    example, 180–182
    frequency scaling, 187–188
    hardware, 187–190
    integers, 183
    interrupt handlers, 186–187
    parameters, 184–185
    profiling, 176–179
    rules, 175–176
    subroutines, 185
cache, 10, 193–194
    architecture, 31–33
    coprocessor, 39
    instructions, 188
    Thumb, 189–190
cache hit, 39, 194
cache lines, 188, 189, 194
cache miss, 32, 39, 194

`calcfreq`, 177
calculation unit, 37
cameras, 47, 50
capes, 24
`CBNZ`, 110, 117, 231
`CBZ`, 110, 117, 231
`CC`, 63
central processing unit (CPU), 6–7
    Acorn, 5
    alignment, 186
    Apple Computer, 6
    arithmetic instructions, 125–127
    cache, 31
    floating point numbers, 17
    frequency, 195
    heat, 12
    licenses, 12
    MMU, 45–47
    mobile devices, 21
    mobile phones, 21
    pipeline, architecture, 37–39
    register, architecture, 30
    Technical Reference Manual, 11
    unsigned integers, 17
`char`, 166
`CHIP_Init()`, 90
CISC. *See* Complex Instruction Set Computing
`CLZ`, 131, 224
`CMN`, 132, 230
`CMP`, 114, 132, 230
CodeSourcery suite, 77, 119
Colossus, 29–30
comments, 61
Community Edition, DS-5, 27
comparison instructions, 131–132, 153, 229–230
compiler, 27, 68, 77, 104–105, 119
    assembly language, 57–58
    C optimization, 176, 186
    embedded systems, 25–26
Complex Instruction Set Computing (CISC), 19–21
`cond`, 116
condition codes, assembly language, 62–66
condition flags, CPSR, 36
conditional branches, 69, 114

conf_ssd1306.h, 98
conf_sysfont.h, 98
context switch, 40
coprocessor, 39–40, 194–195
    assembly instructions, 141–142
    Thumb-2, 117
copy protection, 60
Core i7, 20
Core War, 57
Cortex series, 25–26, 30, 40, 49,
    208–213
Cortex-A, 9, 11, 22, 48, 209–211
    bootloader, 170
    Thumb, 111
Cortex-A5, 210
Cortex-A7, 210
Cortex-A8, 24, 30, 210
Cortex-A9, 210–211
Cortex-A12, 211
Cortex-A15, 211
Cortex-A50, 211
Cortex-A53, 25–26, 203, 211
Cortex-M, 9, 11, 93, 118, 178, 212–213
    Arduino Due, 23
    ARMv6-M, 202
    Atmel, 96
    cache, 32
    exceptions, 113
    initialization, 87
    multiplication hardware, 48–49
    Silicon Labs, 86
    Thumb, 111–113
        instructions, 234–245
    Thumb-2, 116
    vector tables, 45
    Versatile Express, 22
Cortex-M0, 90, 111, 212–213
Cortex-M0+, 90, 93, 96, 111, 213
Cortex-M1, 213
Cortex-M3, 213
Cortex-M4, 213
Cortex-R, 9, 211–212
Cortex-R4, 137, 212
Cortex-R5, 137, 212

Cortex-R7, 212
CP10, 195
CP11, 195
CP14, 29, 40, 195
CP15, 40, 179, 195
CPSID, 234
CPSIE, 234
CPSR. *See* Current Program Status Register
CPU. *See* central processing unit
CPY, 226
cs, 63
Current Program Status Register (CPSR),
    35–37, 42, 43, 65, 183
Curry, Chris, 3
cycle counter, 179

D

D register, 147–148
D20 Xplained Pro, 95–101
Data Abort exception, 41, 43, 169–170
data cache (D-cache), 32, 189
data types, NEON, 147, 154–155, 215
DBX. *See* Direct Bytecode eXecution
D-cache. *See* data cache
DDR memory, 30, 57, 83
debugging, 10, 159–174
    ARM1176, 173
    bootloaders, 163
    breakpoints, 161, 170, 171
    coprocessor, 39, 40
    CP14, 29, 40, 195
    Data Abort exception, 169–170
    division by zero, 168–169
    DS-5, 27, 167–168
        profilers, 178
    ELF, 77
    embedded systems, 26
    EmbeddedICE, 160–161
    examples, 165–169
    infinite loop, 165–167
    interrupt controllers, 163
    JTAG, 47, 160–161
    Lauterbach Trace32, 26

loops, 162–163
MMU, 174
Monitor mode, 44
optimization, 174
routines, 163
serial line, 170–172
64-bit, 172–173
stack frames, 162
stepping, 161–162
types, 162–163
unknown exceptions, 167–168
vector catch, 162
vector tables, 173
watchpoints, 161
Denx Software, 79, 102–103
Development Studio 5 (DS-5), 26–27,
     167–168, 178
DIGIC, DSP, 47
digital signal processing (DSP), 47–48,
     109, 118
Direct Bytecode eXecution (DBX),
     48, 201
dirty cache, 33, 188
DISPLAY_Init(), 91
division
     assembly instructions, 136–137
     C optimization, 183–184
     by zero, debugging, 168–169
DIY NAS boxes, 24
DMB, 110, 213
DS-5. See Development Studio 5
DSB, 110, 213
DSP. See digital signal processing

E

early termination, 48
Eclipse IDE, 27
EFM32, 87, 89, 178
ELF. See Executable and Linkable Format
else, 167
ELT. See Emergency Locator Transmitter
embedded systems, 13–28
     Android, 25

bootloader, 56–57
CISC, 19–21
Compiler, 26
compiler, 25–26
debugging, 26
definition, 15
development environments, 26–27
evaluation boards, 23–24
floating point numbers, 18
GCC, 25–26
Linux, 24–25
operating system, 24–25
optimization, 17–19
processor, choosing, 21–22
RISC, 19–21
SoC, 15–16
Sourcery CodeBench, 26
system programming, 16–17
Versatile Platform Baseboard, 79
Y2K, 18–19
EmbeddedICE, 47, 48, 160–161
Emergency Locator Transmitter (ELT), 20
energy efficiency
     ARM926EJ-S, 10
     big.LITTLE, 50–51
     Cortex-M, 11
     EFM32, 89
     SoC, 16
Energy Micro, 178
energyAware Profiler, 178
ENIAC, 30
EOR, 131, 229
EQ, 62, 116
evaluation boards, 22, 23–24, 90
exception modes, 43
exceptions, 195
     architecture, 40–43
     Cortex-M, 113
     Data Abort, 41, 43, 169–170
     MMU, 168
     PC, 168
     Prefetch Abort, 41, 43
     Reset, 41
     Thumb-2, 116

exceptions (*Continued*)
    Undefined Instruction, 43
    unknown, 167–168
Executable and Linkable Format (ELF), 77–79, 81, 105
EXT2, 102
extend instructions, 231–233
Exynos Octa, 11–12

F

FAT, 102
FAT32, 103
FIQ, 37, 41, 44, 186
firmware, 79, 170
flash memory, 170–172
Flash Micro, 95
floating point numbers, 9, 17, 18, 48
Floating Point Unit (FPU), 86, 93, 118
for, 182–183
FPGA, 16, 49, 213
FPU. *See* Floating Point Unit
Freescale, 6, 16, 22, 160
frequency, CPU, 195
frequency scaling, 22, 187–188

G

Game Boy Advance, 107–108
games, reverse engineering, 59–60
GCC. *See* GNU C Compiler
GDB Debugger, 165
GE, 63
Gecko, 86
getio, 177
GFX Monochrome - System Font, 98
gigahertz syndrome, 21
GLIB_drawLine, 93
global variables, 185
GNU C Compiler (GCC), 25–26, 80, 104–105
GNU Debugger, 163–165
GPIO, 24, 87, 91, 178
gprof, 177

GPU, 16, 103
grayscale, NEON, 156–158
GRUB2, 79
GT, 64, 116

H

hard macro license, 7
hardware
    branch prediction, 39
    C optimization, 187–190
    Cortex-M, 11
    floating point numbers, 9
    initialization, 74
    mobile phones, 50
    multiplication, 200, 207
    optimization, 113
    profiler, 178
    Vector Floating Point, 39
Harvard cache, 32
Harvard Mark I, 56
Hauser, Hermann, 3
heat, 12, 22
Hello, world!, 74–76, 79–81
Hertz, 195
hexadecimal dump, 78
HI, 63
Hiapad Hi-802, 16
high vectors, 44
hit rate, 188
Hopper, Grace, 56
Hyp mode, 44

I

I-cache. *See* instructional cache
ICEs. *See* In-Circuit emulators
#ifdef, 155
If-Then, 116–117
immediate values, 66, 115, 124
iMX 6, 16
iMX SoC, 22
iMX51, 160
In-Circuit emulators (ICEs), 47, 48, 160–161

industrial systems, 22
infinite loop, 165–167
initialization
    Atmel, 97
    Cortex-M, 87
    DDR, 57
    hardware, 74
    STK3200, 90
    STK3800, 87
instructional cache (I-cache), 188
instructions. *See also* assembly instructions;
    Reduced Instruction Set Computing; Single
    Instruction Multiple Data
    arithmetic, 125–127, 152–153, 202,
        221–224
    assembly language, 61
    bitfield, 117
    branch, 132–135, 231
    cache, 188
    CISC, 19–21
    comparison, 131–132, 153, 229–230
    extend, 231–233
    jump, 80
    load, 227–228
    logical, 130–131, 229
    MIPS, 22, 196
    movement, 122–125, 226
    NEON, 215–219
    parallel arithmetic, 224–225
    saturating arithmetic, 127–129, 230
    store, 228–229
    Thumb, 107–109, 189–190, 234–245
    Undefined Instruction, 42
integers, 168
    C optimization, 183
    signed, 215
    unsigned, 17, 18, 147, 215
Intel, 20, 21, 47
interleaves, NEON, 148–150
internal RAM, 31
interrupt controllers, 163
interrupt handlers, 39, 74, 174, 186–187, 196
interrupt masks, 37
interrupts, 40, 88, 196

interworking, Thumb, 113, 134–135
intrinsics, NEON, 154–156, 220
I/O, 23, 24, 93, 178, 202
iOS, 25
IP, 7, 34
IRQ, 37, 41, 44, 91, 189
ISB, 110
IT, 110

J

Java runtime, 25
Jazelle, 48, 108, 196, 201
JFFS2, 102
J-Link, 165, 178
Joint Test Action Group (JTAG), 10, 47,
    160–161, 196
jump instruction, 80

K

Keil series, 22
kernel.c, 105
kernel.img, 104

L

label, 8–9, 61
lanes, NEON, 146–147, 216
Last In, First Out (LIFO), 31
Lauterbach, 26, 57, 178
LDM, 139, 227, 228
LDMFD, 118
LDMIA, 115, 141
LDR, 66, 69, 124, 129, 227
LDRB, 129, 227
LDRBT, 227
LDRD, 227
LDREX, 228
LDRH, 129, 227
LDRSB, 129, 227
LDRSH, 227
LDRT, 227
LE, 64

licenses, 85–86
    CPUs, 12
    SoC, 16
    synthesizable, 7, 49, 197–198
LIFO. *See* Last In, First Out
LILO, 79
link register (LR), 35, 70, 115
Linux, 20, 24–25, 103
load and store architecture, 30, 148
load instructions, 227–228
`loader.bin`, 104
logical instructions, 130–131, 229
loops
    debugging, 162–163
    infinite, 165–167
    register, 182–183
Lorenz cipher code, 29
LR. *See* link register
`LR_<mode>`, 42
`LS`, 63
`LSL`, 67, 139–140
`LSR`, 67, 140
`LT`, 64, 116

M

machine code, 53
`main`, 99
Mali graphics processor, 12
manufacturer documentation, 11
mathematics, 70, 125–127
`MCR`, 84, 142
`memcpy`, 130, 152
memory, 30. *See also* cache; *specific types*
    Cortex-M, 11
    mapping, 83–85
    NEON, vectors, 154–155
    RISC, 107
    stack, 31
    Thumb, 110
    vector tables, 44–45
    Y2K, 18
memory bottleneck, 31
Memory LCD, 90–93

Memory Management Unit (MMU), 10, 20, 24,
    26, 43, 83–85
    architecture, 32, 45–47
    assembly language, 57
    coprocessor, 39, 40
    D-cache, 189
    debugging, 174
    exceptions, 168
Memory Protection Unit (MPU), 32, 40, 43
`MI`, 63
Million Instructions per Second (MIPS), 22, 196
Minecraft, 24, 103
MIPS. *See* Million Instructions per Second
`MLA`, 135–136, 222
MMU. *See* Memory Management Unit
`mmuloop`, 85
mobile devices, 11–12, 21, 107
mobile phones, 21, 50, 56–57, 78–79
Mojang, 24
Monitor mode, 44
`MOV`, 66, 67, 114, 226
    assembly instructions, 122, 125
    Thumb-2, 116
`MOV pc, lr`, 135
movement instructions, 122–125, 226
`MOVT`, 123, 125
`MOVW`, 123, 125
Moxa, 22
MPU. *See* Memory Protection Unit
`MRC`, 40, 85, 141–142
`MRS`, 110, 142–143, 226
`MSR`, 110, 142–143, 226
`-mthumb`, 119
`MUL`, 135, 222
multiplication, 48–49, 200, 207
    assembly instructions, 135–136
    NEON, 153, 157
`MVN`, 66, 122, 226
`myfunc`, 119

N

naming conventions, 7–11
NAND flash memory, 170–172

NE, 62, 116
NEG, 123
NEON, 145–158
    addressing, 151–152
    alignment, 185
    arithmetic instructions, 152–153
    assembly instructions, 152–153, 216–219
    C, 153–158, 220
    comparison instructions, 153
    coprocessor, 39
    CP11, 195
    data loading and storing, 148–152
    data types, 147, 215
    DSP, 48
    grayscale, 156–158
    instructions, 215–219
    interleaves, 148–150
    intrinsics, 154–156, 220
    lanes, 146–147, 216
    load and store architecture, 148
    memcpy, 152
    multiplication, 153, 157
    register
        64-bit, 146
        128-bit, 147–148, 196
    SIMD, 50, 145, 195, 196
    VLD, 146
nested interrupt handler, 187
non-tested interrupt handler, 187
NOP, 142–143, 234
-nostartfiles, 105
NV, 62

O

Objective-C, iOS, 25
OLED display, 98–99
128-bit, 92, 200
    NEON, 147–148, 196
<op>, 61
operating system, 24–25, 50, 177–178
optimization. See also C optimization
    assembly language, 60
    debugging, 174

embedded systems, 17–19
    hardware, 113
ORR, 124, 125, 131, 229
out-of-order execution, 39, 197
output buffer, 79
overclocking, 24, 104

P

parallel arithmetic instructions, 224–225
parameters, C optimization, 184–185
PC. See Program Counter
Pentium, 20
performance
    ARM926EJ-S, 10
    RISC, 107
Performance Monitor Unit, 179
Peripheral Event System, 95
Peripheral Touch Controller, 96
physical address, 45
pipelines, 37–39, 197
PKHBT, 233
PKHTB, 233
PL, 63
PLD, 228
PLDW, 228
POP, 35, 115, 141
post-index addressing, 68, 130
power. See also energy efficiency
    DS-5, 27
    frequency scaling, 22
    transistors, 21
PowerDebug, 26
PowerPC, 20
PowerTrace, 26
precalc.calcfreq, 177
Prefetch Abort exception, 41, 43
pre-index addressing, 68, 129
printf, 166
privileged modes, 40, 42–43, 45, 142, 169
processor, 7, 30. See also central processing unit;
    coprocessor
        determining, 8–9
        embedded systems, 21–22

processor (*Conitnued*)
- GCC, 25
- integers, 168
- interrupts, 40
- jump instruction, 80
- labels, 8–9
- MMU, 45–47
- numbering, 8
- register, 54
    - architecture, 33–35
- Thumb, 113
- U-Boot, 102

profiling
- bare metal system, 178–179
- C optimization, 176–179
- Cortex-M, 178
- cycle counter, 179
- GPIO, 178
- operating system, 177–178

Program Counter (PC), 35, 115, 168
Programmer's Model, ARM926EJ-S, 10
PROTO1, 96
PSR, 142–143
PUSH, 35, 115, 141

Q

Q register, 147–148
QADD, 128, 222
QDADD, 128–129, 222
QDSUB, 129, 222
Qemu, 79, 80
QSUB, 128, 222

R

r0 to r15 register, 33–34
RAM, 21
- assembly instructions, 124–125
- Cortex-R4, 212
- internal, 31
Raspberry Pi, 23–24, 103–105
RCT. *See* Runtime Compilation Target
recovery, bootloader, 78–79

Redcode, 57
Reduced Instruction Set Computing (RISC)
- assembly instructions, 121
- embedded systems, 19–21
- memory, 107
re-entrant interrupt handler, 187
register, 197
- addressing modes, 66–68
- banked, 33, 44
- CPSR, 35–37, 42, 43, 65, 183
- CPU, architecture, 30
- D, 147–148
- IP, 34
- Lauterbach Trace32, 26
- loops, 182–183
- LR, 35, 70, 115
- MMU, 85
- MOV, 67
- NEON
    - 64-bit, 146
    - 128-bit, 147–148
- processor, 54
- Q, 147–148
- r0 to r15, 33–34
- SCTRL, 113
- subroutines, 185
- Thumb-1, 114
- Update Status Register, 114–115
relative branches, 69
RESET, 83, 113
Reset exception, 41
REV, 233
REV16, 233
reverse engineering, games, 59–60
REVSH, 233
RFE, 234
RISC. *See* Reduced Instruction Set Computing
ROR, 140, 239
routines, debugging, 163
RRX, 140, 239
RS-232, 171
RSB, 126–127, 222
RSC, 127, 222
RTC, 87–88, 92

RTC_CompareSet, 88
RTC_IRQHandler, 88
Runtime Compilation Target (RCT), 108

S

Samsung, 11–12
saturating arithmetic instructions, 127–129, 230
SAX, 225
SBC, 126, 222
SBFX, 117
SCTRL register, 113
SDIV, 82, 137, 239
segfault, 42
Segger, 178
SegmentLCD_Number, 89
SEL, 234
serial line, debugging, 170–172
SETEND, 234
7420 system, 22
signed integers, 215
Silicon Labs
    Gecko, 86
    STK3200, 89–95
    STK3800, 85–89
    Wonder Gecko, 86–87, 89–90
Single Instruction Multiple Data (SIMD), 197
    ARMv6, 202
    DSP, 47
    NEON, 50, 145, 195, 196
SiP. See System in Package
16-bit
    ARM7TDMI, 108
    Thumb, 49, 107–108, 116
64-bit
    ARMv8, 12, 203
    debugging, 172–173
    multiplication hardware, 48
    NEON register, 146
SMALD, 223
SMLA, 223
SMLAD, 223, 240
SMLAL, 136, 223, 240
SMLAW, 223

SMLSD, 223, 240
SMLSLD, 223, 240
SMMLA, 224, 240
SMMLS, 224, 241
SMMUL, 224, 241
SMULL, 136, 172, 223, 241
SMULW, 223
SMUSD, 223
snprintf, 100
SoC. See System on a chip
Sourcery CodeBench, 26
SPSR_<mode>, 42
SRAM, 31
SRS, 234
SSAT, 230
SSAT16, 230
stack
    architecture, 31
    assembly instructions, 140–141
    backtrace, 166–167
    subroutines, 185
    Thumb-1, 115
stack frames, 162
stack pointer, 34–35
stalls, 39, 188
start.elf, 104
startup.o, 81
status flags, 114–115
stepping, 161–162
STK3200, 89–95
STK3800, 85–89
STM, 138–139, 229
STMDB, 115
store instructions, 228–229
STR, 69, 130, 170, 228
STRB, 130, 228
STRBT, 228
STRD, 228
STREX, 229
STRH, 130, 170, 228
StrongARM, 201, 206–207
STRT, 228
SUB, 126, 222
SUB8, 225

SUB16, 225
subroutines, 31, 119, 141, 185
subsystems, 33–40
Supervisor Call (SVC), 42, 43
Supervisor mode, 43
SVC. *See* Supervisor Call
SVC, 142–143, 234
SXTAB, 232
SXTAB16, 232
SXTAH, 232
SXTB, 232
SXTB16, 232
SXTH, 232
synthesizable license, 7, 49, 197–198
System in Package (SiP), 16
System mode, 43
System on a chip (SoC), 11, 15–16, 22, 197
system_init(), 97

T

Tag_CPU, 77
Tahiti, 20
TBB, 231, 242
TBH, 231, 242
TCM. *See* Tightly Coupled Memory
Technical Reference Manual, 11
technologies, 47–50
TEQ, 132, 229
Texas Instruments, 22
32-bit, 12, 18, 37
    alignment, 185
    assembly instructions, 123–125
    processor register, 33
    Thumb, 49, 107–108, 116, 189
    vector tables, 44
Thumb
    architecture, 49
    ARM7, 47
    ARM7DMI, 10
    cache, 189–190
    calculation unit, 37
    compiler, 119
    Cortex-A, 111

Cortex-M, 111–113
    exceptions, 42
    instructions, 107–109, 189–190, 234–245
    interworking, 113
        branch instructions, 134–135
    memory, 110
    processor, 113
    RESET, 113
    16-bit, 107–108
    32-bit, 107–108, 189
    vector tables, 44
    writing for, 118–119
Thumb-1, 113–115
    ARMv6-M, 202
Thumb-2, 108, 109, 115–118
    ARM1156T2-S, 111
    ARMv6-M, 202
ThumbEE, 108
tick, 41
Tightly Coupled Memory (TCM), 39
TLB. *See* Translation Lookaside Buffer
Trace32, 26, 57, 178
transistors, 19, 21
Translation Lookaside Buffer (TLB),
    46–47, 189
translation tables, 46, 83, 84
TrustZone, 49–50, 198
TST, 132, 229

U

UAL. *See* Unified Assembler Language
UART, 171–172
UBFX, 117
U-Boot, 79, 102–103
UDIV, 137
UMAAL, 222, 243
UMLAL, 136, 222
UMULL, 136, 172, 222
Undefined Instruction, 42
Undefined Instruction exception, 43
Undefined mode, 43
Unified Assembler Language (UAL), 121
unified cache, 32

unknown exceptions, 167–168
unsigned integers, 17, 18, 147, 215
Update Status Register, 114–115
USAD8, 225
USADA8, 225
USAT, 230
USAT16, 230
User mode, 43
UXTAB, 233
UXTAB16, 233
UXTAH, 233
UXTB, 232
UXTB16, 232
UXTH, 232

V

VAR embedded systems, 25
VC, 63
vector catch, 162, 168
Vector Floating Point, 48
vector tables, 44–45, 173, 198
vectors, NEON, 151, 154–155
Versatile Express boards, 22
Versatile Platform Baseboard, 79
VFP, 39, 195
VHDL, 10
Virtex-7, 20
virtual address, 45

virtual memory, 46
VLD, 146
VLSI, 5
Von Neumann cache, 32
VREV, 153
VS, 63
VSHRN, 157
VxWorks, 25

W

watchpoints, 161
Wilson, Sophie, 4
Wind River, 25
Wonder Gecko, 86–87, 89–90
write-back cache, 32–33, 188
write-cache strategy, 32–33
write-through cache, 32–33, 188

X

x86, 20, 21
XBMC, 24
Xilinx, 20
XScale, 22, 208

Y

Y2K, 18–19

Printed in the United States
By Bookmasters